The Moral Animus
of David Hume

University of Delaware Press Awards

General John Burgoyne
By Richard J. Hargrove

Time and the Artist in Shakespeare's English Histories
By John W. Blanpied

*Small Georgian Houses in England and Virginia:
Origins and Development through the 1750s*
By Daniel D. Reiff

Shakespeare's Comedies: From Roman Farce to Romantic Mystery
By Robert Ornstein

Elegy by W. S.: A Study in Attribution
By Donald W. Foster

The Moral Animus of David Hume
By Donald T. Siebert

The Moral Animus
of David Hume

Donald T. Siebert

DELAWARE

Newark: University of Delaware Press
London and Toronto: Associated University Presses

Associated University Presses
440 Forsgate Drive
Cranbury, NJ 08512

Associated University Presses
25 Sicilian Avenue
London WC1A 2QH, England

Associated University Presses
P.O. Box 488, Port Credit
Mississauga, Ontario
Canada L5G 4M2

The paper used in this publication meets the requirements
of the American National Standard for Permanence of Paper
for Printed Library Materials Z39.48-1984.

Library of Congress Cataloging-in-Publication Data

Siebert, Donald T.
  The moral animus of David Hume / Donald T. Siebert.
    p.   cm.
  Includes bibliographical references.
  ISBN 0-87413-367-X (alk. paper)
  1. Hume, David, 1711–1776—Ethics.   2. Hume, David, 1711–1776—
Religion.   I. Title.
  B1499.E8S54   1990
  192—dc20   88-40581
                                                                        CIP

To the Memory of

Irvin Ehrenpreis,

Best Teacher and Friend

Contents

Preface

MOST modern studies of Hume have concentrated on the philosophy he advanced in *A Treatise of Human Nature*, the *Enquiries Concerning Human Understanding* and *Concerning the Principles of Morals*, and the *Dialogues Concerning Natural Religion*. Of these works, certainly the *Treatise* has been the one most carefully scrutinized and annotated, even in spite of the fact that late in his life Hume repudiated his magnum opus and advised his readers to look elsewhere for his philosophy. Although it would be wrongheaded to take Hume at his word and ignore the *Treatise*, many students of Hume have ignored everything but the *Treatise*, or at the least they have largely neglected his supposedly non-philosophic writings, such as the various essays, dissertations, and the multivolume *History of England*. This book redresses this imbalance, introducing readers almost for the first time to the writings to which he devoted the largest part of his life and on which he presumably intended his reputation and achievement to rest.

Unlike other broad discussions of Hume's thought, this study treats the *History of England* as a primary document. While including the strictly philosophical works in its purview, this study also considers, in addition to the *History*, the less read essays and dissertations, in particular *The Natural History of Religion*, as well as Hume's correspondence. There are many excellent studies of Hume as an epistemologist or metaphysician, or even as a moral philosopher; there are very few, on the other hand, of Hume as a moralist. Indeed, many students of Hume might well deny that he had a practical moral philosophy, and rarely has the term "moralist" been applied to him.[1] I am chary of nomenclature, though, and will admit that "moralist" may fit Hume as ill as the many and often conflicting labels applied to him: empiricist, rationalist, idealist, skeptic, infidel, theist, naturalist, positivist, nominalist, associationist, phenomenologist. This litany suggests how little such epithets serve us and how valuable it may be to explore the ways in which Hume's practical moral philosophy shapes and informs his work. I am concerned with examining

Hume's central values and ideas, viewed within an eighteenth-century context or milieu, and discovering what explains his passions and commitments, with understanding the pronounced moral animus of his teaching, with accounting for his appeal to intelligent people of his own generation, and with suggesting the grounds of his enduring importance.

Hume's attitudes toward religion, comprising a significant part of this book, are bound to offend some religious people. Because there have been few careful readers of all the *History of England,* many are not aware of how vitriolic and insistent a critic of religion Hume could be. Indeed, authorities such as Ernest Mossner, Donald Livingston, and J. C. A. Gaskin have insisted on Hume's fundamental theism—what Mossner calls Hume's "religion of man"; Livingston, Hume's "genuine, or philosophical, theism"; and Gaskin, allowing Hume a next-to-nothing theism, "attenuated deism."[2] Whatever we get in any of these defenses of Hume's "faith" does not resemble anything one would normally call religious belief. But I am more concerned with Hume's treatment of popular religion than with his definition of an ideal quasi-religion for the enlightened few. What we shall discover is that behind Hume's antagonism to popular religion lies a surprising recommendation of certain religious forms as a way of controlling the dangers of theological zeal. Hume suggests, perhaps paradoxically, that more primitive religious forms serve civilization better than the supposedly more advanced modern forms. This attitude is part of Hume's thoroughgoing worldly morality, as this study makes clear. Hume had sound philosophical reasons for his suspicion of religion, however much he may have viewed the subject from an unsympathetic outsider's perspective. Even those who deplore his religious skepticism as a serious liability may well grant that Hume nonetheless provides revealing insights into the problems caused by *homo religiosus,* indeed into the very nature of spiritual belief.

Few people have read many fascinating and brilliant parts of Hume's works because these passages are buried in formidably lengthy works such as the *History of England.* Accordingly I have quoted copiously from Hume because I want him to do what he can do best for himself: to argue his views in his own forceful words. Throughout I explore various meanings implicit in those words. My approach to Hume is different from most other interpreters in that I seek meaning in Hume's tone and style—indeed in a complex of embedded codes—as much as in the surface of his text.[3] If in so doing I force his meanings too far, sufficient passages of Hume himself remain so that all may read him for themselves. Even better would be a reader's determination to go beyond snippets to engage Hume in whole text—and perhaps first of all in the *History of England,* not in the *Treatise of Human Nature.*

Work for this book was begun during a 1981 sabbatical and helped along by a 1985 summer research grant and two research-and-productive scholarship awards: for this assistance I wish to thank the University of South Carolina. I am also grateful to those who offered suggestions for improving the book: to Lewis White Beck, Irvin Ehrenpreis, and Ernest Mossner, who read individual chapters, and to Eve Tavor Bannet and George Brauer, colleagues at South Carolina, who read the entire typescript. Not least of all I want to thank my wife Joan, whose patient encouragement I could not have done without.

My approach to Hume is that of a student of the eighteenth century rather than a specialist in philosophy, and I am particularly fortunate to have had great teachers who shaped my understanding of eighteenth-century culture: David French, Martin Battestin, Ralph Cohen, Leopold Damrosch, and Irvin Ehrenpreis. I am grateful to each, but especially to the last named, to whom this book is dedicated. As was always his way, Irvin Ehrenpreis encouraged me in my work on this subject, and in his last letter to me he said, "You must write more about Hume." He died before the book was completed, and I can only hope that he would not have been displeased with what I have done here. To him my debt, gratitude, and affection are beyond my ability to express.

Abbreviations for Hume's Works

D   *Dialogues concerning Natural Religion*, in *The Nat-
             ural History of Religion*, ed. A. Wayne Colver,
             and *Dialogues concerning Natural Religion*, ed.
             John Valdimir Price (Oxford: Clarendon,
             1976).

E   *Essays, Moral, Political, and Literary*, ed. Eu-
             gene F. Miller (Indianapolis: Liberty Classics,
             1985).

EHU   *An Enquiry concerning Human Understanding*, in
             *Enquiries Concerning Human Understanding and
             Concerning the Principles of Morals*, ed. L. A.
             Selby-Bigge, 3d ed. revised by P. H. Nidditch
             (Oxford: Clarendon, 1975).

EPM   *An Enquiry concerning the Principles of Morals*, in
             Enquiries (cited above in *EHU*).

First *Enquiry*   = *EHU*

H   = *History*

History   *The History of England, from the Invasion of Julius
             Caesar to The Revolution in 1688*, 6 vols. (In-
             dianapolis: Liberty Classics, 1983). While
             there is no standard text of Hume's *History*,
             this recent edition is the one of choice. Super-
             vised and introduced by William B. Todd, it is
             based on the 1778 edition incorporating
             Hume's last corrections, and it returns the
             History to the original six-volume format, re-
             grettably abandoned in 1763 for commercial
             reasons (see *History* 1:xxii). Todd's introduc-

13

tion also displays important variants between the first and the 1778 editions.

L   *The Letters of David Hume,* 2 vols., ed. J. Y. T. Greig (Oxford: Clarendon, 1932).

MOL   *My own Life.* Hume's brief autobiography appears in most editions of his works. My text is that reprinted by Ernest C. Mossner in *The Life of David Hume,* 2d ed. (Oxford: Clarendon, 1980), pp. 611–15.

NHR   *The Natural History of Religion,* ed. Colver (cited above in *D*).

NL   *New Letters of David Hume,* ed. R. Klibansky and E. C. Mossner (Oxford: Clarendon, 1954).

Second *Enquiry*   = *EPM*

T   = *Treatise*

Treatise   *A Treatise of Human Nature,* ed. L. A. Selby-Bigge, 2d ed. revised by P. H. Nidditch (Oxford: Clarendon, 1978).

Works   *The Philosophical Works of David Hume,* 4 vols., ed. T. H. Green and T. H. Grose (London: Longmans, Green, and Company, 1875).

The Moral Animus
of David Hume

Introduction: Hume's Shaping Moral Imagination

> Be a philosopher; but, amidst all your philosophy, be still a man.
>
> *—EHU*

DAVID Hume is justly regarded as one of the great British philosophers—perhaps without peer—and indeed one of the preeminent philosophers of the world. That is the judgment of the twentieth century. In his own day and well through the nineteenth century, he was regarded as a great historian. Moralist, however, is a label not commonly applied to him. John B. Stewart in *The Moral and Political Philosophy of David Hume* insists that although Hume was a moral philosopher, he was not "a moralizing philosopher."[1] In *The English Moralists*, Basil Willey finds that as a moralist, if that term even applies, Hume is sadly lacking:

> Hume is not, as some earlier and later moralists have been, a man earnestly wrestling with the problem of how to find a rationale for right conduct. It never occurs to him that the agreeable or the useful can change to their opposites according to the state of our spiritual growth. He *knows* what is useful and agreeable; and so, instead of teaching us what we should do, and on what principles we should do it, he simply tells us, with great urbanity, what we are doing already.[2]

Apparently Hume is not, to use the eighteenth-century definition of a "moralist" provided by Samuel Johnson in his *Dictionary*, "one who teaches the duties of life." Nor is he a moralist in the tradition of Montaigne, La Bruyère, La Rochefoucauld, or even Johnson himself—one who in probing the psychology of everyday living helps us to begin knowing ourselves. Hume simply does not fit the ready mold of the moralist.[3]

Hume never called himself a moralist. Nonetheless, much of his writing not only advances a theory of ethics—something no one would deny—but also deals in questions of practical morality: what values in life can be defended, and how? What social forces shape the individual? If individual morality is culture-specific in the main, then what moral codes do various cultures foster and which codes are most defensible? Hume is confessedly not a systematic moralist, and some of the ethical positions he takes are not very conventional: that our duty is in some circumstances to commit suicide would be an extreme example. In any case, however, he does not teach the whole duty of man as an eighteenth-century reader might expect. Moreover, to say that Hume ever teaches morality can be misleading. Indeed, as I will demonstrate in chapter 4, he is quite doubtful that morality is capable of being taught, even though he recommends certain conditions that can shape moral behavior. That doubt itself is part of his moral stance. Hume might be seen, to employ a fashionable idiom, as the moralist as self-deconstructionist.

In one of his well-known letters to Francis Hutcheson, he seems deeply concerned at Hutcheson's criticism that the moral part of the *Treatise* lacks "a certain Warmth in the Cause of Virtue." Hume goes to great lengths in excusing this deficiency, one he implicitly recognizes. He argues that the metaphysician and the moralist can be compared respectively to the anatomist and the painter. The work of each is different—and they are mutually exclusive. The anatomist does not present the grace and nobility of the human being, as does the painter, but he can give the painter "very good Advice." It is in the role of anatomist/metaphysician that Hume has written the *Treatise of Human Nature*. That, contends Hume, is the reason he has avoided open moralizing, a tendency to declamation that would have rendered his work ineffective: "otherwise I must despair of ever being servicable to Virtue." Yet Hume is still not satisfied with being a cold anatomist, a mere ethical metaphysician:[4] "I hope these Reasons will satisfy you; tho at the same time, I intend to make a new Tryal, if it be possible to make the Moralist & Metaphysician agree a little better" (*L*, 1:32–33). We might suspect Hume of simply trying to appease Hutcheson, a moralist in holy orders, were it not that Hume later did what he promised. In the *Enquiry Concerning the Principles of Morals* (1751), based on the ethical theories of the *Treatise* but incorporating significant new material, both emotional and exhortatory, Hume does successfully become both anatomist and painter.[5] Although philosophers do not regard this work as his most important, it is revealing that Hume himself thought it "incomparably the best" of all his writings (*MOL*, 613).

It may be argued further that Hume wanted to abandon metaphysics to pursue what we might call more relevant subjects. There are many explanations for the famous "Advertisement" printed posthumously in the edition of 1777, which repudiated the *Treatise* and directed the reader to the collected works of that edition as solely "containing his philosophical sentiments and principles." Some Humeans attribute this repudiation to petulance and misjudgment: Hume was irritated and chagrined over the failure of the *Treatise* to attract any favorable notice, and he had a mistaken notion that he ought to be known as an elegant man of letters and not an ungentlemanly pedant—that ridiculous metaphysician so embarrassingly identified with himself at the end of the *Treatise*, Book 1. But whatever the explanation and however misguided were Hume's reasons, most of his work after 1740 is not concerned with what many regard as "pure" philosophy. Instead, much of it is ethical, broadly construed. Even the *Dialogues Concerning Natural Religion*, ranked second to the *Treatise* by philosophical consensus, is not particularly metaphysical or epistemological. Significantly, it takes the classical form of a discussion among enlightened and truth-seeking gentlemen. The *Dialogues* ultimately is a morally didactic work, understood within the assumptions developed in the discussion of moral skepticism in chapter 4, teaching by the example of fashioned selves. It holds that several religious hypotheses have a certain degree of possibility but little degree of plausibility and none of certainty. We must suspend judgment, realizing that neither a metaphysical nor a celestial answer will ever likely be ours. Dignity, courage, flexibility, toleration, and serenity are all, however, human responses within our grasp.

Undeniably the work that occupied more of Hume's time than any other, in research and composition as well as in a series of revisions made up until his death, is a work of practical morality: the voluminous *History of England from the Invasion of Julius Caesar to The Revolution of 1688*.[6] That this *History* is an effective vehicle of moral instruction will become obvious as the study unfolds. Again and again we shall see Hume looking at the heroes and wretches of history, seeking to understand what made some noble and others base. Moral precepts are foremost among the many lessons of Hume's Clio.

It is fitting that in the pages of his *History* we find what may be Hume's most candid autobiographical confession. Writing of the adulation given Thomas à Becket after his martyrdom, Hume observes with bitterness:

It is indeed a mortifying reflection to those who are actuated by the love of fame, so justly denominated the last infirmity of noble minds, that the wisest legislator and most exalted genius, that ever reformed or enlightened the world, can never expect such tributes of praise, as are lavished on the memory of pretended saints, whose whole conduct was probably, to the last degree, odious or contemptible, and whose industry was entirely directed to the pursuit of objects pernicious to mankind. It is only a conqueror, a personage no less intitled to our hatred, who can pretend to the attainment of equal renown and glory. (*H*, 1:336–37)

Hume takes a key phrase from Milton's "Lycidas"—"*Fame . . . / That last infirmity of Noble mind*" (ll. 70–71)—in a passage lamenting that a young poet's sacrifice and merit should go unrewarded on earth. Through his ostensible concern with Edward King, whose untimely death occasioned "Lycidas," Milton voices his own sense of neglect and uncertain vocation. By his allusion Hume expresses a similar emotion. Can one doubt that Hume's rise to the language of poetry, his angry soliloquy protesting misplaced values, is called forth by a noble mind who would himself love that fame of reforming and enlightening the world? The enlightenment spoken of here is not the crabbed reasoning of *A Treatise of Human Nature*. Hume is surely thinking of ethical enlightenment and reform—"re-form" brought about by the reshaping power of the moral imagination—a creative force pervading the *History of England*. Even on his deathbed he was still envisioning himself as a reformer of mankind, though by then he had to concede, in a mood of jocular cynicism, that such a lofty goal was far beyond the reach of any single life's work.[7]

Immediately after the outburst provoked by Becket's apotheosis, Hume remarks on two details of Henry II's reign, both resulting from the king's overanxiety "to express his zeal for religion" and thus to placate the archbishop. One involved a special tax on all subjects to free the Holy Land from Saladin, an enterprise Hume scarcely regarded as worthwhile—or moral, as I will show later in chapter 2. The other fact was yet more disturbing. Thirty German heretics, ignorant and harmless, came over to England and were "burned on the forehead, and then whipped through the streets . . . [and] after they were whipped, they were thrust out almost naked in the midst of winter, and perished through cold and hunger; no one daring, or being willing, to give them the least relief. . . . They seem to have been the first that ever suffered for heresy in England" (*H*, 1:337–38). Juxtaposed with the holy life and the beatification of St. Thomas of Canterbury is an ugly reality of holy wars and religious persecution. In shaped narratives like this one Hume becomes an outspoken and eloquent moralist.

Thus I shall argue that Hume's *History* projects a moral vision by its ability to reshape the past, to impose meanings on that past, creating patterns that imply a corresponding beauty of human nature—all too seldom instantiated in human life, it is true, but nonetheless capable of being discovered, indeed created in the fiat of narrative, by the historian's moral imagination. That the historian can so emplot the past is itself proof of the dignity and worth of human nature. The eighteenth-century assumptions that encumber and limit Hume's *History* are apparent to us in the late twentieth century, but his work transcends such ideological blind spots and becomes one of the classic texts in our Western tradition.

Speaking of such classic texts, though not naming Hume's, Hayden White observes (following Paul Ricoeur) that these works are "worthy of study and reflection long after their scholarship has become outmoded and their arguments have been consigned to the status of commonplaces. . . ." In its ability to dramatize the past, to impose a form of narrative upon it, Hume's *History* creates a significance, indeed a truthfulness, that the chaos of factuality did not have before:

> The authority of the historical narrative is the authority of reality itself; the historical account endows this reality with form and thereby makes it desirable by the imposition upon its processes of the formal coherency that only stories possess. . . . In this world, reality wears the mask of a meaning, the completeness and fullness of which we can only imagine, never experience. Insofar as historical stories can be completed, can be given narrative closure, can be shown to have had a plot all along, they give to reality the odor of the ideal. . . . [Thus] Has any historical narrative ever been written that was not informed not only by moral awareness but specifically by the moral authority of the narrator?[8]

As will become apparent, I will ground the moral efficacy of Hume's *History* on the inevitable moral function of narrativity itself.

At the beginning of his career, again in the letter to Francis Hutcheson, Hume wrote, "Upon the whole, I desire to take my Catalogue of Virtues from *Cicero's Offices*, not from the *Whole Duty of Man*" (*L*, 1:34). The contrast suggests much about Hume's ethical teaching, not that his views derive in a straight line from Cicero's *De Officiis* or conversely reject every precept enjoined by this extremely popular manual of Christian piety, reputedly the work of Bishop Richard Allestree. Indeed a critic bent on perversity might argue that the *Offices* and the *Whole Duty* enforce a remarkably similar code of conduct—or at least similar catalogues of virtues. Both agree that duty to the gods, or God—the difference is admittedly great—is primary, that otherwise one should be honest, plaindealing, considerate of one's neighbors, loyal to one's family and friends, exercising moderation and self-control in all things. On particular points the two are surprisingly close. One should not make conflicting promises that result in breaking one's word, but in such a difficulty one should break the promise that involves the least harm. When obliged to correct one's children, one should never punish in anger. One should not profit by another's ignorance or need: the marketplace doctrine of *caveat emptor* does not permit the seller to deceive the buyer, even by simply withholding unsolicited information. Of course the two moral guidebooks differ on several critical points. Cicero applauds suicide in certain cases and justifies the murder of one's best friend if that friend is a tyrant (1.31.112; 3.4.19); the *Whole Duty*, as might be expected, categorically condemns this violation of the sixth commandment as the most heinous of crimes, "of the deepest dye, a most loud crying Sin."[9] And the pious Allestree roundly denounces such sins as pride and adultery that hardly claim the notice of Cicero. The reader may recognize in this contrast the kind of game in relativistic ethics that Hume himself plays in "A Dialogue." (See chapter 4.) Nonetheless, with a few egregious exceptions like these, the two apparently opposed works on practical ethics come very close to detailing the *same* "Catalogue of Virtues," despite Hume's insistence on their differences.

Where the two appear to coincide best, however, there are significant differences that Hume would not fail to appreciate. Consider more closely the apparent agreement on the obligation of a seller never to cheat a buyer, even if indirectly. Cicero rests his case on the fundamental harm such deceit does to society:

> *tamen naturae lege sanctum est. Societas est enim (quod etsi saepe dictum est, dicendum est tamen saepius), latissime quidem quae pateat, omnium inter omnes, interior eorum, qui eiusdem gentis sint, propior eorum, qui eiusdem civitatis.* [nevertheless it is forbidden by the moral law. For there is a bond of fellowship—although I have often made this statement, I

must still repeat it again and again—which has the very widest application, uniting all men together and each to each.][10]

We see that Cicero's reasoning is high-minded and rational. Allestree, on the other hand, reasons very differently. It is shameful, he says, that Christians should be guilty of what even "sober Heathens" would avoid—an argument from pride that one would expect him normally to condemn. "Yet besides this, there want not other; among which, one there is of such a Nature, as may prevail with the arrantest Worldling, and that is, that this Course does not really tend to the enriching of him; there is a secret Curse goes along with it, which, like a Canker, eats out all the Benefit was expected from it." And he cites biblical passages preaching that such trickery does not pay. It is "the arrantest Worldling" indeed to whom this calculating argument is addressed. What sullies Allestree's teaching most, however, is his use of divine wrath and punishment as the ultimate argument. The cheat will finally cheat himself of heaven. Even should he go undetected by the world, the devil, that greatest cheat of all, will claim his soul: "So thou that art gaping to swallow up thy poor Brother, art thyself made a Prey to that great Devourer" (pp. 255–58). As his title makes plain, Allestree appeals "especially [to] the Meanest Reader"; Cicero, if not exclusively to philosophers, at least to his son, a student of philosophy. Perhaps Allestree considered that he could not convince his lowly reader with noble arguments, while Cicero on the other hand enjoyed the advantage of confidence in his reader. Nevertheless, these differences in tone and assumption help to gloss Hume's remark to Hutcheson. Appealing to the basest model of human nature, the *Whole Duty* evokes the atmosphere of a prisonhouse; the *Offices* speaks instead to an ideal of human freedom and dignity.

Thus it is not so much in their literal catalogs of virtues but rather in how they justify these catalogs that the two works differ so markedly. They do not speak to the same audience; they most certainly do not share the same vision of what human life can and should be. If both state that one's obligation to the divine is the highest of duties, the Christian guidebook obsessively devotes the first five and the longest of its seventeen chapters to that obligation, not to mention a lengthy section later on duties owed to the ministers of God. Cicero's mention of one's obligation to the immortal gods seems by contrast pro forma. More importantly, Cicero's gods do not ask an individual to do anything contrary to reason or nature. To be virtuous by the wise pagan's teaching does not require one to give up anything that people normally value. But to follow the *Whole Duty*'s exhortation one must often obey the commandments of God in spite of reason and nature: "Now examine thyself by this. . . . Dost thou make it thy constant and greatest care to keep God's Commandments? To obey him in all Things; earnestly labouring to please him to the utmost of thy Power, even to the forsaking of what is dearest to thee in this World?" (p. 18) According to the *Whole Duty*, pleasing God is frequently not expedient in any sense of the word—sometimes it is contrarational—but in Cicero's eminently reasonable world, expediency *(utile)* and moral good *(honestum)* are always identical—a belief notable in Hume's ethics as well. To be sure, this noble expediency may sometimes cost one personal advantages, but this cost is amply repaid by its ultimate benefit to human society, that cosmopolitan ideal to which many systems of ethics appeal. Cicero's point of reference, after the obligatory bow to the immortal gods, is always *this* life and *this* world. How important to Hume that assumption is, will be the subject of this book.

In ordering my chapters, I begin with the Humean premise that the passions are the foundation of morality, and in chapter 1 I deal with Hume's place in that complex of eighteenth-century ideas surrounding that ubiquitous figure, the man of feeling, and discuss Hume's distinctive reshaping of that figure. In chapter 2 I concentrate on what for Hume is an especially problematic aspect of human psychology, religious belief, and explore its manifestations, and I suggest his prescription for a religion that is not in conflict with the morality that Hume recommends. In chapter 3 I present Hume's answer to the threat posed by spiritual zeal—that answer being salvation by physical reality—and deal with the pervasiveness in Hume's *Weltanschauung* of the things of this world and their implications for his ethics. In chapter 4 I am concerned with the dynamic strategies by which Hume teaches his cherished mitigated skepticism. And in chapter 5 I demonstrate how Hume's often neglected autobiography functions, much like his *History*, to define and exemplify the shaped self of Hume's moral ideal.

1

In Search of the Hero of Feeling

It seems arrogant to pretend to Genius or Magnanimity, which are the most shining Qualities a man can possess. It seems foppish & frivolous to pretend to bodily Accomplishments. The Qualities of the heart, lye in a medium & are neither so shining as the the one, nor so little valu'd as the other. I suppose the Reason why Goodnature is not more valu'd is its Commonness, which has a vast Effect on all our Sentiments. Cruelty and Hardness of Heart is the most detested of all Vices.

—*L* (1743)

Upon the whole . . . it seems undeniable, *that* nothing can bestow more merit on any human creature than the sentiment of benevolence in an eminent degree.

—*EPM* (1751)

The first Quality of an Historian is to be true & impartial; the next to be interesting. If you do not say, that I have done both Parties Justice; & if Mrs Mure be not sorry for poor King Charles, I shall burn all my Papers, & return to Philosophy.

—*L* (1754)

The Sentimental Hume

"REASON is, and ought only to be the slave of the passions, and can never pretend to any other office than to serve and obey them" (*T*, 415), Hume says in perhaps the most controversial sentence of *A Treatise of Human Nature*.[1] Still, whether this pronouncement is to be taken as literal truth or rhetorical exaggeration, there is no need to question the centrality of passion in both Hume's epistemology and ethics. Little attention has been paid, however, to more popular ramifications of Hume's theories of the passions. To what extent is this philosophical emphasis on feeling manifest in his other writings and in his life? How does Hume stand in regard to that pervasive eighteenth-century movement,

25

sensibility, whose flood of tears spread to literature and the other arts, to criticism, and to ethical writing?[2] Was Hume in the popular sense of the word a sentimentalist, a devotee of *sensibilité*? There is much to suggest that he was, and he would probably not have objected to such a label.

Calling himself "a Man of Humanity," Hume could glow with pleasure when his travels revealed the prosperity and happiness of "so considerable a Part of Mankind as the Germans" (*L*, 1:126). In the company of Rousseau he found perfect occasions to exercise his sentimental faculties, as he tells Hugh Blair:

> But Judge of my Surprize, when [Rousseau] sat down suddenly on my Knee, threw his hands about my Neck, kiss'd me with the greatest Warmth, and bedewing all my Face with Tears, exclaim'd, *Is it possible you can ever forgive me, my Dear Friend. . . . I love you, I esteem you. . . .* I hope you have not so bad an Opinion of me as to think I was not melted on this Occasion: I assure you I kissd him and embrac'd him twenty times, with a plentiful Effusion of Tears. I think no Scene of my Life was ever more affecting. (*L*, 2:30)

Hume was so pleased with this "scene" that he also described it to the Comtesse de Boufflers and told her she need not keep the story a secret: "Please to tell this story to Madame la Marechale de Luxembourg. . . . I also allow you to tell it to Madame de Barbantane, and to such of her female friends as you think worthy of it. I scarce know a male who would not think it childish" (*L*, 2:36). The afterthought reinforces the impression that however pleased he was with himself, Hume regarded his sentimental reaction as extreme even for a man of feeling. After the break with Rousseau, Hume complains, "Unhappy Man! to deprive me so cruelly of the delicious Pleasure I felt in serving him." (*L*, 2:87). If in these examples Hume seems more than a little self-indulgent, it is but just to remember that he consistently sympathized with others and took pleasure in helping them. One thinks of his efforts in behalf of the blind poet Thomas Blacklock or his self-effacing recommendations of William Robertson's *History of Scotland*, a competitor with his own *History of England*.[3] As he told a friend, it is one of the "greatest Pleasures [of power] to be serviceable to Merit in Distress" (*L*, 2:220).

Not only in his personal life but also in his writings one finds passages of undoubted sentimental inspiration. In one of his early essays we discover Eugenius, a stock figure of the man of feeling. Eugenius marries "the virtuous and beautiful *Emira*," whose memory after her death is kept ever alive by the requisite tribute of tears. Moreover,

> he preserves her Picture with the utmost Care, and has one Picture in Minature, which he always wears next to his Bosom. . . . He has left Orders in his last Will, that, in whatever Part of the World he shall happen to die, his Body shall be transported, and laid in the same Grave with her's: And that a Monument shall be erected over them, and their mutual Love and Happiness celebrated in an Epitaph, which he himself has compos'd for that Purpose. (*E*, 541)

In the *History of England* our hearts are sometimes wrenched by an appeal to sentimental plot, as when a "young maid," exchanging her virtue for her brother's life, finds the next morning that her ravisher has had the brother hanged outside the bedroom window: "Rage and despair and indignation took possession of her mind, and deprived her for ever of her senses" (*H*, 6:462–63). When Lord Stafford faces beheading for his alleged complicity in the Popish Plot, "the executioner himself was touched with sympathy. Twice he lifted up the ax, with an intent to strike the fatal blow; and as often felt his resolution fail him. A deep sigh was heard to accompany his last effort, which laid Stafford for ever at rest" (*H*, 6:395).[4] Surely the ultimate triumph of pity occurs when the executioner cannot do his brutal duty. One thinks of the very sentimental Polly Peachum dreaming, in the *Beggar's Opera*: "I see [Macheath] at the tree! The whole circle are in tears!—even butchers weep! Jack Ketch himself hesitates to perform his duty, and would be glad to lose his fee by a reprieve" (1.12.7–10).

Likewise *An Enquiry Concerning the Principles of Morals*, regarded by Hume as "incomparably the best" (*MOL*, 613) of his writings, turns out to be the most sentimentally textured as well. At one point Hume professes to be so enraptured by human goodness that he forgets his main purpose is to analyze, not "paint, in their true colours, all the genuine charms of the social virtues. These, indeed, sufficiently engage every heart . . . ; and it is difficult to abstain from some sally of panegyric, as often as they occur in discourse or reasoning" (*EPM*, 177). It is the necessary reminder that no man is qualified to recommend virtue who does not feel its power, a power that sometimes makes the good completely forget self-interest and self-control, as when kindly Parson Adams in Fielding's *Joseph Andrews* (chapter 12) lets his beloved, hand-copied Aeschylus expire in the hearth while he capers about in ecstasy at the happy reunion of Fanny and Joseph. In fact the basic argument of the second *Enquiry* is that one must feel the beauty of moral choices for them to become a way of life. Certainly, Hume finally admits, reason can find specious justifications for iniquity, but his Conclusion rests on the emotional plea that the human heart will not usually be content with the merely selfish choice of life (*EPM*, 282–84).

From such evidence it would seem undeniable that Hume was a sentimentalist, but there are difficulties in applying the label to him. The examples chosen thus far make the identification fit, but we could find counterevidence. To be sure, Hume never repudiated the assumptions of sensibility, yet there is something in the spirit of Humean philosophy fundamentally opposed to sentimental values. Consider these statements in the *Treatise:*

> Women and children are most subject to pity, as being most guided by that faculty. The same infirmity . . . makes them pity extremely those, whom they find in any grief or affliction. (*T,* 370)

> Let us remember, that pride and hatred invigorate the soul; and love and humility infeeble it. (*T,* 391)

> by *pride* I understand that agreeable impression, . . . when the view either of our virtue, beauty, riches or power makes us satisfy'd with ourselves: . . . by *humility* I mean the opposite impression. (*T,* 297)

> I believe no one, who has any practice of the world . . . will assert, that the humility, which good-breeding and decency require of us, goes beyond the outside, or that a thorough sincerity in this particular is esteem'd a real part of our duty. (*T,* 598)

Such remarks sound a bit like Nietzsche, tempered somewhat by the calculating gentility of Lord Chesterfield. What man of feeling, or for that matter anyone more tolerant than the most supercilious snob, would ever say, "Nothing has a greater tendency to give us an esteem for any person, than his power and riches; or a contempt, than his poverty and meanness" (*T,* 357)? Or is the following not the observation of a Hobbist?—"Moralists or politicians" can do nothing to correct "the selfishness and ingratitude of men. . . . All they can pretend to, is, to give a new direction to those natural passions, and teach us that we can better satisfy our appetites in an oblique and artificial manner, than by their headlong and impetuous motion" (*T,* 521).

Certainly it is unfair to hold up these *obiter dicta* from Hume's youthful and somewhat indiscreet *Treatise* as representative, but they do suggest something about Hume's philosophy that is out of keeping with typical manifestations of sentimentalism.[5] By and large, the stock man of feeling both exhibits and honors certain qualities that are absent in Hume's list of merits: meekness in attitude, humility in station, melancholy in mood, weakness and passivity in situation. Usually the sentimental hero is more acted upon than acting; the sentimental object of pity is customarily someone poor, infirm, very old, very young, female, or eccentric—sometimes even a helpless animal. These aspects undergo marked changes in Hume's practice of sensibility. His hero is by contrast proud and dignified; distinguished by birth, fortune, talents; dominating and self-controlled; superior to his fate, even though that fate involves his own death. For the spectator he becomes paradoxically an even greater object of sympathy than a more helpless victim because he shows what human nature is capable of. The spectator shares in this triumph, shedding tears of joy, not pity.

In the next section I review the background in Hume's writings for this conception of sensibility and amplify the assumptions behind it. In the section following that I show Hume applying these ideas as practical exercises in cultivating sensitivity, that catalyst of morality. In the final two sections I analyze Hume's discovery of the hero of feeling.

Theoretical Assumptions

Reason and passion both play a role in moral action. Hume never derogates reason's function: reason sorts out and clarifies our experience, allowing us to compare and judge; it shows us the utility of moral action. But virtuous behavior would be improbable had we not some innate moral sense, some natural propensity to prefer and even love that beauty and utility that reason shows us:

> The end of all moral speculations is to teach us our duty; and, by proper representations of the deformity of vice and beauty of virtue, beget correspondent habits, and engage us to avoid the one, and embrace the other. But is this ever to be expected from the inferences and conclusions of the understanding, which of themselves have no hold of the affections or set in motion the active powers of men? They discover truths: but where the truths which they discover are indifferent, and beget no desire or aversion, they can have no influence on conduct and behaviour. What is honourable, what is fair, what is becoming, what is noble, what is generous, takes possession of the heart, and animates us to embrace and maintain it. . . .

> Extinguish all the warm feelings and prepossessions in favour of virtue, and all disgust or aversion to vice: render men totally indifferent towards these distinctions; and morality is no longer a practical study, nor has any tendency to regulate our lives and actions.
>
> [The final sentence or determination of moral judgment] depends on some internal sense or feeling, which nature has made universal in the whole species. (*EPM*, 172–73)

If the reason or understanding is prerequisite, this internal sense or feeling is the trump card assuring the actualization of virtue.[6]

One quality this internal sense or feeling is particularly drawn toward is the usefulness of an action or thing. Now utility is bound up with the determinations of reason, but it is also at the basis of our emotional responses. In other words, we cannot help approving of and even loving what is useful and despising what is not. It is worth noting that this emphasis on utility would imply that our strongest emotional reactions center on beautiful scenes and comely, energetic people, not on anything ugly or weak. In Hume's thinking such scenes and persons suggest usefulness, and usefulness is connected with beneficence. Consider, for example, the scene Hume presents to illustrate how a favorable emotional response is triggered:

> We enter . . . into a convenient, warm, well-contrived apartment: We necessarily receive a pleasure from its very survey; because it presents us with the pleasing ideas of ease, satisfaction, and enjoyment. The hospitable, good-humoured, humane landlord appears. . . . His whole family, by the freedom, ease, confidence, and calm enjoyment, diffused over their countenances, sufficiently express their happiness. I have a pleasing sympathy in the prospect of so much joy, and can never consider the source of it, without the most agreeable emotions. (*EPM*, 220–21)

Although we learn that all this prosperity and happiness had been threatened but not destroyed by a larger-than-life villain, described in some of Hume's most risibly hyperbolic language as one "who had enslaved provinces, depopulated cities, and made the field and scaffold stream with human blood" (*EPM*, 221)—this melodramatic evil is included only to demonstrate the opposite reaction of horror and indignation.

Thus the admirable individual is characterized by active benevolence—that is, by beneficence—and Hume's celebration of his actions tends toward apotheosis: "Upon the whole, then, it seems undeniable, *that* nothing can bestow more merit on any human creature than the sentiment of benevolence in an eminent degree; and *that* a *part*, at least, of its merit arises from its tendency to promote the interests of our species, and bestow happiness on human society" (*EPM*, 181). He is "like the sun, an inferior minister of providence [who] cheers, invigorates, and sustains the surrounding world" (*EPM*, 178).

Sympathy is the term Hume uses to describe the connection between the internal sense or feeling and whatever it responds to.[7] Every kind of emotion we witness in others is capable of being transferred to us by the power of sympathy: "In general, it is certain, that, wherever we go, whatever we reflect on or converse about, everything still presents us with the view of human happiness or misery, and excites in our breast a sympathetic movement of pleasure or uneasiness" (*EPM*, 221).[8] And no emotions are stronger or more contagious than those associated with benevolence, with "a generous concern for our kind and species. These, wherever they appear, seem to transfuse themselves, in a manner, into each beholder, and to call forth, in their own behalf, the same favourable and affectionate sentiments, which they exert on all around" (*EPM*, 178). This sympathy makes possible what we might call the physiology of sentimentality: "The tear naturally starts in our eye on the apprehension of a warm sentiment of this nature: our breast heaves, our heart is agitated, and every humane tender principle of our frame is set in motion, and gives us the purest and most satisfactory enjoyment" (*EPM*, 257).

But sympathy is not automatic or always efficacious, and this is an aspect and feeling that has a particular bearing on our discussion. Too weak an emotional impression may produce hatred or contempt, not benevolence or love, and too strong an impression—that is, one that is overwhelming and traumatic—may be self-defeating, resulting in either inattention or horror (*T*, 386–89):

> Thus we find, that tho' every one, but especially women, are apt to contract a kindness for criminals, who go to the scaffold, and readily imagine them to be uncommonly handsome and well-shap'd; yet one, who is present at the cruel execution of the rack, feels no such tender emotions; but is in a manner overcome with horror, and has no leisure to temper this uneasy sensation by any opposite sympathy. (*T*, 388)

As Foucault has said, the presumably didactic function of public torture and execution up through the eighteenth century could sometimes backfire on the executioner and the state: even to spectators accustomed to spectacles of cruelty, there were limits that could be disastrously transgressed.[9] Certainly in the artistic rendering of such material there would seem to be a decorum of sentimental spectacle, and those who use the powers of sensibility to teach morality—the poets, orators, dramatists, and historians—must take great care. They must ensure that the emotional impression is strong—and this is the province of the imagination—but they cannot risk destroying noble sentiments by an excess of misery and horror.

Used well, however, nothing can equal the power for moral education wielded by these dramatizers of human emotion. Although Hume does not present a systematic aesthetics of sensibility, it is possible to infer his premises. First, our nature predisposes us to respond with pleasure to any scene of human happiness and beneficence or to respond with indignation at what might oppose them. As long as the impression is neither too weak nor too horrible, any clear representation of passion will be likely to move us:

> No passion, when well represented, can be entirely indifferent to us; because there is none, of which every man has not, within him, at least the seeds and first principles. It is the business of poetry to bring every affection near to us by lively imagery and representation, and make it look like truth and reality: A certain proof, that, wherever that reality is found, our minds are disposed to be strongly affected by it. (EPM, 222–23)

It is not mere verisimilitude that Hume seeks. The truthfulness of the representation is a criterion of its success: "If we bring those subjects nearer: If we remove all suspicion of fiction and deceit: What powerful concern is excited" (EPM, 224). Indeed, the representations Hume regards as most moving always have as a referent the "actual" past—the narratives of ancient oratory and history, for example, and never the manifest fictions of novels and romances.

Yet he concedes that witnessing a distressing event would not by itself give aesthetic pleasure or evoke moral sentiment. That is partly attributable to the danger of excess mentioned before, but it is also related to another criterion of sentimental art, one perhaps more important than any other:

> The indifferent, uninteresting stile of Suetonius, equally with the masterly pencil of Tacitus, may convince us of the cruel depravity of Nero or Tiberius: But what a difference of sentiment! While the former coldly relates the facts; and the latter sets before our eyes the venerable figures of a Soranus and a Thrasea, intrepid in their fate, and only

moved by the melting sorrows of their friends and kindred. What sympathy then touches every heart! (*EPM*, 223)

This quality of style is what Hume most often refers to as eloquence. Precisely what such an abstraction means to him is difficult to pin down—artistic heightening, shaping, emotive language, or what postmodern theory would subsume under the concept of narrativity itself: the metaphor of Tacitus's pencil gives a hint, but there are some indications in the Second *Enquiry*, "Of Tragedy," and in his own practice in the *History of England* of what makes something eloquent. As in the example above of Tacitus's Soranus and Thrasea, eloquence shows us what human nature is capable of, and that truly admirable characters are superior to their pathetic situation. Eloquence involves the ability of human genius to create beauty out of suffering, a beauty that dignifies human nature and so touches a chord deep within us: "The impulse or vehemence, arising from sorrow, compassion, indignation, receives a new direction from the sentiments of beauty" (*E*, 220). Because horror can overwhelm sympathy, however, the artist must ensure that the spectator is not too close to the suffering that is being transfigured by eloquence: to "an afflicted parent" one would not, "with all the force of elocution," speak of "the irreparable loss" of a "favourite child"; likewise in his history Lord Clarendon avoids the death of Charles I because of its nearness to him and his readers—a subject that "another age would regard as the most pathetic and most interesting, and, by consequence, the most agreeable" (*E*, 223–24).[10]

One other aspect of sentimental aesthetics is social reinforcement: that is, how the effect of any moving scene will be increased if the spectator has a sense of participating with others in the whole experience. The theater is therefore ideally suited to heightening sensibility: "A man, who enters the theatre, is immediately struck with the view of so great a multitude, participating of one common amusement [i.e., serious entertainment or reflection]; and experiences, from their very aspect, a superior sensibility or disposition of being affected with every sentiment, which he shares with his fellow-creatures" (*EPM*, 221)[11] This endorsement of the theater's power and the example of Tacitus's eloquence call to mind that for Hume a scene best calculated to have sentimental power would be crowded with people, including the object of compassion, those dear to him or her, the other participants, and of course the spectators. For Hume sentiment is definitely an experience of strong social participation, as indeed sentiment's origin in sympathy would lead one to expect. He would appear to have little appreciation of solitary pathos: for him no saints brooding through a dark night of the soul.

Thus our human nature would seem to make sentimental experience inevitable and constant, and the only factor preventing our lives from being a great orgy of sensibility would be the availability of heartless scoundrels to make somebody unhappy in the first place. Physical evil, of course, can be relied on to cause pathos, but moral evil is more commonly the antagonist in most sentimental art. But if our nature makes universal benevolence the order of the day, where will the persecutors, tyrants, and other villains be found to play their necessary role in an art of tears? Hume does not deny the existence of these wretches; no one can. His insistence, however, on innate benevolence puts him into some difficulty. In the second *Enquiry,* where he feels most obliged to persuade his reader that this moral sense is part of human nature, he wishes to believe that absolute evil can never inhere in a human character. "A creature, absolutely malicious and spiteful, were there any such in nature, must be worse than indifferent to the images of vice and virtue. All his sentiments must be inverted" (*EPM,* 226).[12] Later he seems to hedge—"Let us suppose a person originally framed so as to have no manner of concern for his fellow-creatures" (*EPM,* 235)—but his basic position is to regard either a congenital sadist or a moral neuter as a hypothetical case, as a "fancied monster" (*EPM,* 235). Even Nero, the most depraved example of humankind, cannot be regarded as totally devoid of a moral sense (*EPM,* 227). Thus we must recognize a strong tendency in Hume to dignify human nature. Even at the worst, some benevolence is part of every human being: "It is sufficient for our present purpose, if it be allowed, what surely, without the greatest absurdity cannot be disputed, that there is some benevolence, however small, infused into our bosom; some spark of friendship for human kind; some particle of the dove, kneaded into our frame, along with the elements of the wolf and serpent" (*EPM,* 271).[13]

Thus Hume, though granting the rare capacity of natural man for malice, wishes nonetheless to present human nature in the best possible light, as he does in the early essay "Of the Dignity or Meanness of Human Nature" (1741). Even if people can fall short of their moral capacity, they are more likely to excel in virtue if encouraged, even flattered:

I must . . . be of opinion, that the sentiments of those, who are inclined to think favourably of mankind, are more advantageous to virtue, than the contrary principles, which give us a mean opinion of our nature. When a man is prepossessed with a high notion of his rank and character in the creation, he will naturally endeavour to act up to it, and will scorn to do a base or vicious action, which might sink him below that figure which he makes in his own imagination.[14] (*E*, 81)

In the *History of England* we find him blaming Charles II, not for being the "merrie monarch" but rather for cynicism: "he had a heart not very capable of friendship, and he had secretly entertained a very bad opinion and distrust of mankind" (*H*, 6:189). Surely part of Hume's moral teaching is that virtue, and benevolence as central to it, may be innate, but it must be buttressed by reason and nurtured by words of praise. This encouragement of benevolence is the goal of moral art, including ethics and history.

Then how does Hume deal with those who are obviously not benevolent? What has become of their innate moral sense? In part he explains that people vary a good bit in their sensibility to moral impressions, just as they vary in their sensitivity of taste, whether it be to food or beautiful art. Yet different degrees of sensibility can hardly account for a Nero or even a Cromwell. In these cases the moral sense has been smothered by some overriding force— madness for Nero, which Hume terms "fear and resentment" (*EPM*, 227), and religious fanaticism for Cromwell. We see Hume sharing that assumption common to benevolists that man's innate goodness is often perverted by cultural, historical factors.[15]

Notably in the *History* he takes care to identify the most pernicious enemies of benevolence: barbarity, stemming from ignorance and a primitive mode of life; political factionalism; and worst of all, religious zeal. The Irish barbarian Hugh O'Neale "was noted for the vices of perfidy and cruelty, so common among uncultivated nations" (*H*, 4:315). The unfortunate Edward II was finally regarded with sympathy because "it was impossible, that the people, however corrupted by the barbarity of the times, still farther inflamed by faction, could for ever remain insensible to the voice of nature" (*H*, 2:171). But religious zeal is the most pandemic cancer destroying benevolence. Such fanaticism takes many twisted forms of expression, perverting the innate nobility of man, as we see in this remarkable description of the victorious crusaders:

> After a siege of five weeks, they took Jerusalem by assault; and, impelled by a mixture of military and religious rage, they put the numerous garrison and inhabitants to the sword without distinction. Neither arms defended the valiant, nor submission the timorous: No

age or sex was spared: Infants on the breast were pierced by the same blow with their mothers, who implored for mercy: Even a multitude, to the number of ten thousand persons, who had surrendered themselves prisoners, and were promised quarter, were butchered in cool blood by those ferocious conquerors. The streets of Jerusalem were covered with dead bodies; and the triumphant warriors, after every enemy was subdued and slaughtered, immediately turned themselves, with the sentiments of humiliation and contrition, towards the holy sepulchre. They threw aside their arms, still streaming with blood: They advanced with reclined bodies, and naked feet and heads to that sacred monument: They sung anthems to their Saviour, who had there purchased their salvation by his death and agony: And their devotion, enlivened by the presence of the place where he had suffered, so overcame their fury, that they dissolved in tears, and bore the appearance of every soft and tender sentiment. So inconsistent is human nature with itself! And so easily does the most effeminate superstition ally, both with the most heroic courage, and with the fiercest barbarity! (H, 1:250)

It is a passage of savage irony, displaying brutal warfare waged to serve the Prince of Peace, merciless slaughter to gain forgiveness and salvation, and heartlessness immediately succeeded by the "tears . . . of every soft and tender sentiment." We see that Hume's treatment of sensibility can have a polemical edge, and in the next sections we shall see that particular animus as another dimension of his efforts to distinguish the hero of feeling.

One should bear in mind that Hume's theory and practice of sensibility are not divorced from his moral philosophy. As he emphasizes again and again in the second *Enquiry,* sensibility is the basis of morality; the moral individual is perforce marked by a fine sensibility. However, Hume's definition of virtue is not that of most moralists in his age, and so that sensibility he identifies and recommends has its own distinctive form. At the end of the *Enquiry* he personifies Virtue in a way, he claims, in which she has not often been viewed: "The dismal dress falls off, with which many divines, and some philosophers, have covered her; and nothing appears but gentleness, humanity, beneficence, affability; nay even, at proper intervals, play, frolic, and gaiety" (*EPM,* 279).[16] The "*useful* or *agreeable*," according to Hume, can be the only standard of virtue. Cleanthes, the fictional "model of perfect virtue" in the *Enquiry,* is distinguished by these characteristics: honor and humanity, success in the world, wit and good manners, cheerfulness and serenity, and finally, greatness of mind *EPM,* 269–70). Cleanthes does not resemble the typical saint, nor very much the typical man of feeling. His tranquillity seems at odds with the excesses of sensibility; his worldliness and enterprise are far removed from the humility, vulnerability, and passivity often associated with sentimental characters; his confident cheerfulness differs from that pleasing melancholy that seems to bless the sentimental man more than any other trait. In Gray's *Elegy*, almost the locus classicus of sentimental idealism, among the speaker's distinctions, such as poverty, obscurity, and piety—not one of which, we might also note, fits Cleanthes—there is one more of particular significance: "*And* [not *But*] *Melancholy marked him for her own*" (*Elegy* l. 120). Back to Burton's *Anatomy of Melancholy* and through Milton's "Il Penseroso" runs the tradition of the melancholy, thus sensitive and benevolent, man. Hume has no use for melancholy in his definition of the man of feeling.

Even more noteworthy is Hume's inclusion of greatness of mind among the other hallmarks of his moral ideal. He devotes a long section of the *Treatise* to a defense of this trait, and it caps the list of Cleanthes' virtues. To Hume no merit seems more inspiring than this one, and almost all his heroes, certainly all who seem capable of exciting strong emotions, show "greatness of mind," the actual phrase he most often uses. Consider his description of

> philosophical tranquillity, superior to pain, sorrow, anxiety, and each assault of adverse fortune. . . . [This attitude carries] a grandeur with [it], which seizes the spectator, and strikes him with admiration. And the nearer we can approach in practice to this sublime tranquillity and indifference . . . the more secure enjoyment shall we attain within ourselves, and the more greatness of mind shall we discover to the world. (*EPM*, 256)

His use of the word "sublime" in this and other such passages would suggest that Hume actually recognizes two sources of emotional response, indeed two distinct kinds of sensibility—the pathetic and the sublime.[17] The pathetic is the kind of feeling generally associated with sensibility. The sublime on the other hand represents a kind of emotion that Hume wants to add to the complex of sentimental experience. Note the following analysis of poetry's function: "It is observable, that the great charm of poetry consists in lively pictures of the sublime passions, magnanimity, courage, disdain of fortune; of those of the tender affections, love and friendship; which warm the heart, and diffuse over it similar sentiments and emotions" (*EPM*, 259). Soon after, Hume calls "this talent itself of poets, to move the passions, this pathetic and sublime of sentiment." Clearly he is not content with merely the pathetic—the softer, gentler, and more domestic emotions. The very juxtaposition of these two kinds of passion—one great and one small—and the use itself of the word "sublime," with all its richly favorable connotations in eighteenth-century aesthetics, imply the superiority of the sublime.

Consider how in the following passage Hume seems to give equal credit to both ancient and modern ideas of merit, perhaps even suggesting, as he normally would, a kind of progress:

> Among the ancients, the heroes in philosophy, as well those in war and patriotism, have a grandeur and force of sentiment, which astonishes our narrow souls, and is rashly rejected as extravagant and supernatural. They, in their turn, I allow, would have had equal reason to consider as romantic and incredible, the degree of humanity, clemency, order, tranquillity, and other social virtues, to which . . . we have attained in modern times. . . . Such is the compensation, which nature, or rather education, has made in the distribution of excellencies and virtues, in those different ages. (*EPM*, 256–57)

Hume normally ascribes a superiority in sentiment to the moderns and in consonance with his age regards primitive virtues with suspicion. In this particular instance, however, the attractions of the rugged ancients proved too strong. One can see in Hume's language where his sympathies lie. Can one believe that the greatness of "heroes," the "grandeur and force of sentiment," on the one hand, remain in balance with "humanity, clemency, order, tranquillity" on the other? There is the suggestion that we moderns with "our narrow souls" have no longer an ability to experience the highest sensibility. And Hume's choice of the word "romantic" to distinguish modern achievements is revealing, for he always uses the word to imply contempt. Without question he found very moving that greatness of mind so common in ancient poetry and history.

Nonetheless, Hume was not on the side of Ancients over Moderns. He considered history progressive and normally much preferred the situation and culture of modern Europe to any other imaginable. It is just that among the ancients are found the greatest number of larger-than-life heroes. Their very remoteness makes them the stuff of legends and mythology, of obvious exaggeration and embellishment. Hume was too much of a skeptic not to concede, even while praising these heroes of old, that they were impossible ideals: "These pretensions [i.e., claims], no doubt, when stretched to the utmost, are by far too magnificent for human nature" (*EPM*, 256). Yet we may nevertheless be stirred by such magnificence, by a greatness to which human nature may aspire. His own portrayal of the hero of feeling shows how.

As a summation, let us sketch this figure whose embodiment in historical characters we shall see later in the chapter. He, or she, exhibits the usual qualities of Humean virtue discussed before, such as worldly prominence, wit, and of course tender sensibility, but one quality is outstanding—greatness of mind. Since this greatness is revealed only by adversity, the hero will always be tested by some conflict that usually ends with his death. Greatness of mind is established by two criteria. The first is that the hero never surrenders to weakness or abject despair. In the essay "Of Tragedy," this superiority to adversity becomes the touchstone of heroic behavior, and it is also a source of tragic emotion. Hume blames religious art in particular for representing "such horrible subjects as crucifixions and martyrdoms, where nothing appears but tortures, wounds, executions, and passive suffering, without any action or affection." Instead Hume prescribes a rather more pleasing and, for him, moving spectacle: "Even the common sentiments of compassion require to be softened by some agreeable affection, in order to give a thorough satisfaction to the audience. The mere suffering of plaintive virtue, under the triumphant tyranny and oppression of vice, forms a disagreeable spectacle" (*E*, 224). What Hume is saying is paradoxical, perhaps: essentially it is more moving to see a hero scorn and thereby overcome his suffering than to see him overwhelmed by it. Even as early as the *Treatise*, while discussing another subject, Hume put his finger on this paradox:

> A man, who is not dejected by misfortunes, is the more lamented on account of his patience; and if that virtue extends so far as utterly to remove all sense of uneasiness, it still farther encreases our compassion. When a person of merit falls into what is vulgarly esteem'd a great misfortune, we form a notion of his condition; . . . entirely overlooking that greatness of mind, which elevates him above such emotions, or only considering it so far as to encrease our admiration, love and tenderness for him. (*T*, 370)

But greatness of mind does not end with the hero's fortitude, a stance that might make him appear cold and inhuman. If superior to his own suffering, in the climactic moment of his own trial he responds deeply to the grief and suffering of others, and this is the second criterion that distinguishes greatness of mind. This quality will appear prominently in the great scenes of Hume's own sentimental writing.

The Generous Tears of History

Of all Hume's works, it can be argued that the *History of England* is his only attempt at practical moral instruction. To be sure, the second *Enquiry* contains paeans to virtue and luminous examples of noble conduct, but it lacks a quality that Hume considered indispensable for complete emotional impact: what he usually terms making a reader "interested" in the fortunes of others, a sense of the word that means being caught up in or emotionally concerned and involved with the fortunes of others.[18] At the end of his essay "Of History," for instance, he recommends that genre for its ability to inculcate virtue better than poetry, philosophy, or common life. Poetry sometimes does not distinguish vicious from virtuous passion; philosophy is either cold and abstract or cleverly heterodox; common life obscures perspective, making every experience egocentric. "But . . . the historians have been, almost without exception, the true friends of virtue, and have always represented it in its proper colours. . . . The writers of history, as well as the readers, are sufficiently interested in the characters and events, to have a lively sentiment of blame or praise; and, at the same time, have no particular interest or concern to pervert their judgment" (*E*, 567–68).

It would seem that pure sympathy, unimpeded by personal or factional bias, is the common experience of both historian and reader, and we have already considered the moral benefit of sympathy. There is a passage in the second *Enquiry* even more emphatic in its recommendation of true history as a vehicle of moral instruction:

> There is no necessity, that a generous action, barely mentioned in an old history or remote gazette, should communicate any strong feelings of applause and admiration. Virtue, placed at such a distance, is like a fixed star, which, though to the eye of reason it may appear as luminous as the sun in his meridian, is so infinitely removed as to affect the senses, neither with light nor heat. Bring this virtue nearer, by our acquaintance or connexion with the persons, or even by an eloquent recital of the case; our hearts are immediately caught, our sympathy enlivened, and our cool approbation converted into the warmest sentiments of friendship and regard. (*EPM*, 230)

In his letters we find Hume thinking of historical subjects in terms of their capacity to be "interesting." For that reason he counseled William Robertson to abandon his plans to write on Charles V—"your hero . . . is not very interesting"—but highly praised Robertson's portrayal of Mary, Queen of Scots, precisely for being "interesting."[19] And it is significant that Hume himself began writing history with the subject he chose: "I esteem this Period [the Stuart era], both for signal Events & extraordinary Characters, to be the most interesting in modern History" (*L*, 1:193). Clearly all of Hume's theoretical principles, his own conception of history, as well as his choice of subject support the use of history for moral education. Now let us see how he used the power of sympathy in his historical writings to shape his readers' sensibility.[20]

We have seen that viewing human life with complete sympathy and understanding is the source of moral perception. The first goal of the historian is to illustrate by his own example how such a vision is achieved. He must himself be an individual of large views and wide experience, of reason to be sure, but most of all, of tender sensibility. Fully convinced of what he says, he takes on the power of the ancient orator, who "by the force of his own genius and eloquence, first inflamed himself with anger, indignation, pity, sorrow; and then communicated those impetuous movements to his audience" (*E*, 104). He must express horror at human cruelty and self-deception, as Hume does at the Jerusalem massacre. He must respond with sincere but elevated feeling at scenes of "noble courageous despair" (*E*, 224), shedding "a generous Tear for the Fate of Charles I, and the Earl of Strafford" (*MOL*, 613).

Most exemplary of all, he will look with magnanimous sympathy on the misfortunes of even those whose principles and conduct he deplores. Although it may not have required of Hume much of an effort to pity the "misguided" Archbishop Laud, as "this old infirm prelate" became victim to the "vengeance and bigotry" (*H*, 5:458) of the Puritan extremists, it costs rather more to sympathize with the regicides when their turn comes to receive more deserving punishment:

> The general indignation, attending the enormous crime, of which these men had been guilty, made their sufferings the subject of joy to the people: But in the peculiar circumstances of that action, in the prejudices of the times, as well as in the behaviour of the criminals, a mind seasoned with humanity, will find a plentiful source of compassion and indulgence. (*H*, 6:160)

In fact, the entire *History of England* will not yield one instance of Hume exulting over the misfortunes or punishment of any person, even those he obviously disliked. The treatment of James II is particularly touching. James may have been inflexible and bigoted, Hume may have rejoiced at the Glorious Revolution dethroning him, but in a wave of compassion stirred by the plight of the king, deserted by officers sworn to defend him and even by some closest to him like his daughter Anne, Hume's sympathy takes him to the king's side:

> He burst into tears, when the first intelligence of [her desertion] was conveyed to him. . . . The nearer and more intimate concern of a parent laid hold of his heart; when he found himself abandoned in his uttermost distress by a child, and a virtuous child, whom he had ever regarded with the most tender affection. "God help me," cried he, in the extremity of his agony, "my own children have forsaken me!" It is indeed singular, that a prince, whose chief blame consisted in imprudences, and misguided principles, should be exposed, from religious antipathy, to such treatment as even Nero, Domitian, or the most enormous tyrants, that have disgraced the records of history, never met with from their friends and family. (H, 6:513)

One might well term this the stance of the humane, weeping historian. Hume shows himself moved by the spectacle of the forsaken king and encourages his readers to resist "religious antipathy" and to share his compassion for James.

Again and again Hume guides the reader's response by his own example, insisting all along that humane feeling supersedes every other consideration. Take this apology for what some might regard as extraneous or unnecessary—that is, Hume's inclusion of the duke of Ormond's elevated sentiment at the loss of his son, the illustrious earl of Ossory: "These particularities may appear a digression; but it is with pleasure, I own, that I can relax myself for a moment in the contemplation of these humane and virtuous characters, amidst that scene of fury and faction, fraud and violence, in which at present our narration has unfortunately engaged us" (H, 6:411).[21] What matter the form or decorum of history, when noble feelings are aroused? Hume seems almost to renounce his task of recording the history of those times because it would appear to threaten the tender sensibility of a good man. At the very least he must celebrate those examples of moral greatness he finds.[22]

For contemporary readers Hume's History often had the effect he desired. Philosophes like Friedrich Grimm may have praised it for its intellectual detachment: "M. Hume proves by his example that the writing of history belongs by right to the philosophers, exempt from prejudice and from passion."[23] Yet more common readers admired it for its passion, for its stirring inculcation of morality, for its ability to make the reader emotional. As she writes to Hume, the Comtesse de Boufflers claims, at least, to have come under his power: "Je ne say point de termes qui puissent vous rendre ce que jeprouve en lisant cet ouvrage. Je me sens attendrie, transportée, et l'émotion quil me cause est en quelque facon penible par sa continuité. Il eleve l'ame, il remplit le coeur de sentimens dhumanite et de bienfaisance. . . . Il anime d'un noble emulation, . . . en un mot c'est une source feconde de morale et dinstructions, presentées avec des couleurs si vives qu'on croit les voir pour la premiere fois." ["I know no words to express how I felt while reading that work. I was moved, transported, and the emotion which it engendered is, in some manner, painful in its continuance. It elevates the soul and fills the heart with sentiments of humanity and benevolence. . . . It animates the reader with a noble emulation. . . . In a word, it is a rich mine of morality and of instruction, presented in colors so bright, that we believe we see them for the first time."][24] Had he described the ideal reaction to his *History,* Hume could probably not have said it better himself.

On a rather less elevated plane, we can go to Hume's ebullient young countryman James Boswell, for whom a period of illness had provided the opportunity to become Hume's pupil: "I have now one great satisfaction, which is reading Hume's *History.* It entertains and instructs me. It elevates my mind and excites noble feelings of every kind." The circumstances surrounding Boswell's response may well devaluate his noble enthusiasm: the youthful rake had been forced to abstain from all high living and social intercourse while recovering from a bout of gonorrhea, apparently contracted from his liaison with the fair actress Louisa, an arrangement from which he had "expected at least a winter's safe copulation."[25] Yet we need not doubt the sincerity of Boswell's testimony. Perhaps in its own amusing way the story reminds us of the frequent gap between emotional rhetoric and reality. Still, if we never live up to the glorious visions of a sentimental humanity, who is to say that some degree of compassion and nobility— sentiments that may not otherwise have come to the fore—is not the product of a literature of tears?

At this point we might well pause and ask ourselves precisely how the emotionalism generated by Hume's *History,* or by any other kind of sentimental literature for that matter, is supposed to shape the sensibility of others. The first difficulty comes of course in saying precisely what we mean by morality, and perhaps we must abandon from the outset the word "precisely" in discussions of this nature. We are talking primarily of Hume's own morality, a conception whose outline will require the rest of this book to suggest, even though his general moral preferences and opinions are familiar to any student of Hume or to anyone who reads through something like the second *Enquiry*.

But back to the initial question: how would emotionalism in literature contribute to morality, as Hume understood morality? Hume never spelled out the answer. In his day the assumption that strong feelings were somehow always virtuous was rarely challenged. Still, we can arrive at a working explanation of why sentimental writing is didactic. On the premise that our natural passions are to be valued and trusted, Hume's *History* provides a kind of laboratory in which those passions can be isolated and strengthened, while all the factors that inhibit or pervert those passions can be identified and marked, we might say, with warning labels. Hume believed that we will inevitably pity and help those in need, tolerate those who differ from us, work to make existence more comfortable and satisfying for ourselves and others, and finally even entertain a vision that human civilization is perfectible and that human beings are wonderfully capable of sacrifice and love—all this on the condition that people are not distracted or corrupted by some form of intellectual blindness, some ideological mania, or by distrust and fear, which are for Hume the sins of little faith. To put the matter simply, admittedly oversimply, I think that Hume saw history—a literature whose "truth" we are more apt to believe prima facie than any other kind—as making it possible for us to feel pity and love as we look on someone like James II, despite all else, and as showing us the dignity, the beauty, that life is capable of rising to in spite of apparent defeat, a vision implicit in his portrayal of the hero of feeling, as described in the final sections of this chapter.

There are two sides to Hume's genius. One is the philosophical theorist who gives us a universe whose pattern we cannot understand and whose future we cannot predict, a universe of inexplicably ricocheting billiard balls and botched worlds created by third-rate gods; the other is the shaping historian and moralist who argues for the nobility of human nature by appealing to human emotion, who encourages us to see that whatever and wherever divinity might be it must be enacted in human terms. And Hume himself indicated the priority and indeed the relation of the two sides: "Be a philosopher; but, amidst all your philosophy, be still a man" (*EHU*, 9).

Embodiments of Heroic Sensibility

In this and the concluding section we shall consider Hume's efforts to exploit the sentimental dimensions of certain historical figures. No creature of flesh and blood ever makes a perfect hero, but we shall see Hume making the most of his material, shaping it for didactic purposes. We meet four types of heroic sensibility: Mary, Queen of Scots; Charles I; the earl of Strafford; and, in the last section, the marquess of Montrose. It is not surprising that all but Mary are part of the Stuart volumes, that period Hume called "the most interesting in modern History" (*L*, 1:193).[26]

From her time to the present, the life of Mary, Queen of Scots, has inspired partisan biography, bitter controversy, not to mention romantic and emotional legends and art. Hume's attitude toward Mary is complex, marked by some ambivalence.[27] He thought the evidence implicated her in her husband's murder and perhaps also in plots against Queen Elizabeth's life. Hence she was stained by enormous guilt. But she was a charming and beautiful woman, a queen of signal accomplishments and distinguished royal connections. She possessed spirit and courage—certainly, greatness of mind. No wonder he would find her sympathetic, especially at her execution, an event contrived with duplicity by Elizabeth and her courtiers, and with doubtful legality. My focus will be on that event, replete with the drama of both tender and dreadful emotion and with lessons of morality.

The account of Mary's execution runs some eight pages in the *History* (*H*, 4:245–52), and Hume follows his sources fairly closely, particularly John Strype, William Camden, and Samuel Jebb.[28] His version of the story may therefore appear to be the usual one. If, for example, one were to compare Hume's account with that of William Robertson, who wrote and published his independently in the same year as Hume did, there would appear no egregious differences in narration. As a matter of fact, in letters Hume praised Robertson's account of Mary—"her singular catastrophe is rendered truly lamentable and tragical; and the reader cannot forbear shedding tears for her fate, at the same time he blames her conduct" (*L*, 1:344)—and he even defended Robertson's handling of this delicate subject:

I cannot agree that Robertson is guilty of any Inconsistence. Why might not Mary be seduced into many Imprudences & even some Crimes; & yet possess many Accomplishments which, joined to her singular Misfortunes, render her a proper Object of Compassion? I know of no Story more pathetically wrote than that of Anthony & Cleopatra by Plutarch; yet these were far from being innocent Persons. It is a singular and a very commendable Piece of Art in our Friend, to make the Princess an interesting Object, even while he represents her criminal.[29]

Such a defense certainly suggests that Hume would present the very same Mary as Robertson. Not so, however. Closer examination reveals that Hume has de-emphasized or suppressed certain details, given others greater prominence, and added interpretive commentary. These touches urge the narrative toward that thematic conclusion and emotional effect Hume desires.

Religious detail saturates the whole episode. As many would see it, Mary was a martyr to Roman Catholicism, and her own strong religious faith was undoubtedly a mainstay during her trying ordeal. Protestant accounts like those of Robertson do not honor her as a martyr but do fully report her devout Catholic observances, including her prayers, and her use of prayer beads and an ornate ivory crucifix. Hume by contrast downplays the Catholic detail. Mary's frequent prayers and holy ejaculations are either unmentioned or briefly paraphrased, in spite of the fact that these details are prominent in Hume's sources. Hume does include the consecrated host sent to Mary by the Pope, but that detail highlights her "want of a priest and confessor" (H, 4:247), heartlessly denied her by the Protestant agents of Queen Elizabeth. He does mention the crucifix at one point, but its presence allows him to reflect on the malice of the earl of Kent, who calls it "that popish trumpery" (H, 4:250), and on Mary's superiority to the earl's baiting. Still, unless there is some didactic advantage in including references to Mary's religious beliefs and practices, Hume makes as little of her faith as he can. In the other accounts Mary quiets her people with the sign of the cross; in Hume the cross disappears as she puts "her finger upon her lips, as a sign of imposing silence upon them; and having given them her blessing, desire[s] them to pray for her" (H, 4:251). And at the fatal moment, head on the block, when all sources record her saying the psalm "In thee, O Lord, do I trust, let me never be confounded" and the prayer "Into thy Hands, O Lord, I commend my Spirit," Hume writes instead, "She laid herself down, without any sign of fear or trepidation; and her head was severed from her body. . . ."

(*H*, 4:251).[30] It is not that Hume entirely suppresses the fact of Mary's devotion, but he certainly makes it more subdued and rational—and less zealously Catholic, less central.

One aspect of the religious dimension serves his purpose very well, however. If he minimizes the queen's Catholic martyrdom, he magnifies the extreme Protestant zeal that hardens men's hearts and thus warps their moral sense. Hume never misses a chance to play up the cruel piety of the two earls and of the dean of Peterborough, provided her instead of a Catholic priest. The dean attempts to instruct her in the ways of the true Protestant faith, a malicious torment in her last hour. Hume may have slighted the text of Mary's prayers and devotions, but he includes a long paraphrase of the dean's "unseasonable exhortation," as found in Strype, and Hume observes: "The terms, which he employed, were, under colour of pious instructions, cruel insults on her unfortunate situation; and besides their own absurdity, may be regarded as the most mortifying indignities, to which she had ever yet been exposed" (*H*, 4:249). The harangue of the dean continues until "even the two earls perceived, that it was fruitless to harass her any farther with theological disputes; and they ordered the dean to desist" (*H*, 4:250). Most sources do not give the dean's speeches at all, and the Protestant clergyman Robertson even regards the dean's ministrations as seemly and compassionate: "Then the dean of Peterborough began a devout discourse, suitable to her present condition, and offered up prayers to Heaven in her behalf."[31] Hume of course has a polemical intention in his presentation. He wishes to stress how insidious and repellent spiritual zeal can be. It threatens and sometimes poisons benevolence; it makes people inhumane.

And who could be unmoved by this scene of pathos and sublimity? Hume fully exploits the sentimental potential of the story. Sighs and tears abound as the retainers of Mary, the tender-hearted spectators, the historian, and the reader look on this great drama. Indeed, Hume frames the scene of execution with a crowd of spectators whose sympathetic responses presumably echo in the hearts of historian and reader alike—by implication, in every uncorrupted heart:

> She then passed into another hall, where was erected the scaffold, covered with black; and she saw, with an undismayed countenance, the executioners, and all the preparations of death. The room was crowded with spectators; and no one was so steeled against all sentiments of humanity, as not to be moved when he reflected on her royal

dignity; considered the surprising train of her misfortunes, beheld her mild but inflexible constancy, recalled her amiable accomplishments, or surveyed her beauties, which, though faded by years, and yet more by her afflictions, still discovered themselves in this fatal moment. (*H*, 4:249)

The foregoing passage stands on one side of the execution scene. On the other side stands this:

[The executioner] instantly held [her head] up to the spectators, streaming with blood and agitated with the convulsions of death: The dean of Peterborow alone exclaimed, "So perish all queen Elizabeth's enemies:" The earl of Kent alone replied "Amen:" The attention of all the other spectators was fixed on the melancholy scene before them; and zeal and flattery alike gave place to present pity and admiration of the expiring princess. (*H*, 4:251)

The image is terrible, perhaps overwhelming enough to threaten a sympathetic response.[32] (But it is worth considering, too, that Hume's readers were more accustomed to public executions and their attendant horrors than we are.) Yet the image could have been more terrible still, for Hume has excluded certain details found in his sources that are bizarre, even grisly: the three strokes of the ax needed to sever the head; the dropping of the head by accident, the executioner grasping a wig instead of Mary's hair; and his displaying her head on a platter. Jebb (p. 357) also includes this detail: "Her little dog was observ'd to have crept under her cloaths, and would not be remov'd but by force; and afterwards would not depart from the body, but came and lay between the head and shoulders." In sentimental literature one might well expect a touch like this, and we may wonder why Hume rejected it. But Hume wants nothing to detract from the awful solemnity of the scene. He clearly does what he can to heighten Mary's dignity, an effect that would be overpowered by this macabre imagery. Mary deserves a dramatic clean stroke of the ax, not a clumsy, horrible butchery. Likewise, before describing the execution, Hume displays "her beauties, which, though faded by years, and yet more by her afflictions, still discovered themselves in this fatal moment." Consider how different she appears in Strype (p.558): she was ". . . of stature tall, of body corpulent, round-shouldered, her face fat and broad, double-chinned, with hazel eyes, . . . [and with] borrowed hair."

But Hume does make the final image strong enough to drive home a moral. Other accounts mention the dean's and the earl's exclamations somewhat routinely, as if their voiced approval were a matter of course and necessity. Here is Jebb (p. 357): "The Executioner lift up the Head, and said, *God save the Queen*; and the Dean replied, *So let Queen Elizabeth's enemies perish*. The Earl of Kent approach'd the body, and said in a lower voice, *May such end happen to all the Queen's and the Gospel's enemies*." Hume's version is generally true to his sources, but he has taken some license with details. From the chorus he removes the executioner, whom we may suppose a blind instrument of cruelty. Hume concentrates the heartless emotion of revenge in the two religious tormentors, shortening their speeches, giving the dean the holy prayer and the earl a simple but wonderfully ironical "amen." Hume's addition of "alone" after each response emphasizes that the bigoted dean and earl are the only ones indifferent to this drama. As every other human creature reacts with natural emotion, the indifference of these zealots is especially vivid and chilling.

One other aspect of Mary's final hours Hume must have found very moving. She comports herself with that dignity, self-possession, and courage that Hume refers to as "greatness of mind" and to which he attributes the sublime power of heroic sensibility. Hume did not of course invent this characteristic of Mary; all sources portray her as resigned, courageous, and even cheerful.[33] But Hume was surely stirred by this behavior, and his version magnifies it. Surrounded by servants who are beside themselves with grief, she consoles them. During the last supper, "her wonted chearfulness did not even desert her," Hume stresses, and "she comforted her servants under the affliction which overwhelmed them" (*H*, 4:246). Hume is quite careful that Mary show no sign of weakness or faintness of heart. In Strype (p. 558) she "wept bitterly, and became silent" when informed of her death sentence and impending execution, but Hume ignores this detail. When she must lean for support on the guards, as Strype and Camden report, Hume adds that it was "because of an infirmity in her limbs" (*H*, 4:247), making her deserve our compassion all the more. Her only loss of temper comes when the earl of Kent persists in refusing to allow servants "to attend her at her death." " 'I am cousin to your queen,' cried she, 'and descended from the blood-royal of Henry VII. and a married queen of France, and an anointed queen of Scotland.' " But this spirited outburst is obviously not from weakness but rather from affronted greatness: ". . . her mind, which had fortified itself against the terrors of death, was affected by this indignity, for which she was not prepared" (*H*, 4:248–49). By contrast, in Jebb (p. 352) her tearful protest sounds merely like a woman's tactic to get her way. And without doubt Mary controls the scene of execution, for she is always undismayed, sometimes indifferent, superior to the importunities and insults of her persecutors, taking charge, as it were, of the proceedings, even capable of a bon mot as she prepares to meet her death: "She now began, with the aid of her two women, to disrobe herself; and the executioner also lent his hand, to assist them. She smiled, and said, That she was not accustomed to undress herself before so large a company, nor to be served by such valets" (H, 4:250–51).

It all fits Hume's formula for greatness of mind. A character remains superior to adversity and is moved only by the grief of others. In this light it is interesting to examine how Hume retouches one of the most heart-rending scenes in this drama. Most accounts record that Mary's steward Sir Andrew Melvil met her on the way to the hall of execution, fell down on his knees bewailing her fate, and was comforted by Mary, who joined him in weeping. It is a picture of great sentimental possibility, but Strype (pp. 559–60) provides the most detail, including the speeches of Melvil and Mary. Hume transcribes all of Strype's moving account, heightening it with stage directions like the initial description of Melvil:

> Here she also found Sir Andrew Melvil, her steward, who flung himself on his knees before her; and, wringing his hands, cried aloud, "Ah, Madam! unhappy me! what man was ever before the messenger of such heavy tidings as I must carry, when I shall return to my native country, and shall report, that I saw my gracious queen and mistress beheaded in England?" His tears prevented farther speech; and Mary too felt herself moved, more from sympathy than affliction. "Cease, my good servant," said she, "cease to lament: Thou hast cause rather to rejoice than to mourn. . . ." [Then follows a long speech taken from Strype, with a few stylistic changes.] After these words, reclining herself, with weeping eyes, and face bedewed with tears, she kissed him. "And so," said she, "good Melvil, farewel: Once again, farewel, good Melvil; and grant the assistance of thy prayers to thy queen and mistress." (H, 4:247–48)

The poses of the actors—Melvil on his knees; Mary reclining, weeping, and embracing her steward—illustrate that exaggerated style of eighteenth-century acting and history painting that would mark the great scene. Hume is faithful to Strype, but he improves him. Take Mary's final speech in Strype (p. 560): "And so dissolving herself again into tears, said, Good Melvin [sic], farewell. And with her eyes and her cheeks all besprinkled with tears, as they were, she kissed him; saying again, Farewell, good Melvin, and pray for thy mistress and queen." Hume adds Mary's reclining position and moves the interruption of more tears and a farewell kiss to a point before the speech, thus concentrating the incantatory repetition and realizing a poetical chiasmus: "good Melvil, farewel: once again, farewel, good Melvil. . . ." Most striking of all, here is a heroic woman, herself facing a horrible death, having to comfort a man. She weeps, too, but "more from sympathy than affliction." How revealing it is that this comment is entirely Hume's interpolation, rounding off for him a picture of true greatness of mind.[34]

It is of significance, finally, that Queen Mary was not a figure Hume had treated very sympathetically at all until her execution. And even after writing his account of Mary, he apologized for being swayed by sympathy. To his fellow historian Robertson, he wrote: "I am afraid, that you, as well as myself, have drawn Mary's character with too great softenings. She was undoubtedly a violent woman at all times" (*L*, 1:299). His handling of her execution thus indicates how sensitive he was to the possibility of "interesting" scenes, especially those involving the great emotions, and how he made his *History* a vehicle of the great scene.

His treatment of Charles I has been viewed as the centerpiece of his sentimental or sympathetic characterizations.[35] Hume himself so identified his Charles when he remarked in *My own Life* that he had been maligned as the "Man who had presumed to shed a generous Tear for the Fate of Charles I, and the Earl of Strafford" (*MOL*, 613), or when in letters he admitted: "I did indeed endeavour to paint the King's Catastrophe . . . in as pathetic a manner as I cou'd: And to engage me, needed I any other Motive, than my Interest as a Writer, who desires to please & interest his Readers?" (*L*, 1:222) (Also see the third epigraph to this chapter or the comment earlier in the chapter about Clarendon's avoidance of Charles's execution.) And many readers have found the story of Charles extremely touching and inspiring.[36] It is a fitting tribute that Louis XVI, upon learning of his death sentence, requested a copy of Hume's Charles I, as Louis's valet Cléry reports: '*Le roi m'ordonna de chercher dans la bibliothèque, le volume de* l'Histoire d'Angleterre *où se trouve la mort de Charles I*er: *il en fit la lecture les jours suivants.*" ["The king ordered me to look in the library for the volume of the *History of England* where the death of Charles I is found: he spent the following days reading it."][37] Louis would appear to be using Hume's narrative as a script for his own imminent tragic performance. Hume's shaping of an historical hero becomes the prototext of another historical self-fashioning.

As with Mary, Queen of Scots, Charles I was not Hume's perfect hero, even though he approved of Charles's character decidedly more than he did Mary's. For one thing, despite his unjustified reputation as a Tory historian, Hume was in fact very appreciative of the liberty wrested from the king's hand by the fractious Parliament. He hated the Parliament's hypocrisy and double-dealing, but he recognized and celebrated this age for giving birth to a strong House of Commons, the cornerstone of an enlightened, balanced government.[38] Hence despite the many other factors making him sympathetic with Charles, politically the best Hume could do is excuse him for being the enemy of liberty. As a leader Charles was far from being ideal; he lacked foresight, discretion, and the ability to act with vigor and decision. Charles was not totally passive and weak, else he would surely have been damned in Hume's eyes, but his activity was ill-timed, his strength evident only under severe trial. Even his moral qualities, though unquestionably praiseworthy, were for Hume's liking too "tinctured with superstition" (H, 5:542), with too deep and doctrinaire a religiosity. (Admittedly, Hume had trouble responding favorably to extremely religious people.) Of course, Hume did not make light of Charles's sincere faith. At best he fashioned it to his own specifications: "The great source whence the king derived consolation amidst all his calamities, was undoubtedly religion; a principle, which, in him, seems to have contained nothing fierce or gloomy, nothing which enraged him against his adversaries, or terrified him with the dismal prospect of futurity. . . . He reposed himself with confidence in the arms of a being, who penetrates and sustains all nature" (H, 5:517–18). Such religious belief Hume could tolerate, but this credo sounds more like that of a latitudinarian or deist, not of Charles, as Hume surely knew. Thus Hume found much that would prevent the king from being his hero. As Hume pronounces in the character sketch, Charles "deserves the epithet of a good, rather than of a great man" (H, 5:542).[39]

Nevertheless, Charles was a king, a king with many eminent graces, talents, and personal qualities to recommend him. He may have had too grandiose a sense of royal prerogative, but he had acquired that hauteur from a long tradition in English government and especially from the practices of both Elizabeth and his father. His royal magnificence and power were threatened by a few popular leaders who were honorable and eloquent but by many more who were rude, fanatical upstarts. Hume may have been on the side of English liberty against royal prerogative, but he was certainly no Leveller. He respected patrician taste and values; he distrusted and often despised the *mobile vulgus*. The very thought of a noble and virtuous king being abused and finally murdered by low-born, half-mad extremists—religious hypocrites, to make matters worse—would be more than sufficient to make him join the royalist camp. What man of sensibility, of Hume's kind of sensibility, could resist shedding "a generous Tear" for such a king? It was not that Hume was recommending Charles as an ideal monarch; rather he was making him a very sympathetic figure. To shed a generous tear would be an act of great virtue, as Hume's account demonstrates.

Hume goes out of his way to make Charles sympathetic, and no scene is more heart-wrenching than that of an afflicted parent with his children. Charles is perfect in this role. Even in prosperity, his "domestic tenderness" (*H*, 5:282) is his salient virtue: "When we consider Charles as presiding in his court, as associating with his family, it is difficult to imagine a character at once more respectable and amiable. A kind husband, an indulgent father, a gentle master, a stedfast friend. . . ." (*H*, 5:220). When the king's fortunes change, Hume does not neglect to include scenes of him protecting his wife and caressing his children. Before his execution, we find him with his youngest son and daughter, the others having fled across the Channel (*H*, 5:539). Or in the army's captivity,

> his children were once allowed to visit him. . . . He had not seen the duke of Gloucester, his youngest son, and the princess Elizabeth, since he left London . . . nor the duke of York, since he went to the Scottish army before Newark. No private man . . . more passionately loved his family, than did this good prince; and such an instance of indulgence in the army was extremely grateful to him. Cromwell, who was witness to the meeting of the royal family, confessed, that he never had been present at so tender a scene. . . . (*H*, 5:504–05)

Hume does not describe the king's paternal affection directly: instead he registers it in the eyes of Oliver Cromwell. Is it not poignant that the arch-villain of the story should himself be present to verify the pathos? Under normal circumstances, and certainly later in time, no tender feeling could reach Cromwell's heart, steeled by ambition and religious zeal. But here is a scene so touching that for one moment even Cromwell is affected. The point is precisely that those uncorrupted by politics or religion would naturally pity King Charles. One does not have to be a royalist or Jacobite to do so. The humane historian everywhere leads his gentle reader to the desired response.

For Hume the sublime of feeling is stirred by greatness of mind. If Charles was far from ideal as a hero of action, he did possess this quality, or at least Hume's narrative by its reminders and interpolations ensures that he does. If greatness of mind is revealed only by extreme difficulties and suffering, then the hard lot of Charles had at least this compensation: "The resources of this prince's genius encreased in proportion to his difficulties; and he never appeared greater than when plunged into the deepest perils and distresses" (H, 5:384). As Hume never tires of insisting, from the time of the king's capture to his trial and execution, "the king . . . sustained, by his magnanimous courage, the majesty of a monarch" (H, 5:535). For example, Hume obviously admires the king as he calmly continues to play chess after just having received word that the Scots had betrayed him to the English army, and when he later receives the English commissioners with "the same grace and chearfulness, as if they had travelled on no other errand, than to pay court to him" (H, 5:490).[40] According to Hume, Charles knew how to play his part well: "It is confessed, that the king's behaviour, during this last scene of his life, does honour to his memory; and that, in all appearances before his judges, he never forgot his part, either as a prince or as a man" (H, 5:537). *Prince* and *man* sum up the duality of great emotion for Hume—the sublime and the pathetic.

And greatness of mind, as we have seen, is manifest when a hero is moved, not by his own suffering, but by the grief of others. In the following story, where the king appears most "justly the object of compassion," we find him both superior to his suffering and afflicted only by the misfortune of his supporters:

> The condition of the king, during this whole winter, was, to the last degree, disastrous and melancholy. . . . perhaps in no period of his life was he more justly the object of compassion: His vigour of mind, which, though it sometimes failed him in acting, never deserted him in his sufferings. . . . The affectionate duty . . . of his more generous friends, who respected his misfortunes and his virtues, as much as his dignity, wrung his heart with a new sorrow; when he reflected, that such disinterested attachment would so soon be exposed to the rigour of his implacable enemies. (H, 5:479)

It is hard not to suspect that Charles must have occasionally felt sorry for himself, too, but Hume's account would not seem to admit that possibility. Hume is careful to script the right part for his historical characters.

Hume's way of writing history is to shape the historical fact for a desired instructive or emotional impact. Several of the most sublime passages of sensibility clearly reflect this shaping. One passage records the king's reaction to the death of one of his heroic supporters, Sir Charles Lucas. It is meaningful that immediately preceding this episode is the story of Lucas's and his comrade Sir George Lisle's courageous indifference to their summary execution, and this statement honoring Lisle: "Thus perished this generous spirit, not less beloved for his modesty and humanity, than esteemed for his courage and military conduct." Then, "soon after, a gentleman appearing in the king's presence, clothed in mourning for Sir Charles Lucas; that humane prince, suddenly recollecting the hard fate of his friends, paid them a tribute, which none of his own unparalleled misfortunes ever extorted from him: He dissolved into a flood of tears" (*H*, 5:529). Heroic service to the king elicits a stirring and wholly fitting response. In this particular instance Charles is the very hero of feeling, and a hero of Hume's creation. Hume's source, Bulstrode Whitelocke, says only, "At the sight of a gentleman in mourning for Sir Charles Lucas, the king wept."[41]

The description of Charles's bidding his youngest son farewell is also instructive. The situation itself is pathetic, as the king attempts to warn a young child about the gravity of impending events:

> Holding [the young duke] on his knee, he said, "Now they will cut off thy father's head." At these words, the child looked very stedfastly upon him. "Mark! child, what I say: They will cut off my head! and perhaps make thee a king: But mark what I say: Thou must not be a king, as long as thy brothers, Charles and James, are alive. They will cut off thy brothers' heads, when they can catch them! And thy head too they will cut off at last! Therefore I charge thee, do not be made a king by them!" The duke, sighing, replied, "I will be torn in pieces first!" So determined an answer, from one of such tender years, filled the king's eyes with tears of joy and admiration. (*H*, 5:539)

Even the king is moved by this reflection in his small son of the king's own greatness of mind. By now it should not be surprising that Charles's "tears of joy and admiration," provoked by this "determined" answer, are Hume's own construction. His source says only, "Which falling so unexpectedly from one so young, it made the King rejoice exceedingly."[42]

As final sign of Hume's emotional involvement—by his own confession, his "Interest"—in writing the life of Charles, let us examine his version of what followed the king's beheading. Using the "words cannot describe" formula common among writers of overblown passion, he states, "It is impossible to describe the grief, indignation, and astonishment, which took place, not only among the spectators, who were overwhelmed with a flood of sorrow, but throughout the whole nation." The rapid transformation among the people from disloyalty and animosity, to love and adoration, wrought by the king's "misfortunes and magnanimity, his patience and piety" throughout his ordeal, had amazing results:

> On weaker minds, the effect of these complicated passions was prodigious. Women are said to have cast forth the untimely fruit of their womb: Others fell into convulsions, or sunk into such a melancholy as attended them to their grave: Nay some, unmindful of themselves, as though they could not, or would not survive their beloved prince, it is reported, suddenly fell down dead. (*H*, 5:540–41)

It is hardly characteristic of Hume, the philosopher or the historian, to publish miracles or to encourage credulity. Admittedly, he protects himself to some degree by his phrasing: "women are said" and "it is reported." But the passive voice and the absence of any documentation allow Hume to entertain the possibility that these stories were true; they were believed; they were part of the historical tradition. At any other time Hume would have rejected such miracle-mongering with scorn. Can one imagine that this passage in the *History* was written by the same man who wrote section 10, "Of Miracles," in the first *Enquiry*? In this case, however, the historian's sympathy with his subject compels him to exploit all means of hyperbole. Almost despite himself he is writing the crucifixion of Charles Martyr—yet, we might note, not one of those crucifixions in religious art "where nothing appears but . . . passive suffering, without any action or affection" (*E*, 224). How remarkable an ending to the life of one whom he is not willing to regard a few pages later, when writing more dispassionately about Charles's character, as a great man.[43]

Hume's accounts of both Mary and Charles show the extent to which he would go in developing the emotional dimensions of figures who were far from being truly heroic. Particularly in the case of Charles, Hume clearly shapes historical fact for sentimental purposes and in so doing becomes emotionally caught up in the hero of his own creation. Thus very much unlike himself in cooler, more reflective moments, Hume becomes something of an hagiographer, fervently displaying the cataclysm of regicide.

History, of course, does not normally furnish many examples of great characters whose lives also have emotional associations. The Earl of Strafford is another case in point. Hume's strong sympathy with him undoubtedly stems in part from his being, like Charles and Laud, the victim of Puritan wrath. That is not the whole of it, however. Strafford's life, even as Hume relates it, would seem to offer little evidence of greatness. Certainly there was no blemish either, for he was an honorable man who loyally served his king. But his exit from the stage has everything Hume could require in a powerful drama, like the kind he analyzes in "Of Tragedy." Hume presents Strafford eloquently exonerating himself and pointing tearfully at his children, his only cause of anguish and concern. Strafford has the magnanimity to offer himself as a sacrifice for his king, urging Charles to agree to his execution. During his walk to the scaffold, Strafford passes "the aged primate [Laud] dissolved in tears," himself expecting a similar death. But "Strafford, still superior to his fate, moved on with an elated countenance, and with an air even of greater dignity than what usually attended him." Hume must have been pleased to record that only "his mind, erect and undaunted," supported him: he lacked the usual consolations of glory, compassionate spectators—and, we wonder, religion?[44] But Hume finishes by calling Strafford "one of the most eminent personages that has appeared in England" (*H*, 5:326–27). That encomium derives from the strength of Hume's sympathy. Hume appears eager to find a true hero of feeling.

The Hero of Feeling

In the second *Enquiry* Hume had posited a kind of character so lofty and noble that like the heroes of old this figure, subsuming the smaller emotions into the great, becomes almost superhuman:

> The epithets *sociable, good-natured, humane, merciful, grateful, friendly, generous, beneficent,* or their equivalents, are known in all languages, and universally express the highest merit, which *human nature* is capable of attaining. Where these amiable qualities are attended with birth and power and eminent abilities, and display themselves in the good government or useful instruction of mankind, they seem even to raise the possessors of them above the rank of *human nature*, and make them approach in some measure to the divine. (*EPM*, 176)

Later he talks of courage in a way that surprisingly makes it the most stirring emotion to witness:

> this quality has a peculiar lustre, which it derives wholly from itself, and from that noble elevation inseparable from it. Its figure, drawn by painters and by poets, displays, in each feature, a sublimity and daring confidence: which catches the eye, engages the affections, and diffuses, by sympathy, a like sublimity of sentiment over every spectator. (*EPM*, 254)

Such magnificent courage seems far removed from the usual emotions of sensibility, but my purpose has been to argue in this chapter that Hume enlarged the complex of what eighteenth-century sentimentalists considered inspiring emotion. For Hume there is a great dimension as well as a little dimension of sensibility. And the great or sublime of sensibility radiates from what could be termed a hero of feeling.

Are there any such giants in Hume's *History*? Hume was not writing mythology, at least ostensibly, but now and then something resembling a demigod rises from his pages. William Wallace, a Scot "revered as the deliverer of his country," is one such character. Hume confesses that the legend of Wallace is probably a romantic fabrication: "[His] valourous exploits are the object of just admiration, but have been much exaggerated by the traditions of his countrymen." A few lines later his countryman Hume gives this much-exaggerated characterization of Wallace: "He was endowed with gigantic force of body, with heroic courage of mind, with disinterested magnanimity, with incredible patience, and ability to bear hunger, fatigue, and all the severities of the seasons" (*H*, 2:125–26). We note also that Hume's customary term "greatness of mind" has swollen into "heroic courage of mind." Later on, true to the spirit of Scots legend, not fact, Hume repeats the noble speech of Wallace to Robert Bruce, which words inspired Bruce to become another fabled Scottish hero. In a footnote Hume admits that the incident is probably apocryphal, "authors of good credit" agreeing that Bruce was not even near Wallace at the time (*H*, 2:131n.). Nonetheless, Hume decides to follow the Scottish instead of the more reliable English historians in immortalizing Robert Bruce (*H*, 2:131–40). Sometimes, as we have seen, Hume will abandon his normal care in establishing historical truth to tell a morally invigorating story. It is hard not to follow the hero of feeling where he leads.

The figure approaching this eminence most nearly is another

Scot, "the gallant marquess of Montrose" (*H,* 6:24). Here is a hero almost ready-made for Hume's purpose. Everything would seem to set him off as a different kind of being from the dwarfs of the modern age. One would have to search among the sublime ancients for his type. In France he "became acquainted with the famous cardinal de Retz; and that penetrating judge celebrates him in his memoirs as one of those heroes, of whom there are no longer any remains in the world, and who are only to be met with in Plutarch" (*H,* 6:20). It is an invaluable endorsement of Hume's own characterization.

We need not follow Montrose through his fortunes or attend him during his final days, betrayed by a friend, vilified, persecuted, and barbarously executed by the Scots Covenanters. The ingredients of his glory are what we have seen before: dignity, eloquence, wit, cheerfulness, honor; concern for others, especially his king, before himself; and most of all, undaunted courage. His fate moves the people to tears, but not the Covenanters, inflamed by bigotry and zeal. As a focal point of sublime emotion, Montrose simply appears loftier than any other figure in Hume's *History.* His defiance of his tormentors assumes the form of heroic sentiment: " 'For my part . . . I am much prouder to have my head affixed to the place, where it is sentenced to stand, than to have my picture hang in the king's bed-chamber. So far from being sorry, that my quarters are to be sent to four cities of the kingdom; I wish I had limbs enow to be dispersed into all the cities of Christendom, there to remain as testimonies in favour of the cause, for which I suffer.' " Montrose turns that sentiment into poetry on the night before his execution, "a signal monument of his heroic spirit, and no despicable proof of his poetical genius" (*H,* 6:24). So that Montrose may be the perfect hero, Hume does not say that Montrose's eight-line poem is actually a prayer that his Maker finally recover the scattered parts of his body and "raise [him] with the just."[45]

Indeed, this cynosure begins to resemble some mythic creation of the epic. Montrose excels Hume's other exemplars of heroic sensibility in his contempt for the enemies who attempt to triumph over him. He far surpasses the others in the dominance of his character. It is a Hume swept away in admiration who applies the last brush strokes to the hero's portrait:

> Thus perished, in the thirty-eighth year of his age, the gallant marquess of Montrose; the man whose military genius, both by valour and conduct, had shone forth beyond any, which, during these civil

> disorders, had appeared in the three kingdoms. The finer arts, too, he
> had, in his youth, successfully cultivated; and whatever was sublime,
> elegant, or noble touched his great soul. Nor was he insensible to the
> pleasures either of society or of love. Something, however, of the *vast*
> and *unbounded* characterized his actions and deportment; and it was
> merely by an heroic effort of duty, that he brought his mind, impatient
> of superiority, and even of equality, to pay such unlimited submission
> to the will of his sovereign. (*H*, 6:24–25)

One could almost think that Achilles himself had stepped into
British history, and in cultivation and elegance Montrose in fact
eclipses the Greek. The "gallant marquess" embodies both the
sublime and pathetic of sensibility, but "the *vast* and *unbounded*"
mark him primarily as a sublime hero of feeling.

Nevertheless, that Hume would so fervently glorify a martial
hero, even one that scintillating, may seem to conflict with some
of his other values. There are other places in the *History* where he
suggests that these heroes have been overpraised, considering
what disruption and bloodshed they bring about: "The unhappy
prepossession, which men commonly entertain in favour of ambition, courage, enterprize, and other warlike virtues, engages generous natures, who always love fame, into such pursuits as
destroy their own peace, and that of the rest of mankind" (*H*,
5:51). But ten years before in the *Treatise* he had given a hint of
how this kind of hero could be put to use in the writing of history:

> Heroism or military glory, is much admir'd by the generality of man-
> kind. They consider it as the most sublime kind of merit. Men of cool
> reflection [like Hume, normally, one must imagine] are not so san-
> guine in their praises of it. The infinite confusions and disorder,
> which it has caus'd in the world, diminish much of its merit in their
> eyes. . . . But when we fix our view on the person himself, who is the
> author of all this mischief, there is something so dazling in his
> character, the mere contemplation of it so elevates the mind, that we
> cannot refuse it our admiration. The pain, which we receive from its
> tendency to the prejudice of society, is over-power'd by a stronger and
> more immediate sympathy. (*T*, 600–601)

Hence we might see Hume as not so much glorifying the warrior
Montrose as employing that hero's inevitable attraction in the
service of didactic history. Hume recognizes the power that the
sentimental sublime exercises on the human sensibility, and he
exploits that power again and again.

Just as Hume cites Alexander the Great with admiration in his

Enquiry on morals, he adds sublime passions to those emotions of pathos customarily associated with sentimentalism. Hume could not resist the attraction of what I have termed the sublime of sensibility. Moreover, this unusual manifestation of sensibility is a natural complement to a moral system whose embodiment, Cleanthes of the second *Enquiry*, is so quintessentially the man of the world, a paragon of social grace and enterprise. Yet Cleanthes remains lackluster, his merit wanting the burnish of action. The dazzling Montrose may be seen as a flesh-and-blood Cleanthes who has been magnificently tested and proven. Clearly, Hume's morality is informed with assumptions that stem from eighteenth-century benevolism. Clearly, too, Hume enlarged those assumptions to embrace ideas not usually part of the literature of feeling.

2

Religion and the "Peace of Society"

Upon the whole, I desire to take my Catalogue of Virtues from *Cicero's Offices*, not from the *Whole Duty of Man.*

—*L* (1739)

I have frequently had it in my Intentions to write a Supplement to *Gulliver,* containing the Ridicule of Priests.

—*L* (1751)

The worst speculative Sceptic ever I knew, was a much better Man than the best superstitious Devotee and Bigot.

—*L* (1751)

I believe I shall write no more History; but proceed directly to attack the Lord's Prayer & the ten Commandments & the single Cat[echism]; and to recommend Suicide & Adultery: And so persist, till it shall please the Lord to take me to himself.

—*NL* (1757)

Homo Religiosus

Hume's quarrel with religion is well-known.[1] In the *Dialogues Concerning Natural Religion* he subjected theological arguments, whether a priori or a posteriori, to a devastating scrutiny and whittled away the basis for any belief in a God who is more substantial than a mere possibility of a First Cause bearing *"some remote Analogy to human Intelligence"* (*D*, 260).[2] As we gather from the stimulating interplay of disputants in that work, Hume enjoyed the challenge of such argumentation; it was a subject that he could pursue with detachment and serenity of mind. Hume's real objection to religion, however, was not that it failed of proof, its conviction relying finally on faith, not reason. That was surely a matter about which he could afford to be indifferent or even amused. Rather, Hume's quarrel with religion stems from his claim that piety is an enemy of morality, and indeed the main enemy. This charge is iconoclastic, because the usual recommendation of religion, even by those who reject it otherwise, is that at least it makes people moral: Cleanthes advances this defense in the *Dialogues* (*D*, 251). Yet Hume attacks even this last bulwark of religious belief. Even on his deathbed he shocked James Boswell by his contempt for all aspects of religion, including its vaunted morality. According to Boswell's *Journal*, "He then said flatly that the morality of every religion was bad, and, I really thought, was not jocular when he said that when he heard a man was religious, he concluded he was a rascal, though he had known some instances of very good men being religious. This was just an extravagant reverse of the common remarks as to infidels."[3]

For a decade and a half—roughly from the late 1740s through the early 1760s—Hume was obsessed with religion and its relation to civilization. During these busy years he found other subjects for his pen, but religion dominated his writing. The second *Enquiry, A Natural History of Religion* (henceforth *NHR*), and the *Dialogues concerning Natural Religion* (written but not published during these years) come to mind. In the *History of England* (1754–62) likewise religion becomes a major concern. *NHR* and the *Dialogues* of course deal directly with religion; they are separate philosophical examinations of the subject, each in a different mode. But whether in the direct exposition of *NHR* or with the evasive irony of the *Dialogues*, Hume seems to reach no conclusion about religion and society. What is religion's place, if any? Is there a way to make religion useful or at least render it harmless? In both works Hume washes his hands of the problem. In *NHR* Hume and the enlightened reader "happily make [their] escape into the calm, though obscure regions of philosophy" (*NHR*, 95), where they may enjoy "a manly, steddy virtue, . . . [the] calm sunshine of the mind," before which "these spectres of false divinity never make their appearance" (*NHR*, 91). In the *Dialogues* we are left to choose between an anemic rational theology that cannot be proved or a revealed theology that is irrational and absurd. On such an untenable position the debate ends, with the youthful Pamphilus casting his vote for what he admits is the less probable but more comforting "truth" of Cleanthes' traditionalism. What hope is there, Hume seems to imply?

When writing the *History of England*, however, it was not as easy for Hume to play the philosopher and detach himself from the sticky problems involving religion in society. Such problems crop up again and again, and they insist on practical answers. The historian Hume was dealing with that majority of mankind whom the philosopher Hume would sometimes as soon forget. And the historian could not help seeing how this majority's actions, so often directed by crazed spiritualism, threaten the "calm sunshine of the mind," that retreat of philosophical indifference. Accordingly, the *History of England* suggests answers to this problem that will be found nowhere else in Hume's writings. I could not disagree more, then, with the opinion of Victor Wexler that "Hume failed to treat religion as a legitimate motive in influencing the course of English history . . . [and in the Middle Ages] paid only cursory attention to the role of religion and religious institutions."[4] I mean to demonstrate the contrary. Hume's practical discussion of the religious problem as well as its recommended solution will be the subject of this chapter.

Before I pursue that subject, however, it may be useful to examine the problem itself. Why indeed should religion bulk so large in human affairs? What explains its centrality in human experience and its power to change the course of history? For his answer Hume points to the very essence of human psychology: the fear of existence; ignorance of causes; the resulting desperation to find security in a hostile universe. Hume is therefore pessimistic that religious belief will simply disappear once philosophy brings its light, even in the unlikely event that clergymen should lose interest in proselytizing and intimidating helpless men and women. Religion's "root strikes deeper into the mind, and springs from the essential and universal properties of human nature" (*NHR*, 92). Hume emphasizes in *NHR* that it is one thing for physico-theologians, deists (Hume refers to them as genuine theists), and theodicean apologists to point upward to the splendor of Newtonian order, to the fiat of universal law and harmony celebrated by Alexander Pope:

> Nature, and Nature's Laws lay hid in Night.
> God said, *Let Newton be!* and All was Light.[5]

Mankind in fact is more disposed to look downward at the events of life, shrouded in darkness. People suffer pain and disappointment and dread the future, especially death. They sense mysterious and invisible power and anxiously seek some means of placating it: "No wonder, then, that mankind, being placed in such an absolute ignorance of causes, and being at the same time so anxious concerning their future fortunes, should immediately acknowledge a dependence on invisible powers, possest of sentiment and intelligence" (*NHR*, 34). This whole disposition of mind exacerbates their suspicions and fears and leads them to grasp any supposed remedy, however selfish or unworthy of reason, which promises to protect them. It is not a situation calculated to bring about that Humean ideal of a civilization marked by openmindedness, toleration, cheerfulness, service to others, and an enterprising concern with the things of this world.

Thus Hume speaks in *NHR*. In the *Dialogues* Philo stresses that this frantic search for protection does not finally result in happiness or peace of mind. "We find the tremendous [that is, causing trembling] Images to predominate in all Religions . . . [and] the Terrors of Religion commonly prevail above its Comforts." It is "no wonder" that religion-inspired fear "disjoints the ordinary Frame of the Mind, and throws it into the utmost Confusion . . . , [producing] that Gloom and Melancholy, so remarkable in all devout People" (*D*, 257–59). Furthermore, in the *History* we see the tangible result of this fear and melancholy as primitive pagans stand in awe of omens and chants, Roman Catholics tremble before relics and images, and Protestant extremists poison life itself with vainglorious sanctity and holy rage. Hume never doubts religion's power, even if for him that power is almost always malign. Perhaps the only "miracles" Hume records with any credulity involve that power. That irresistible military force assembled by William the Conqueror on the shores of Normandy was nearly undermined by religious terror: "These bold warriors, who despised real dangers, were very subject to the dread of imaginary ones." (*H*, 1:154). The only antidote for their debilitating fear was the delusion that Heaven had switched sides to favor them. Religion's ability to defeat reasonable expectations, indeed to determine history, will become apparent as this chapter unfolds.

Forms of Religion

Although Hume viewed all forms of popular religion with suspicion, he did not regard them all with equal hostility. Polytheism and monotheism have votaries with widely differing values and dispositions, and the remarkable variety of monotheisms produces similar divergence. Of the Episcopal Cavaliers and the Puritan Roundheads Hume remarks, "The manners of the two factions were as opposite as those of the most distant nations" (*H*, 6:141).[6] The "genius" (*H*, 5:131) of a particular religion is a concept very prominent in Hume's theory of religion, and it explains his preference of some forms over others.

Religious historians have often heralded the movement from polytheism to monotheism as progress, an emergence from the darkness of ignorance into the light of truth. Not so, Hume. First of all, he argues that there is no clear-cut progress at all, and the explanation of any preference for monotheism is hardly to be found in human reason. All evidence and probability suggest the same conclusion, that man's first religion was a crude, confused polytheism, and only much later did something approaching a more orderly and systematic monotheism develop, but not because of reason so much as because of man's predilection for exaggeration and flattery: fearful and fawning, he must always magnify his god of the moment and so arrives by chance at one mighty deity who displaces the others. The One-God's origin is thus ignoble, to say the least. Again and again we see how "some groveling and familiar notion of superior powers," like gods of sneezing and copulation (NHR, 27, 32n.), leads finally to a more perfect conception of divinity. Unfortunately, however, human beings can never keep their gaze riveted upward toward any spiritually abstract and perfect Creator, and so they sink back to a belief in demons and demigods unworthy of their former elevation. Hume sees popular religion as a cycle, rising and falling, or a "Flux and Reflux," as he terms it in the heading of section 8 in NHR. Thus monotheism's origin is impure, and even its highest reach is gained by a leap from the dirty earth of idiotic polytheism or idolatry, into which it falls again (see NHR, 58).

If the progress into monotheism is doubtful in its finality, it is doubtful even as progress. What comes as a greater shock to the reader of NHR is Hume's suggestion that polytheism may, after all, be the better form. How so? Hume's implicit endorsement of pagan idolatry is based on the light hold which that religion had on the lives of the ancients and on the energy and hope that grew out of Greek mythology, the offspring of a polyphiloprogenitive Zeus. Hume claims that men do not really believe in the absurdities of religious fables and dogma. They may try, but "nature is too hard for all their endeavours, and suffers not the obscure, glimmering light, afforded in those shadowy regions, to equal the strong impressions, made by common sense and by experience" (NHR, 74). But therein lies the difference between the two theisms, between the casually evolved, unsystematic, mythological religions and the scriptural, systematic, scholastic modern forms. The latter place the believer in an awkward position, strait-jacketed by codified dogma—which happens to be even more absurd, says Hume, than pagan beliefs—and thus tormented by doubt and guilt (*NHR,* sections 12–13). The monotheist cannot enjoy confident serenity, that quality *sine qua non* to Humean virtue. His primitive cousin the pagan, on the other hand, wears a much looser, more comfortably fitting religious mantle. Hume in fact repeatedly uses such a metaphor: pagan religion "hung loose upon the minds of men" (*NHR,* 80).[7] It follows that the ancient is happier, for the many fables of his religion, being at least plausible and certainly entertaining, do not make many demands on him or oppress him with guilt; he is freer to make the most of *this* life.

One concludes that Hume does not object to the spirit becoming flesh, as long as it is the flesh of a worldly Jupiter and not of an unworldly Jesus. For that matter, whether frolicking on earth or disporting himself on Olympus, Jove remains very human, quite in contrast to Jehovah, who is often very mysterious and unapproachable. Once again it is the genius of polytheism that gives it a strikingly different complexion from that of monotheism. The ancient mythology to Hume is inherently comical and absurd, and yet it makes for pleasant stories and even great art. It is vivifying and occasionally exemplary. We are hardly apt to give it much credence, but if we did, our mood would be happy and our behavior hedonistic at worst: "the fables of the pagan religion were, of themselves, light, easy, and familiar; without devils or seas of brimstone, or any objects, that could much terrify the imagination. Who could forbear smiling, when he thought of the loves of *Mars* and *Venus,* or the amorous frolics of *Jupiter* and *Pan?*" (*NHR,* 75) Hume laughs at the reason why the *Amphitrion* of Aristophanes was staged at Rome: "The *Romans* supposed, that, like all old letchers, [Jupiter] would be highly pleased with the rehearsal of his former feats of activity and vigour, and that no topic was so proper, upon which to flatter his pride and his vanity" (*NHR,* 41). But how pleasant a representation and how little apt to excite superstitious forebodings! Hume keeps the great Alexander in his place by mordant irony: "One great incitement to the pious *Alexander* in his warlike expeditions was his rivalship of *Hercules* and *Bacchus,* whom he justly pretended to have excelled" (*NHR,* 63). But the point, notwithstanding Hume's superior vantage, is that this "pious" emulation did contribute to human enterprise (as well as to drunkenness, but what of that?) Hume's title for this section is [A comparison of polytheism and theism] "With regard to courage or abasement,"[8] and there is no mistaking his celebration of the courage engendered by polytheism—that is, pagan idolatry.[9]

In one other respect, more important than any other, the genius of polytheism is preferable to all forms of monotheism. Polytheism disposes its votaries to tolerating other expressions of religion. Because of its light and genial hold on the faithful, because of its many gods, its lack of system and doctrine, its whole carelessness and inherent absurdity, its believers are hardly inclined to persecute those who differ from them. When there are many gods, there may be more, and who is to say which are finally more real than others? "The tolerating spirit of idolaters both in antient and modern times, is very obvious to any one. . . . So sociable is polytheism, that the utmost fierceness and aversion, which it meets with in an opposite religion, is scarce able to disgust it, and keep it at a distance" (*NHR*, 60–61). Such happy toleration is not, however, in the nature of monotheism. "Thou shalt have no other gods before me," and the devout believer is not disposed to look kindly on those who worship other gods or the same god in other ways. "The intolerance of almost all religions, which have maintained the unity of god, is as remarkable as the contrary principle of polytheists" (*NHR*, 60).

Overall, when one contrasts polytheism and monotheism one concludes of monotheism that *"corruptio optimi pessima"*—that "the corruption of the best things gives rise to the worst" (*NHR*, 61 n., 62). With such a damning appraisal in mind, we are better prepared to appreciate Hume's treatment of developing monotheism in Great Britain and his surprising preference in his solution to the religious problem of those forms bearing some resemblance to idolatrous worship.

The type of polytheism Hume endorses in *NHR* is the mythology of the ancient Greeks and Romans. There are many factors working in favor of that particular religion in Hume's eyes, not the least of which is that he vastly admired those peoples and their civilization to begin with.[10] Of course to some degree he would have to concede that their religious beliefs made their civilization possible, but in the main Hume seems to have regarded this mythology as a happily adventitious and only modestly important part of their culture. Moreover, since the Renaissance, the literature of that culture, certainly including its mythology, had been the admired study of every educated person. One probably does not read Ovid very long without developing a fondness for the pleasant tales of gods and goddesses, satyrs and wood-nymphs, however silly those stories might seem to the sober mind. Thus belles-lettres combining with that image of a great Mediterranean civilization of enlightened pagans, of Ancients who overshadow the Moderns, would certainly have had something to do with Hume's preference for Greco-Roman mythology over any religion of recent times. Nor should we forget that this form of paganism was dead. It could be held up as a manifest if agreeable fiction to oppose religious forms that still commanded belief and wielded power. And was it not a sly dig at the popular modern religions that a paganism so incredible and ridiculous could be flaunted as superior to any of them?

We should keep these points in mind when we come to examine Hume's treatment of paganism in ancient Britain. His hostility to the druidism of the Celts and his contempt for the pantheon of the ancient Germans might suggest that the recommendation of polytheism in *NHR* is very limited in its application. But in fact Hume's discussion of these two polytheisms is of a piece with his theories concerning the preferability of certain religious forms.

Development in Great Britain

The first religion in the British Isles was druidism. Hume says, "No idolatrous worship ever attained such an ascendent over mankind as that of the ancient Gauls and Britons." Such a remark seems to contradict that discussion of idolatry in *NHR* where Hume observes that idolatrous worship generally has a light hold on mankind. But druidism, we learn, was a sinister and highly unusual type of paganism. It exploited the fear lying at the heart of all religious belief to an extent perhaps never before realized. "Besides the severe penalties, which it was in the power of the ecclesiastics to inflict in this world, they inculcated the eternal transmigration of souls; and thereby extended their authority as far as the fears of their timorous votaries. They practiced their rites in dark groves or other secret recesses." Thus mystery, human sacrifice, and torture all helped to ensure that "no species of superstition was ever more terrible than that of the Druids." Indeed, so powerful was that terror that the druids could secure their treasures in the forests without guards, without locks and keys. Hume remarks wryly that "this steddy conquest over human avidity may be regarded as more signal than their prompting men to the most extraordinary and most violent efforts" (*H,* 1:6).

But what explains why druidism would take a form so out of character with other forms of polytheism—for its extraordinary ability to exploit terror and exercise such despotic power? The answer is that druidism represents priestcraft at its most essential and menacing extreme. The ancient druids "presided over the education of youth; . . . possessed both the civil and criminal jurisdiction" (*H*, 1:5). They were thus able to control all aspects of life, customs and beliefs, and their excommunication of any recalcitrant became a sentence far worse than death. Later we shall see that the most grievous mistake is to allow priests political authority, and this is the lesson implied in the brief treatment of the druids.

The other polytheistic religion treated in the *History* is that of the primitive Germanic tribes who invaded Britain in the middle of the fifth century A.D. and from one of whom, the Angles, derive the words *England* and *English*. These Anglo-Saxons, called just "Saxons" by Hume, practiced a more typical polytheism than the Celts they displaced. Hume speaks slightingly of this Saxon religion, of the chaos of absurd beliefs: of kings reputedly descended from Woden, god of war and principal deity; of sun and moon worship; of reverence for Thor, god of thunder; of images, sacrifices, spells, and enchantments; of a paradise of perpetual feasting and intemperance—all marked by "the wildest extravagance." It was indeed "a superstition . . . of the grossest and most barbarous kind," but despite these superlatives of hauteur, Germanic polytheism was distinguished from the Celtic in important respects: ". . . being founded on traditional tales, received from their ancestors, not reduced to any system, not supported by political institutions, like that of the Druids, it seems to have made little impression of its votaries, and to have easily resigned its place to the new doctrine [Christianity], promulgated to them" (*H*, 1:26–27). Germanic paganism was in fact remarkably similar to the polytheism described and preferred in *NHR*: it was casually evolved and unsystematic, consisted of traditional tales inculcating national values, was separate from political institutions, and all in all had an extremely light hold on its believers. It enriched and defined the culture of the Anglo-Saxons without controlling their lives or inclining them to hate and fear other religions.

Indeed, these primitive Germans merit the notice of history: "Of all the barbarous nations, known either in ancient or modern times, the Germans seem to have been the most distinguished both by their manners and political institutions, and to have carried to the highest pitch the virtues of valour and love of

liberty; the only virtues which can have place among an un-
civilized people, where justice and humanity are commonly neglected" (*H*, 1:15). Though surely limited by their barbarity, they
nonetheless exhibited two traits high in the catalogue of Humean
virtues, and could "valour and love of liberty" both be possible
among those whose religion overwhelmed them with fear and
dominated every thought and action? It is not surprising that by
contrast the Celts were prey to any invader, Roman or German,
and the Anglo-Saxons themselves, once they had embraced a
form of religion extoling the monkish virtues vilified in the second
Enquiry (*EPM*, 270), would lose both their courage and their
independence (*H*, 1:50ff., et passim.).

Forms of paganism are simply incidental to the treatment of
religion in the *History of England*, because Hume's chief concern is
with the two main forms of Western monotheism, Roman Catholic and Protestant Christianity. And for centuries there was essentially but one form of Christianity, that of the Catholic church.
That this form would be coeval in its development and power
with the Dark Ages, to denominate the medieval period as Hume
himself viewed it, begins to explain Hume's antipathy to Ro-
manism. Hume did not regard the church as necessarily causative
of medieval darkness, but he did see the church as an institution
exploiting and spreading that darkness. Moreover, the knee-jerk
reaction of a person brought up in a staunchly Protestant family
and in an officially Protestant country is always to see anything
papish as anathema. Intellectually Hume was above such prejudices, of course, and he was no sort of Protestant himself, but it is
still inconceivable that either as a philosopher or as a man he
could have viewed what he saw as the mummeries of Catholic
superstition without distaste.

We see this aversion to Catholicism in Hume's early discussions
of religious denominations. His essay "Of Superstition and Enthusiasm" (1741) is a good example. In this work the term "superstition" describes religious practices originating in human fear and
ignorance and requiring "ceremonies, observances, mortifica-
tions, sacrifices, presents, or . . . any practice, however absurd or
frivolous, which either folly or knavery recommends to a blind
and terrified credulity" (*E*, 74). Such a religion gives rise to priestcraft: "Modern Judaism and popery, (especially the latter) being
the most unphilosophical and absurd superstitions which have
yet been known in the world, are the most enslaved by their
priests" (*E*, 619).[11] Although other forms of religion can be in-

cluded under the term "superstition," we note that Catholicism is the most egregious example; moreover, it was conventional in English usage in the eighteenth century for the term "superstition" specifically to mean Catholicism. In any case in this early and theoretical discussion of Catholicism Hume singles out that particular religion as the most pernicious of all. It originates in fear and augments that fear; it makes people weak, melancholy, timorous—enslaved by the priest, who in turn "becomes the tyrant and disturber of human society" (E, 78). The condemnation could not be stronger.

The treatment of Roman Catholicism in the *History* tends to bear out the truth of this characterization, although we shall note important qualifications later. Certainly Catholicism seems everywhere in Hume's presentation a plot against the liberty of mankind and the stability of society. Superstition itself is referred to in one place as "the vice chiefly of weak minds" (H, 2:144). In the setting of the Middle Ages, or more appositely here, the Dark Ages, the reason for the rapid spread of Catholic Christianity as well as for its great power is not hard to find. Hume anticipates Gibbon's satirical explanation of the rise of Christianity found in chapters fifteen and sixteen of *The Decline and Fall of the Roman Empire*. Hume remarks, "The policy of the court of Rome has commonly been much admired; and men, judging by success, have bestowed the highest eulogies on that prudence by which a power, from such slender beginnings, could advance, without force of arms, to establish an universal and almost absolute monarchy in Europe" (H, 1:264). But bringing to mind the helpless situation of people in that age, then we see that scarcely anything could have prevented the establishment of papal authority:

> The stupid people possessed no science or reason, which they could oppose to the most exorbitant pretensions. Nonsense passed for demonstration: The most criminal means were sanctified by the piety of the end: Treaties were not supposed to be binding, where the interests of God were concerned: The ancient laws and customs of states had no authority against a divine right: Impudent forgeries were received as authentic monuments of antiquity: And the champions of holy church, if successful, were celebrated as heroes; if unfortunate, were worshipped as martyrs; and all events thus turned out equally to the advantage of clerical usurpations. (H, 1:265)

What particularly disturbs Hume in his progress through the Middle Ages is what he terms the usurpation of civil authority by the Church of Rome, "the gradual subjection of the kingdom

[England, in this case] to a foreign jurisdiction" (*H*, 1:51). Again and again he expresses indignation that great princes should fawn and grovel before the Roman pontiff, or that an archbishop of Canterbury should dictate terms of obedience to the king of England. Hume's uncharacteristic use of figurative language always signals his emotional involvement in what he writes, and we find that language everywhere in his accounts of the popes. These scheming men "dart spiritual thunder" (*H*, 1:331) at refractory kings, threatening to discharge their "sacred artillery" (*H*, 1:336). One pope comes off little better than a pickpocket: "The levying of first-fruits was also a new device . . . by which his holiness thrust his fingers very frequently into the purses of the faithful" (*H*, 2:144). Hume may concede of the church's frauds that "it gives less disturbance to society, to take men's money from them with their own consent, though by deceits and lies, than to ravish it by open force and violence" (*H*, 2:70), as the lawless vassals of the king often did, but when both the independence of mankind and the sovereignty of the state are threatened, there can be nothing but alarm at the growing authority of the church.

Hume gives a good deal of attention to the means by which the pope managed to extend his authority over mankind. In every case the strategy was to detach human interests and affections from their normal centers, such as family, social intercourse, material possessions, or national identities. The creation of the monastery was a masterstoke of papal ingenuity, and in the monastery we see that so-called *contemptus mundi* that stands in opposition to Hume's most cherished values. Of all the objections Hume raises to Catholicism, it is quite revealing that he points the finger most at this institution:

> The great encrease of monasteries, if matters be considered merely in a political light [but to Hume there can be no other of equal consideration], will appear the radical inconvenience of the catholic religion [its threat to society]; and every other disadvantage, attending that communion, seems to have an inseparable connection with these religious institutions. Papal usurpations, the tyranny of the inquisition, the multiplicity of holidays; all these fetters on liberty and industry were ultimately derived from the authority and insinuation of monks, whose habitations, being established every where, proved so many seminaries of superstition and of folly. (*H*, 3:227)

Of any of Henry's VIII's achievements, the dissolution of the monasteries was in Hume's eyes the most sagacious and far-reaching. Nothing could more cement the authority of the king against clerical usurpations.

Similar to the institution of monasteries, the celibacy of the clergy transferred human attachments from the world to the Church.

> The Roman pontiff, who was making every day great advances towards an absolute sovereignty over the ecclesiastics, perceived, that the celibacy of the clergy alone could break off entirely their connexion with the civil power, and depriving them of every other object of ambition, engage them to promote, with unceasing industry, the grandeur of their own order. . . . Celibacy, therefore, began to be extolled, as the indispensable duty of priests. (H, 1:91)

Though Hume grants that the doctrine of transubstantiation would appear to justify a requirement for the carnal purity of the celebrant (H, 1:93), he obviously accords that justification little weight, indeed as little as he would give to the truth of transubstantiation itself. To Hume the plain reason for establishing priestly celibacy was the "politics of the Roman pontiffs" (H, 1:217).

Thus by such inventions as monasteries and clerical celibacy the pope ensured the total subjection of the clergy to his own interests, and such a devoted priesthood would prove a fit instrument for the subjugation of mankind. In the previous examination of superstition, it was shown that priestcraft was its particular characteristic and bane. To give a priest full power, what better way than to invest him with the control of human fear and the ability even to create God? Enter the practice of auricular confession and the doctrine of the real presence. Both would ensure the utter dominion of priests over the laity. Hume refers to confession as

> that invention, one of the most powerful engines that ever was contrived for degrading the laity, and giving their spiritual guides an entire ascendent over them. And it may justly be said, that, though the priest's absolution, which attends confession, serves somewhat to ease weak minds from the immediate agonies of superstitious terror, it operates only by enforcing superstition itself, and thereby preparing the mind for a more violent relapse into the same disorders. (H, 3:355)

Hume calls the real presence "that very doctrine, in which, among the numberless victories of superstition over common sense, her triumph is the most signal and egregious" (*H*, 3:261). Hume everywhere scoffs at the notion of a priest creating and then eating God, but he is ready to acknowledge that belief in such a miracle is sure proof that there are in fact no limits to priestly power. Later it will become even more apparent why in Hume's treatment of Catholic practices transubstantiation is almost an *ideé fixe*.

If the power of the church over ordinary human beings was nearly unlimited, it could likewise suspend government and topple kings from their thrones. Enter the highly effective policy of interdict, excommunication, and deposition. In his account of King John's difficulties with the church, Hume devotes some twelve pages to analyzing the subtleties of this papal weapon. This instrument's efficacy derived from the gradations of pressure that the pope could bring to bear on a king, and from the terrible anxiety of "keeping the thunder long suspended" (*H*, 1:429) over the heads of an entire kingdom. In effect the authority, indeed the legitimacy of royal power, could be stripped away step by excruciating step. Hume describes in great detail how the first step, the sentence of interdict against a kingdom, could exacerbate the superstitious fear already prevalent in the human mind, playing upon the very senses with the gloomy symbolism of impending disaster:

The sentence of interdict was at that time the great instrument of vengeance and policy employed by the court of Rome; was denounced against sovereigns for the lightest offences; and made the guilt of one person involve the ruin of millions, even in their spiritual and eternal welfare. The execution of it was calculated to strike the senses in the highest degree, and to operate with irresistible force on the superstitious minds of the people. The nation was of a sudden deprived of all exterior exercise of its religion: The altars were despoiled of their ornaments: The crosses, the reliques, the images, the statues of the saints were laid on the ground; and as if the air itself were profaned, and might pollute them by its contact, the priests carefully covered them up, even from their own approach and veneration. The use of bells entirely ceased in all the churches: The bells themselves were removed from the steeples, and laid on the ground with the other sacred utensils. Mass was celebrated with shut doors; and none but the priests were admitted to that holy institution. The laity partook of no religious rite, except baptism to new-born infants, and the communion to the dying: The dead were not interred in consecrated ground: They were thrown into ditches, or buried in common fields; and their obsequies were not attended with prayers or any hallowed ceremony.

Marriage was celebrated in the church-yards; and that every action in life might bear the marks of this dreadful situation, the people were prohibited the use of meat, as in Lent, or times of the highest penance; were debarred from all pleasures and entertainment; and were forbidden even to salute each other, or so much as to shave their beards, and give any decent attention to their person and apparel. Every circumstance carried symptoms of the deepest distress, and of the most immediate apprehension of divine vengeance and indignation. (H, 1:425-26)

Hume once exclaimed hyperbolically that "the damnation of one man is an infinitely greater evil in the universe, than the subversion of a thousand million of kingdoms" (E, 595). Here it would seem that the subversion of one kingdom could involve the damnation of its entire population. One can appreciate the depth of Hume's outrage that the church would employ so terrible a weapon—even if for him that weapon was imaginary—for the sake of temporal gain.

If interdict did not bring the ruler to his knees, then would succeed his own excommunication, next the absolution of his subjects' loyalty and their own excommunication, and finally his deposition, with his own kingdom offered to another prince for the taking. Hume marvels at "the artifice of the court of Rome" by which superstitious fear could be so extensively manipulated (H, 1:428-30). King John proved stubborn and shortsighted, but he was at last forced to beg the pope's mercy. Hume records every "ignominious" and "humiliating" detail of John's capitulation. Resigning his kingdom "to God, to St. Peter and St. Paul, and to pope Innocent and his successors in the apostolic chair,"

John did homage to Pandolf as the pope's legate, with all the submissive rites which the feudal law required of vassals before their liege-lord and superior. He came disarmed into the legate's presence, who was seated on a throne; he flung himself on his knees before him; he lifted up his joined hands, and put them within those of Pandolf; he swore fealty to the pope; and he paid part of the tribute, which he owed for his kingdom as the patrimony of St. Peter. The legate, elated by this supreme triumph of sacerdotal power, could not forbear discovering extravagant symptoms of joy and exultation: He trampled on the money, which was laid at his feet . . .: An insolence,. . . offensive to all the English. (H, 1:432-33, 437)

Hume is clearly indignant at this thought control through a subtle manipulation of symbols, and his elaborate portrayal of the ultimate "triumph of sacerdotal power" serves as a warning of how a religion, basing its control on superstitious fear, could finally overwhelm civil authority itself.

The tendency of the medieval volumes is to present Roman Catholicism as a great, insidious plot to enslave mankind—as individuals and as rulers. It is hard to believe of course in any such masterplan so well orchestrated and carried out, but Hume argues that the ignorance of the times and the inherent anxiety of the human mind made it inevitable that a body of ecclesiastics, possessing superior knowledge, would successfully assert their authority. Hume never gives the medieval church much credit for its learning, but its incorporation of bits of Roman culture, not to mention its adoption of the Latin language itself, could not help raising churchmen above completely ignorant savages.[12] Moreover, the extreme lawlessness, disorder, and violence of the age occasionally prompts Hume to commend the mollifying influence of the church,[13] as hard as it may be to believe that he could ever say anything favorable of medieval Christianity.

Though unwittingly, the church in its cultivation of classical learning made the Renaissance possible—and by implication the very movement that would liberate mankind from the church's own grasp: namely, the Reformation (*H*, 2:518–21). There is one great ecclesiastic who became a patron of the Renaissance, Pope Leo X. Hume praises Leo as "one of the most illustrious princes that ever sat on the papal throne. Humane, beneficent, generous, affable; the patron of every art, and friend of every virtue." (*H*, 3:95). Lest we be too surprised at this commendation, we learn soon enough the grounds for Hume's warmth. How could any pope be so distinguished? Hume offers slender proof—"it is commonly believed"—but nonetheless maintains that Leo had too much elegant learning and penetration to believe in the truth of Catholic doctrine! In fact Hume excuses Leo's "scheme of selling indulgences" because his "generous and enterprizing temper"— always Humean epithets of the highest praise—forced him to seek revenue for his "projects, pleasures, and liberalities." Besides, since he was above any belief in sacerdotal nonsense, why should he not use the frauds of his predecessors for more beneficial ends? It also turned out that, though not foreseen by Leo, the selling of indulgences precipitated the Reformation (*H*, 3:137–39).

Given the state of Europe in the Middle Ages, suffering the bondage of a corrupt and power-hungry Church, we would expect Hume to herald the Reformation with unbounded joy. True, it would mean the substitution of one kind of zealous monotheism for another, but in theory, at least, Protestantism represents the spirit of liberty and innovation, of resistance to tyranny, whether ecclesiastical or civil. In his essay "Of Enthusiasm and Superstition," enthusiasts, the extreme Protestants, do receive a kind of backhanded praise. Being marked by a passion for independence, their zeal finally subsides into moderation and toleration, once the fury of enthusiasm has spent itself; because their religion is formless and individualistic, the erstwhile fanatics soon cool off and become indifferent to anything save the common affairs of life (E, 75–79). This tendency away from the pernicious otherworldliness of medieval Catholicism, coupled with the bent toward religious and civil freedom, would surely make Protestantism a welcome alternative for Hume.

In that light, Hume can welcome the change. He commends John Wycliffe for having "the honour of being the first person in Europe, that publicly called in question those principles, which had universally passed for certain and undisputed during many ages," even if "affairs were not yet fully ripe for this great revolution [the Reformation]; and the finishing blow to ecclesiastical power was reserved to a period of more curiosity, literature, and inclination for novelties" (H, 2:326, 328–29). He has many reservations about Henry VIII, but he must view with great approval Henry's break with Rome and the establishment of the Church of England. And when the English face a new threat to their freedom, not from the Church of Rome any more but rather from the monarch, Hume grudgingly allows that the spirit of Protestantism preserved English liberty. "So absolute, indeed, was the authority of the crown, that the precious spark of liberty had been kindled, and was preserved, by the puritans alone; and it was to this sect, whose principles appear so frivolous and habits so ridiculous, that the English owe the whole freedom of their constitution" (H, 4:145–46; cf. H, 4:123ff.).

Thus Puritans might deserve praise for libertarian principles, but we see in this last quotation a strong distaste for them. Protestantism might be recommended in the abstract, but its extreme represents many liabilities. As a cure for either superstition or royal prerogative, it became as bad as the disease. In a long discursive passage Hume later relegated to a note with the statement that the discussion contains views too important to eliminate completely, there are some interesting qualifications to his crediting the Puritans with preserving English liberty. He says that civil liberty "reaped more advantage than honour" from its association with the Puritan cause, and he speaks of the "superstition" retained by Anglicanism in language showing considerable approval: "The genius of the church of England, so kindly to monarchy, forwarded the confederacy [of royal and ecclesiastical authority]; its submission to episcopal jurisdiction; its attachment to ceremonies, to order, to a decent pomp and splendor of worship; and in a word, its affinity to the tame superstition of the catholics, rather than to the wild fanaticism of the puritans" (*H,* 5:558–59). "Order,. . . decent pomp and splendor," "the tame superstition of the catholics"? What has become of Hume's aversion to the "ceremonies, observances . . . which either folly or knavery recommends to a blind and terrified credulity" (*E,* 74) or of his contempt for all forms of idolatry and superstition? Let us look more closely at his account of the Reformation.

It becomes apparent that the Reformation was not the result of any noble or laudable effort in man to free himself from error and to worship his God in a more seemly manner. That great hero of the Reformation, Martin Luther, does not emerge from Hume's narrative as anyone to admire. Luther's initial objection to the selling of indulgences resulted from the petty resentments of a "fiery temper." Having once stumbled into his successful role as leader of the Reformation, he found reasons enough to persevere in his efforts: "Luther, a man naturally inflexible, vehement, opinionative, was become incapable, either from promises of advancement, or terrors of severity, to relinquish a sect, of which he was himself the founder, and which brought him a glory, superior to all others, the glory of dictating the religious faith and principles of multitudes" (*H,* 3:139). And in his succeeding explanation of why the Reformation so quickly made converts Hume underlines the reasons: novelty itself, fondness for dispute, the mad zeal of the reformers, the intoxicating rapture of every believer at being the special favorite or even prophet of God: "the rapid advance of the Lutheran doctrine, and the violence, with which it was embraced, prove sufficiently, that it owed not its success to reason and reflection" (*H,* 3:140).

Not the triumph of reason but rather of one absurdity opposing another. In their zeal to cry up faith as the only pathway to salvation, English reformers asserted

> that the most infallible road to perdition was a reliance on *good works;* by which terms they understood, as well the moral duties, as the ceremonial and monastic observances. The defenders of the ancient religion, on the other hand, maintained the efficacy of *good works;* but though they did not exclude from this appellation the social virtues, it

was still the superstitions, gainful to the church, which they chiefly extolled and recommended. (*H*, 3:214–15)

In both cases social virtue becomes a sacrifice to mere religious interests. Neither side commands respect, though we might note that the ancient religion seems somewhat preferable.[14]

Henry VIII may have freed England from the shackles of Rome, but his reasons were grounded in political and personal expediency and whim, not in any desire to embrace the principles of the Reformation. In fact, the pope had conferred the title "Defender of the Faith" on Henry for attacking Luther in a Latin book. Henry's reason? Luther had spoken "with contempt of Thomas Aquinas, the king's favourite author" (*H*, 3:139), and later he fired the king's resentment by an indecent reply to "his royal antagonist" (*H*, 3:213). Hume observes with a smile that Henry "undertook to combat [Luther's tenets] with weapons not usually employed by monarchs, especially those in the flower of their age, and force of their passions" (*H*, 3:140). Apparently not the expected *ultima ratio regum*.

Indeed, Henry's fancying himself "so great a casuist and divine" (*H*, 3:172) becomes an amusing aspect of this personality, and it lends itself to satirical treatment of Henry's part in the Reformation. There is something almost quixotic in the theological jousts of this Defender of the Faith who enters the lists against Luther and other innovators staunchly fighting for the ancient religion, but often for the most frivolous reasons, like his own blind pride, and ending up because of his marital caprices the founder of the reformed church in England. Consider the following assessment of Henry's position:

> He had early declared his sentiments against Luther; and having entered the lists in those scholastic quarrels, he had received, from his courtiers and theologians, infinite applause for his performance. Elated by this imaginary success, and blinded by a natural arrogance and obstinacy of temper, he had entertained the most lofty opinion of his own erudition; and he received with impatience, mixed with contempt, any contradiction to his sentiments. . . . Separate as he stood from the catholic church and from the Roman pontiff, the head of it, he still valued himself on maintaining the catholic doctrine, and on guarding by fire and sword, the imagined purity of his speculative principles. (*H*, 3:212–13)

Henry's favorite occupation, it would seem, was theological disputation, and in the case of the king's attempt to convert one heretic, Hume renders the affair as if it were a mock battle:

[The king] pressed Lambert with arguments drawn from Scripture and the schoolmen: The audience applauded the force of his reasoning, and the extent of his erudition: Cranmer seconded his proofs by some new topics: Gardiner entered the lists as a support to Cranmer: Tonstal took up the argument after Gardiner: Stokesley brought fresh aid to Tonstal: Six bishops more appeared successively in the field after Stokesley. And the disputation, if it deserves the name, was prolonged for five hours; till Lambert, fatigued, confounded, browbeaten, and abashed, was at last reduced to silence. The king, then returning to the charge, proposed, as a concluding argument, this interesting question, Whether he were resolved to live or to die?

The emphasis here on the concluding *argumentum ad baculum*, doubtless the most persuasive of all Henry's reasoning, displays Hume's contempt for that theological squabbling marking the Reformation.[15] He is less subtle in his comments on certain Protestant divines: "These theologians were now of great importance in the world; and no poet or philosopher, even in ancient Greece, where they were treated with most respect, had ever reached equal applause and admiration with those wretched composers of metaphysical polemics" (*H*, 3:223–24).

Another early hero of the Reformation is John Knox, who is treated as no more than a "rustic apostle" and "ringleader in . . . insults of [the] majesty" of Mary, Queen of Scots (*H*, 4:40–41). Note how contemptuously Hume describes this Reformer: "John Knox . . . had imbibed, from his commerce with Calvin, the highest fanaticism of his sect, augmented by the native ferocity of his own character" (*H*, 4:22). "The political principles of the man, which he communicated to his brethren, were as full of sedition as his theological were of rage and bigotry" (*H*, 4:41). Hume uses the language of Swiftian satire, whose tropes "commerce" and "communicated" suggest something filthy in the holy intercourse of the brethren. In his presentation, Hume skillfully uses Knox's *History of the Reformation in Scotland* not only as a factual source but even more as an incontestable proof of the unsavory features of Knox's personality. He takes his details of the assassination of Cardinal Beaton directly from Knox but remarks on the tone of Knox's account: "The famous Scotch reformer, John Knox, calls James Melvil [obviously in the narrative the most sanctimonious, hypocritical, and bloodthirsty of the assassins] . . . a man most gentle and most modest. It is very horrid, but at the same time somewhat amusing, to consider the joy and alacrity and pleasure, which that historian discovers in his narrative of this assassination: And it is remarkable that in the first edition of his work, these words were printed on the margin of the page, *The godly Fact and Words of James Melvil"* (*H*, 3:374n.). Modern readers of Knox might argue over the degree of "joy and alacrity and pleasure" that Knox displays, or consider the extenuating reasons for it, but one cannot dispute the basic accuracy of Hume's charge; and Knox does say, after the account, "These things we write merrily."[16] Later Hume is indignant that this rustic apostle could treat a gentle, charming, and beautiful queen with disrespect or could remain unmoved by her tears.[17] He is, however, often more amused than indignant at the repeated examples of Knox's hypocritical prudery.[18]

Religious controversy, often erupting into violence and persecution, continued to threaten civil stability through the reigns of Edward VI, Mary, and Elizabeth, but by the first half of the seventeenth century, nothing but religious controversy could seem to explain the events of English history. "Religion can never be deemed a point of small consequence in civil government: But during this period, it may be regarded as the great spring of men's actions and determinations" (*H*, 6:86). That James I would erect a college "to promote controversial divinity" in a period during which no one thought of anything else strikes Hume as an incredible irony (*H*, 5:132). By this point religious polemics, grown epidemic, concerned the extent and form to which the Reformation should be carried in England and Scotland; with the exception of several episodes of hysterical anti-Catholicism during the later seventeenth century that were more political than religious, Roman Catholicism itself was no longer a primary concern. No matter, for wrangling among Protestants could equal any battle of Catholic against Protestant. Hume paints vivid scenes of discord, as pulpits "resounded with faction and fanaticism," while "noise and fury, cant and hypocrisy, formed the sole rhetoric, which, during this tumult of various prejudices and passions, could be heard or attended to" (*H*, 5:295).

Indeed, the "war of the pen preceded that of the sword" (*H*, 5:380), but the war of the sword followed all too soon. The terrible Civil Wars of the 1640s, culminating in the deposition and execution of Charles I, were the product mainly of religious controversy, not the noble efforts of an inspired Commons to oppose an arbitrary, tyrannical king. It is a point that Hume never tires of laboring: "to the disgrace of that age and of this island, it must be acknowledged, that the disorders in Scotland entirely, and those in England mostly, proceeded from so mean and contemptible an origin [as religious controversy]," and "that of the most frivolous and ridiculous kind" (*H*, 5:303n.).

I turn now to the examination of the extreme form of Protestantism, the Puritan movement often contemptuously referred to as enthusiasm or fanaticism in the eighteenth century. In theory at least, Hume preferred enthusiasm to superstition—that is, extreme Protestantism to Roman Catholicism—because enthusiasm is congenial to civil liberty and intellectual independence and fairly short-lived in its effects: once the fumes of enthusiastic delusion have dissipated, once the mad fury has spent itself, the fanatic should be expected to regain his equilibrium because his religion lacks the ritual and structure to prolong his zeal, and he should become moderate, tolerant, and indifferent to anything except the common affairs of life (*E*, 75–79).

So goes the theory. In fact, however, history does not corroborate this hypothesis, or at least the history that Hume perceived from his own congenital and cultural vantage. Hume admits that modern-day enthusiasts appear becalmed, sensible, and law-abiding, but Hume, like Robert Burns later, had had unpleasant encounters with the zealots of the Scottish Kirk, who would have been glad to tyrannize society if the whole Puritan cause had not been so thoroughly discredited by the excesses of their seventeenth-century forebears. It is these excesses that Hume had to consider in the *History,* and this empirical evidence of what enthusiasm is capable of doing to human nature and society forced him to shift away from implicitly endorsing, or even tolerating, this form of Christianity. J. G. A. Pocock's judgment that "the great originality of his history of the Puritan Revolution is his insistence that the fanaticism of the Puritan sects was both an excessive threat to rational freedom and a necessary step toward its establishment" is shrewd, but such a tidy paradox fits Hume the political thinker much better than it does Hume the moralist.[19]

Superstition invests things outside the mind with spiritual significance; enthusiasm—etymologically the word means "possessed by god"—makes the mind itself the dwelling place of the spirit. Superstition seeks out evidence of incarnation—the spirit in objects, god in the flesh; enthusiasm looks inward to emotional evidence of some spiritual reality. This introspective, solipsistic, extremely emotional direction of enthusiasm suggests reasons for its attractiveness and power—and, as we shall see, its danger. It is flattering, as Hume makes clear, for people to regard themselves as "the peculiar favourites" of "their Maker" (*H*, 5:10–11), and gratifying for people to be at liberty to believe whatever their emotions direct, to be absolved by the in-dwelling spirit from any demands made by reason, reflection, or an external moral code. It is not surprising that enthusiasts multiplied rapidly: "Their insurmountable passion, disguised to themselves, as well as to others, under the appearance of holy fervours, was well qualified to make proselytes, and to seize the minds of the ignorant multitude. And one furious enthusiast was able, by his active industry, to surmount the indolent efforts of many sober and reasonable antagonists" (*H*, 5:285). This emotionalism naturally inclined the enthusiasts to elevate extemporaneous preaching over formal prayers and liturgy because this popular "method of address" is "more inflaming and animating" (*H*, 5:240). Hume emphasizes that Puritan preaching was rapturous and fanciful, freed from the decent restraints of the traditional liturgy (*H*, 1:xv).

Rhapsodic ejaculations and theogenic reveries set the Puritans off from ordinary men, from ordinary life. The elect could not abide the heathenish celebrations marking the old, unpurified religion any more than they could brook the old ceremonies and idolatry. Along with the abominations of crosses, surplices, stained glass, and statuary, they proscribed feastdays like Christmas and all the dancing and revelry that were part of them. Merriment in general seemed the devil's inspiration: plays and maypoles went the way of crucifixes, and "horse-races and cockmatches were prohibited as the greatest enormities" (*H*, 6:142). This repudiation of life's pleasure brings the Puritans quite close to the monks, whose negative virtues Hume had censured so vigorously. Commenting on the Presbyterian clergy, not the Romish monks, Hume says, "useless austerities and self-denial are imagined, in many religions, to render us acceptable to a benevolent Being, who created us solely for happiness." (*H*, 5:11). Hume cannot help slyly noting, however, some degree of carnal frailty in the Puritan denial of joy: "Even minced pyes, which custom had made a Christmas dish among the churchmen, were regarded, during that season, as a profane and superstitious viand by the sectaries; though at other times it agreed very well with their stomachs" (*H*, 5:453n). If Hume's portrayal of the humorless Puritans seems too severe, we can turn to Samuel Johnson's *Life of Samuel Butler:* "We [moderns] have never been witnesses of animosities excited by the use of minced pies and plumb porridge, nor seen with what abhorrence those who could eat them at all other times of the year would shrink from them in

December."[20] Of course both Johnson and Hume had rather High Church sympathies—Johnson, in theory and practice; Hume, only in theory.

That the unsociable, dour Puritans could become an amusing spectacle is amply demonstrated by Samuel Butler's *Hudibras*, as both Hume and Johnson note. Hume says that when "Colonel Hewson, from his pious zeal, marched with his regiment into London, and destroyed all the bears, which were there kept for the diversion of the citizens, . . . [the] adventure seems to have given birth to the fiction of Hudibras." But in Hume's assessment of this ludicrous episode we perceive something more ominous than amusement: "bear-baiting was esteemed heathenish and unchristian: The sport of it, not the inhumanity, gave offence" (*H*, 6:142). The irony amuses, but we see how warped this piety was—indeed just as cruel as it was absurd. Likewise, we smile at the wit of Hume's understatement:

The thorough-paced Puritans were distinguishable by the sourness and austerity of their manners, and by their aversion to all pleasure and society. To inspire them with better humour, was certainly, both for their own sake and that of the public, a laudable intention in the court; but whether pillories, fines, and prisons, were proper expedients for that purpose, may admit of some question. (*H*, 5:233–34)

"For their own sake" is understandable, but for "that of the public" reminds us once again that the pall of unsociable gloom cast over life by Puritan manners represented a threat to society at large. Hume does make occasional jests at the Puritans' expense, but the implications of this religious melancholy are finally not ludicrous at all. It would be wrong to imagine Hume simply sharing with Butler a good laugh at these caricatures of human folly.

The worldly, hedonistic royalists laughed at "this fanaticism of the parliamentary armies," Hume observes, "without being sensible how much reason they had to apprehend its dangerous consequences" (*H*, 5:470). The new-model armies whose officers "received inspiration with their commission" (*H*, 5:514) soon gave them reason to dread the holy wrath of fanatics. From wrangling to bloodshed, from speaking noble words to doing foul deeds, from insulting the king to beheading him, from opposing tyranny to becoming tyrants, the Puritans followed a familiar course of revolution. Of all the manifestations of religion Hume had treated in the *History*, this one was the most noxious and repugnant.

"No character in human society is more dangerous than that of the fanatic; because, if attended with weak judgment, he is exposed to the suggestions of others; if supported by more discernment, he is entirely governed by his own illusions, which sanctify his most selfish views and passions" (*H*, 6:113). This pronouncement is a strong warning against the danger that enthusiasm presents to civil stability and morality. From the section on Catholicism we remember the political encroachments of the pope and his priesthood. What of the Puritan clergy? "Scarcely, even during the darkest night of papal superstition, are there found such instances of priestly encroachments, as the annals of Scotland present to us during that period" (*H*, 5:70). And the ultimate consequence of unrestrained enthusiasm is immorality, a refrain heard frequently in the *History:*

> Among the generality of men, educated in regular, civilized societies, the sentiments of shame, duty, honour, have considerable authority, and serve to counterbalance and direct the motives, derived from private advantage: But, by the predominancy of enthusiasm among the parliamentary forces, these salutary principles lost their credit, and were regarded as mere human inventions, yea moral institutions, fitter for heathens than for christians. The saint, resigned over to superior guidance, was at full liberty to gratify all his appetites, disguised under the appearance of pious zeal. And, besides the strange corruptions engendered by this spirit, it eluded and loosened all the ties of morality, and gave entire scope, and even sanction, to the selfishness and ambition, which naturally adhere to the human mind. (*H*, 5:493–94)

The mockery of the biblical idiom—"mere human inventions, yea moral institutions"—reveals how much Hume had come to detest the canting Puritans, whose values gave the lie to everything he held dear.

What explains this rampant immorality in enthusiastic religion? Abstraction from worldly concerns and pleasure, theogenic fantasy, emotional rhapsodies posing as "divine illuminations, and . . . illapses of the Holy Spirit" (*H*, 5:459), all disturbed and even supplanted the innate moral sense. This distraction from social values and interests will be analyzed in the next section. Moreover, this emphasis on subjective, idiosyncratic standards of judgment encouraged hypocrisy among the enthusiasts, a phenomenon that will likewise be treated later. Essentially, though, the enthusiast, sanctifying himself, could not perceive that his actions often violated his religious professions, or even

the dictates of his own heart. And could it not be that the antino-
mianism that ran like a torrent through the creeds of most Puritan
denominations was itself an inevitable cause of flagrant immorality, at least according to Hume? The doctrine of faith-over-works
gave many a satirist a ready handle for ridicule. In *Shamela*, Henry
Fielding later created one Parson Williams, who preaches, according to the account of his obliging paramour, "that those people
who talk of vartue and morality, are the wickedest of all persons.
That 'tis not what we do, but what we believe, that must save
us. . . ."[21] Hume may never have created a satirical caricature like
Parson Williams, but the reasons for his outrage against any
doctrine that would depreciate good works as a means of serving
God are obvious. We saw this objection earlier in the absurdities
of both Protestant and Catholic disputation, and we see it in
Philo's remark in the *Dialogues:* "Amongst ourselves, some have
been guilty of that Atrociousness, unknown to the *Aegyptian* and
Grecian Superstitions, of declaiming, in express Terms, against
Morality, and representing it as a sure Forfeiture of the divine
Favour, if the least Trust or Reliance be laid upon it" (*D*, 254).

Given that enthusiasm was so pernicious a form of religion,
how did it disfigure the heroes of the Puritan rebellion? The
whimsies and contradictions of its greatest hero, Oliver Cromwell, make him more vulnerable to attack than some lesser figures
in the drama, who by Hume's time had been praised for vigorous,
even eloquent opposition to the high-handed court party.[22] Without doubt, all these men raise problems for historical interpretation, and their treatment becomes a touchstone of such polar
oppositions as court-country, royalist-republican, and Tory-Whig.
Hume gives these Puritan leaders their due, because the principles of liberty that they introduced into the fabric of English
government are momentous and, to Hume, salutary. But Hume's
argument has been all along that the political was only incidental
to the religious, and so in his presentation of these men he insists
that their greatness was warped by their religious inspiration.
They became freaks of human history, subjects equally of admiration and revulsion.

Hume never denies that these patriots were actors in perhaps
the greatest drama of English history, perhaps of all history, and
their performance invites comparison with those of ancient heroes:

> Some persons, partial to the patriots of this age, have ventured to put
> them in a balance with the most illustrious characters of antiquity; and

mentioned the names of Pym, Hambden, Vane, as a just parallel to those of Cato, Brutus, Cassius. Profound capacity, indeed, undaunted courage, extensive enterprize; in these particulars, perhaps the Roman do not much surpass the English worthies: But what a difference, when the discourse, conduct, conversation, and private as well as public behaviour, of both are inspected!

And what specifically rendered these great abilities, perhaps the match of any Roman's, so contemptible? It is not hard to guess: while "those noble ancients" became civilized by Greek literature and philosophy, "the whole discourse and language of the moderns were polluted with mysterious jargon, and full of the lowest and most vulgar hypocrisy" (H, 5:304). The moderns represent pointed examples of genius vitiated by enthusiasm.[23]

What religious zeal can do to native virtue and ability is one of Hume's favorite themes. Consider him declaiming almost in the style of ancient oratory:

This was the time, when genius and capacity of all kinds, freed from the restraint of authority, and nourished by unbounded hopes and projects, began to exert themselves, and be distinguished by the public. Then was celebrated the sagacity of Pym, more fitted for use than ornament; matured, not chilled, by his advanced age and long experience: Then was displayed the mighty ambition of Hambden, taught disguise, not moderation, from former constraint; supported by courage, conducted by prudence, embellished by modesty; but whether founded in a love of power or zeal for liberty, is still, from his untimely end, left doubtful and uncertain: Then too were known the dark, ardent, and dangerous character of St. John; the impetuous spirit of Hollis, violent and sincere, open and entire in his enmities and in his friendships; the enthusiastic genius of young Vane, extravagant in the ends which he pursued, sagacious and profound in the means which he employed; incited by the appearances of religion, negligent of the duties of morality. (H, 5:293–94)

The shadows lengthen—from the largely favorable memorial of Pym, only hinting at some threatening, pent-up energy; to the looming power and ability of Hampden, forever clouded by the mystery of his intentions; to the openly dangerous and sinister extremism of St. John and Hollis; and finally to the most disturbing picture of all, "the enthusiastic genius of young Vane," whose truly great talents were enhanced and twisted by religion-inspired insanity.

Much later in the Commonwealth chapters of the *History*, Hume expands this characterization of Sir Henry Vane:

Vane was noted, in all civil transactions, for temper, insinuation, address, and a profound judgment; in all religious speculations, for folly and extravagance. He was a perfect enthusiast; and fancying that he was certainly favoured with inspiration, he deemed himself, to speak in the language of the times, to be a *man above ordinances*, and, by reason of his perfection, to be unlimited and unrestrained by any rules, which govern inferior mortals. These whimsies, mingling with pride, had so corrupted his excellent understanding, that sometimes he thought himself the person deputed to reign on earth for a thousand years over the whole congregation of the faithful. (*H*, 6:128–29)

The description is especially interesting because Hume sees it as the character of the "perfect enthusiast," a schizoid personality split between total competence in governmental affairs and hopeless megalomania in matters religious. It is obvious that the madness brought on by enthusiasm completely negated remarkable abilities. We note in particular that religion essentially destroyed morality, and there is scorn in Hume's language for Vane's self-sanctifying presumption of superiority: "a *man above ordinances, . . .* unlimited and unrestrained by any rules, which govern inferior mortals." We see how seriously Hume took enthusiasm's power to craze mankind: he gives it an almost satirical exposition in an historical narrative. Indeed, this description of a person driven insane by theological whimsies and pride could very well come right out of Swift's *Tale of a Tub.* There is little difference between the wild antics of the Calvinist Brother Jack, "run mad with Spleen, and Spight, and Contradiction,"[24] and the dangerously extravagant fantasies of Brother Vane.

We can now step back and review our examination of religion in Hume's *History of England.* Not surprisingly, no form of religion emerges unscathed, but there is clearly a pattern in Hume's assessment of blame. Any form of religion assuming too much authority in individual human life or in government is most to be feared; conversely, a religion with a light hold on its believers, tending to complement the ordinary pleasures of life and reinforce worldly interests and sympathies, comes very close to meriting Hume's endorsement. In *NHR*, the entertaining polytheism of the ancient Greeks and Romans exemplifies such qualities. Of the rude polytheisms in Britain, druidism represents the noxious form, while Germanic paganism exhibits qualities of the tolerable. When Christianity enters the picture, however, its forms represent the various undesirable characteristics of monotheism noted in *NHR*. Roman Catholicism and, later, Protestantism, especially its extreme manifestations, both receive extensive treatment—and withering censure. Considering Hume's theoretical statements on the two forms, however, one expects a much harsher treatment of the Catholics than the Protestants. A close reading of the *History* reveals instead that extreme Protestants have replaced Catholics as the principal mischief-makers of Christianity, according to Hume.

We see that dealing with the facts of history had forced Hume to change his mind about enthusiasm, that ultimate expression of Protestantism. He can find no evidence that fanatical Puritans would ever have subsided into that toleration, indifference, and worldliness predicted by his theory, had their frenetic heyday not been aborted by external forces. Thus the neat antithesis "Of Enthusiasm and Superstition" (1741), implicitly favoring enthusiasm, had disappeared by the time Hume wrote the *History of England* (1754–62). And even though Hume never withdrew the 1741 essay from his canon, all of his changes in that work reflect a progressive softening of his treatment of superstition. By the time he wrote the *History,* he no longer featured weak, fearful, melancholy, and ignorant devotees of superstition versus hopeful, proud, presumptuous, warmly imaginative, and ignorant fanatics. (We note that only ignorance characterizes both.) Each extreme was absurd, oftentimes dangerous, and those qualities like hope and pride that favor the enthusiasts in any Humean catalogue of virtues were now given only the most unflattering constructions. Likewise, the superstitious were no longer too much blamed for their ceremonies and idolatry, even if they were still charged with priestcraft. With the writing of the *History,* superstition had become less objectionable than enthusiasm.[25]

A possible objection to this interpretation of Hume's shifting attitude might be based on a preface to volume 2 of the *History* that Hume drafted and suppressed in 1756.[26] Here is the critical passage:

> The Idea of an Infinite Mind, the Author of the Universe seems at first Sight to require a Worship absolutely pure, simple, unadorned; without Rites, Institutions, Ceremonies; even without Temples, Priests, and verbal Prayer & Supplication; Yet has this Species of Devotion been often found to degenerate into the most dangerous Fanaticism. When we have recourse to the aid of the Senses & Imagination, in order to adapt our Religion, in some degree to human Infirmity; it is very difficult, & almost impossible, to prevent altogether the Intrusion of Superstition, or keep Men from laying too great Stress on the ceremonial & ornamental Parts of their Worship. Of all the Sects, into

which Christians have been divided, the Church of England seems to have chosen the most happy Medium; yet will it undoubtedly be allowd, that during the Age, of which these Volumes treat, there was a Tincture of Superstition in the Partizans of the Hierarchy; as well as a strong Mixture of Enthusiasm in their Antagonists. But it is the Nature of the latter Principle soon to evaporate and decay; A Spirit of Moderation usually succeeds, in a little time, to the Fervors of Zeal: And it must be acknowledg'd, to the Honor of the present Presbyterians, Independents, & other Sectaries of this Island, that they resemble in little more but in Name their Predecessors, who flourished during the civil Wars; & who were the Authors of such Disorder.

The passage repeats the arguments heard before but appears to look more kindly on the fanatics than Hume in his post-*History* thinking usually does. The passage might even seem to constitute a return to the views of the 1741 essay on the subject. There is, however, a small but significant difference in the phrasing of the two statements. In the earlier essay Hume assures us that the dangerous fury of enthusiasm is always soon exhausted: "When the first fire of enthusiasm is spent, men naturally, in all fanatical sects, sink into the greatest remissness and coolness in sacred matters" (*E*, 77). By contrast in the 1756 passage Hume's confidence has waned, and he inserts the qualifier "usually" in his prediction. True, he does pay court to modern-day Presbyterians and sectaries, but does not this very strain of appeasing flattery tell us how far we can trust this whole preface, and give us a good idea of why he rejected it? The preface simply does not represent the whole truth. He wrote it to placate his critics. In the last paragraph he explicitly states that "these considerations . . . [will] afford a compleat Answer" to those unhappy with his treatment of religious controversy. And who can believe that Hume is sincere at the beginning when he indulges in his usual defensive irony that of course he does not mean to say anything against "true & genuine Piety," which, among other benefits, enforces "all moral Duties," though unfortunately it works its good offices so secretly and silently that it seldom comes to the notice of history? What sort of recommendation of piety is that? All in all, the rejected preface confirms those patterns in Hume's religious thinking that have been our concern, but it does not demonstrate that he had at last made his peace with the fanatics.

There is other evidence that Hume was sensitive to the problems that his treatment of religion might cause him, again in deleted passages, these two toward the beginning of the first volumes to be written and published (in 1754). These passages appear in the first edition, but they disappear thereafter. If Hume's reason for the deletions was to blunt criticism of his hostility to religion, and in particular, to the Reformation,[27] one must regard his efforts as nugatory because what remains plainly expresses the same views. In his introduction to the Liberty Classics edition of the *History,* William B. Todd notes that the first passage deleted asperses the Reformers, while the second derogates the Catholics. Todd concludes, "It must be conceded that Hume here betrays no unwonted partiality and is quite even-handed in his censure" (*H,* 1:xviii). Such is not the case. The first may speak with little respect of the early Reformers' fanaticism, but the second on the Catholics betrays a remarkable partiality for that communion, even despite several harsh words of censure. It is possible to see why.

Consider the passage supposedly taking Catholics to task. It begins with the usual view that the excessive power and usurpations of the medieval church needed to be repressed. Interestingly, Hume ignores the corruptions of the church, such as the selling of indulgences; here his main objection to Rome is political. When the Reformation came, Hume makes apparent that "the sharpness of the remedy," the "offensive zeal" of the Reformers, and the combustion into which all Christendom was thrown gave reasonable people second thoughts. Thus far the summary follows the lines of argument seen earlier, but what follows stresses and clarifies certain aspects of Catholicism that are left only implicit elsewhere in the *History.* Hume refers to Catholic superstition before the Reformation as if it were largely harmless and benign: "like the antient pagan idolatry, the popular religion consisted more of exterior practices and observances, than of any principles, which either took possession of the heart, or influenced the conduct" (*H,* 1:xvi). And he praises the "very generous and enlarged sentiments" of Italian churchmen, led by Pope Leo X, which were gradually ameliorating the worst aspects of Catholicism. It is true that a casual reader might interpret these remarks as pejorative. After all, isn't a religion supposed to play an influential role in life? Isn't a pope expected to believe sincerely in the doctrines of the church? We must remember, however, that Hume had other ideas about religion's place in life.

One gets the impression that Europe would have been better off without the Reformation. The enlightenment brought about by the rediscovery and cultivation of classical letters would have soon made Catholic Christianity as pleasant, harmless, and irrelevant a mythology as that of the ancient world. But the furious zeal of the

Reformers, threatening the very existence of the Church, prompted it to take severe countermeasures. Hume does not equivocate about the terrors of Rome's response: "the dreadful tribunal of the inquisition, that utmost instance of human depravity, is a durable monument to instruct us what a pitch iniquity and cruelty may rise to, when covered with the sacred mantle of religion" (*H,* 1:xvii). One may observe, however, that this harshest reproof of Catholicism also applies to religion in general, not just to Catholicism. In any event, Hume's indictment of the Counter-Reformation is strong, but the Church's extreme reaction was all the fault of the Reformation. "No wonder [the church] was animated with equal zeal and ardor," he says defensively.

The penultimate paragraph begins by explaining the attachment of monarchical government to superstitious forms and ceremonies, splendid in themselves and enforcing "blind submission." Nevertheless, soon Hume is expatiating on the voluptuousness associated with popery in a manner that does not exactly suggest his disapproval:

That delicious country, where the Roman pontiff resides, was the source of all modern art and refinement, and diffused on its superstition an air of politeness, which distinguishes it from the gross rusticity of the other sects. And tho' policy made it assume, in some of its monastic orders, that austere mien, which is acceptable to the vulgar; all authority still resided in its prelates and spiritual princes, whose temper, more cultivated and humanized, inclined them to every decent pleasure and indulgence. Like all other species of superstition, it rouses the vain fears of unhappy mortals, but it knows also the secret of allaying these fears, and by exterior rites, ceremonies, and abasements, tho' sometimes at the expence of morals, it reconciles the penitent to his offended deity. (*H,* 1:xvii)

This is admittedly not the work of a devout apologist for Catholicism; even in Humean terms there is mention of a serious liability—"sometimes at the expence of morals"; nonetheless, these sentences and indeed the whole passage represent Hume's most explicit endorsement of the Catholic religion. Rites take the place of the pagan fiction commended earlier and turn the pre-Reformation church into a utopian model. "Decent pleasure and indulgence" are part of civilized life for Hume, and civilized life generally encourages morality, as I shall show in the next chapter. In Hume's thinking the two are almost inseparable. These worldly princes of the church, themselves awash in sensuality and spokesmen for a religion of material splendor, cannot help being vastly preferable to self-absorbed, gloomy enthusiasts whose rusticity and spiritual pride separated them from the polite values and pleasures of this life. Years ago, in his famous little book *The Heavenly City of the Eighteenth-Century Philosophers*, Carl Becker said that even a dull reader of the *History* could not miss Hume's warning against "the worldly interests and intrigues of priests."[28] However, a sharper reader will notice that the worldly interests of priests are none of Hume's concern. If anything, he applauds their worldliness.

To be sure, this veiled recommendation of Catholicism does not square with much of what Hume says later in the medieval volumes, written last. The gross ignorance and barbarism of the Middle Ages repelled him in the first place, and the spectacle of a church exploiting and fostering such darkness would not likely fill him with joy. However, even when we take into consideration that without doubt he would brand abuses by any religion whenever he saw them, that of course he was not inclined either temperamentally or intellectually to countenance popery, we still must conclude that he was surprisingly moderate in his condemnation of Catholicism. Moreover, unlike the earlier Hume, the Hume who dealt with the facts of history had come to be tolerant of some aspects of superstition. Superstition, for reasons that have been suggested already and will be developed further, is simply preferable to enthusiasm as a religion for the multitudes. Dealing with superstition by itself, he can be severe, but facing a choice between these two extremes of Christianity, he condemns enthusiasm with unrelenting severity.

We see such a tendency in passages remaining in the *History*, such as when he comes close to defending Catholic relics against Protestant ridicule—certainly an astonishing position for Hume to be in: "such fooleries, as they are to be found in all ages and nations, and even took place during the most refined periods of antiquity, form no particular or violent reproach to the catholic religion" (*H*, 3:253). Or when he seems to excuse the selling of indulgences, partly, one suspects, because the practice underwrote Leo X's endowment for the humanities: "The sale of indulgences seems, therefore, no more criminal than any other cheat of the church of Rome, or of any other church. The reformers, by entirely abolishing purgatory, did really, instead of partial indulgences sold by the pope, give, gratis, a general indulgence, of a similar nature, for all crimes and offences, without exception or distinction" (*H*, 3:472). That this statement is part of a footnote added after the first edition supports the argument of this section:

namely, that Hume's mature judgment was to regard the extreme Protestants as the worst of all modern types of Christianity. And here his objection is founded once again on the immorality putatively condoned by the antinomian doctrine.

In any case Hume found the lessons of the Puritan rebellion compelling. If religion's "root . . . springs from the essential and universal properties of human nature" (*NHR,* 92), if a society of the masses is difficult to imagine without some form of religion, then almost any form is better than the enthusiastic. When Hume writes the final chapter in the lives of two Puritans, Vane and Lambert, he notes how Vane suffered his execution—his martyrdom—with a courage engendered by headstrong enthusiasm; he was a rebel to the end. Lambert, who became "dutiful and submissive," was reprieved. "He was confined to the isle of Guernesey; where he lived contented, forgetting all his past schemes of greatness, and entirely forgotten by the nation: He died a Roman Catholic" (*H,* 6:181–82). One smiles at the irony of this old fanatic dying in the arms of the Whore of Babylon, that greatest abomination of right-thinking Puritans. Is it too much to infer that Lambert's conversion marked the return of a settled mind, one no longer mad with zeal and ambition?

Religion: A Virulent Disease

In the preceding sections we have witnessed Hume's largely hostile treatment of various religious forms. He may have come to tolerate certain forms of religion over others, but his general attitude toward any popular religion was at best one of suspicion and wariness. To Hume religion was a virulent disease or poison always threatening the health of the body politic. He consistently speaks of religion's influence in such tropes.[29] Religion is "a malady . . . almost incurable," an "intoxicating poison," an "epidemical frenzy," "a disease dangerous and inveterate"; even in France, most civilized of nations, during the religious civil wars "the theological rage, which had long been boiling in men's veins, seems to have attained its last stage of virulence and ferocity" (*H,* 3:366; 5:348; 6:322; 4:57).[30]

The pessimism of Hume's diagnosis is grounded in what he perceives to be religion's tendency to alter human nature for the worse, to blind reason, to inflame the ugliest passions. The *History of England* features a virtual parade of characters exemplifying religion's corrupting power. Among the enthusiasts, Oliver Cromwell, imagining that the murder of his king was a meritorious deed and under the illusion to his death that he was the savior of his people, is only one instance (*H*, 6:110). And James II, "infected with the catholic superstition" (*H*, 6:521), ignoring his subjects' fervent commitment to Protestantism and inciting them to rebellion, is but another. As Hume observes, we may not be too surprised that religion could blind a prince like James, innately virtuous but mediocre in abilities, but what of the estimable Louis XIV's decision to revoke the Edict of Nantes: "when a prince of so much humanity and of such signal prudence as Lewis could be engaged, by the bigotry of his religion alone, without any provocation, to embrace such sanguinary and impolitic measures . . ." (*H*, 6:471)?

Indeed, the mutual animosity among rival denominations, the lengths of violence to which believers will go to destroy the infidel, are perhaps the most frightening and instructive symptoms of the religious malady. The spirit for Hume becomes most often the spirit of persecution. In the medieval volumes, the persecution of the Jews, until their banishment by Edward I, exposes this repellent side of religion, as cruel jealousy and narrow xenophobia hide behind the face of holy indignation. Later in the *History*, when Catholics and Protestants engage in their internecine persecutions, the maxim emerges that "no human depravity can equal revenge and cruelty, covered with the mantle of religion" (*H*, 3:435). Hume expresses a reluctance to dwell on the "horrid spectacle" of repeated, unvaried cruelties practiced in England's age of persecution, the reign of the Tudors, especially Mary. But he does enumerate "a few instances . . . in order, if possible, to warn zealous bigots, for ever to avoid such odious and such fruitless barbarity" (*H*, 3:439, 437).

So he presents examples of unspeakable cruelty, most commonly of men perishing under the excruciating torture of slow fires. Hume notes that torturers, executioners, and guards—not usually reckoned the most feeling of mankind—often showed mercy strikingly absent in their zealous superiors (e.g., *H*, 3:437). In several cases guards intervene to put an end to a slow death by fire, but no examples are more poignant that these: the refusal by the lieutenant of the tower to stretch the rack farther in the torture of a lady heretic, when Chancellor Wriothesely, "intoxicated with religious zeal, put his own hand to the rack, and drew it so violently that he almost tore her body asunder" (*H*, 3:315); and a woman giving birth at the stake, when a guard, attempting to save the infant, was ordered by the magistrate to throw it back into the flames, "being determined, he said, that nothing should survive which sprang from so obstinate and heretical a parent" (*H*, 3:438). (It is suggestive that Hume does not question an incredible story such as this one when it so strongly supports his argument.)

As we might expect, the historian Hume is apologetic over the recital of these shocking accounts, but he is just as eager to give them such emphasis that their lesson can never be forgotten (*H*, 3:441). Yet these horrible exemples—a mere few of hundreds, as he says, including the burnings of bishops, gentlemen, tradesmen, laborers, and even women and children—assume all the more prominence because of his apologies and demurrers: "This persevering cruelty appears astonishing; yet it is much inferior to what has been practised in other countries" (*H*, 3:441). The lower incidence of persecuting rage among the English is not particularly reassuring. We are ready to accept the conclusion: "Human nature appears not, on any occasion, so detestable, and at the same time so absurd, as in these religious persecutions, which sink men below infernal spirits in wickedness, and below the beasts in folly" (*H*, 3:437).[31]

In the preceding observations, Hume notes with disgust how religious intolerance infects human nature. Holy wars reflect this malignancy on a grand scale, and holding up the Crusades as an object lesson, he pronounces them "the most signal and most durable monument of human folly, that has yet appeared in any age or nation" (*H*, 1:234). For Hume the Crusades exemplify the dangerous mass hysteria resulting from spiritual chicanery. The notion of the Crusades as a noble campaign to free the Holy Land from the savage infidel is a delusion Hume is eager to expose. Instead of sanctified Christian soldiers on the most glorious of quests, Hume presents a rout of disorderly, licentious barbarians, ignorant of their own intentions and of the difficulties of such an undertaking, leaderless and undisciplined, pushing their way first toward Constantinople, then Jerusalem. "Deeming the crusades the only road to heaven," most flocked to the standard of the cross believing that their previous violations of justice and humanity would be instantly expiated. A multitude of three hundred thousand, led by the ignorant charlatan Peter the Hermit, followed a path of rapine and self-destruction. Even the nobility does not fare much better. Although they may have been better trained and equipped and motivated by the specious honor of chivalry, they were in fact mere "adventurers," gratifying "their avarice or their ambition," "fanatical and romantic warriors" pursuing "chimerical projects." Hume diagnoses the "universal frenzy" as an explosive conjunction of abject superstition and the military spirit of feudalism, "and Europe, impelled by its two ruling passions, was loosened, as it were, from its foundations, and seemed to precipitate itself in one united body upon the east" (*H*, 1:234–39).

Derogating the Crusades still further is Hume's portrayal of the Christians as more fanatical—and less civilized and moral—than even the infidels themselves! This irony culminates in the contrast between Richard the Lion-hearted and his Moslem counterpart, Saladin:

> The furious wars, which [Saladin] waged in defense of the barren territory of Judea, were not with him, as with the European adventurers, the result of superstition, but of policy. The advantage indeed of science, moderation, humanity, was at that time entirely on the side of the Saracens; and this gallant emperor, in particular, displayed, during the course of the war, a spirit and generosity, which even his bigoted enemies were obliged to acknowledge and admire. Richard, equally martial and brave, carried with him more of the barbarian character; and was guilty of acts of ferocity, which threw a stain on his celebrated victories.

Hume is obviously writing polemical history, rejecting one of the West's inspiring myths and preferring its enemies to its heroes. The superiority of Saladin is apparent even in death, and his is most of all a moral superiority. He dies renouncing his own claim to greatness and ordering "charities to be distributed to the poor, without distinction of Jew, Christian, or Mahometan" (*H*, 1:393). In this age of frenzied persecution and intolerance, could any Christian be capable of such virtue? The sickening description of the Jerusalem massacre, displaying in bloody tones how the high-minded Crusades were finally to culminate, is the disturbing answer (*H*, 1:250).[32]

Thus we see that Hume views religion as a cancer destroying the moral fiber: this is his most damning accusation.[33] It is one thing to argue that there is no demonstrable connection between religious belief and practice, on the one hand, and morality, on the other. Hume actually contends, instead, that religion corrupts morality, and he preaches this message insistently in the *History* and inculcates it in *NHR* and the *Dialogues*.

In the *History*, the story of the Gunpowder Plot is probably the most pointed exemplum (*H*, 5:25–33).[34] Hume's narrative is heavily didactic throughout. At the beginning he announces: "We are now to relate an event, one of the most memorable, that history has conveyed to posterity, and containing at once a singular proof both of the strength and weakness of the human mind; its widest departure from morals, and most steady attachment to religious prejudices." What seems most shocking is that the conspirators could have been unaffected by the heartless enormity of their plan, sanctified as it was by its goal of restoring in one violent blow the Catholic religion in England: "And it is remarkable, that no one of these pious devotees ever entertained the least compunction with regard to the cruel massacre, which they projected. . . . The holy fury had extinguished in their breast every other motive [but religious service]." Hume accentuates this aspect of the plotters' zeal, dramatically quoting a long speech in which one conspirator enlarges on the pleasure of witnessing Parliament and king blown to pieces. Hume's source is an inflammatory anti-Catholic account, but no matter, for Hume is more intent on satire than objectivity. His presentation resembles Swift's satiric strategy in *Gulliver's Travels,* when Lemuel Gulliver proudly describes the wonders of gunpowder to the horrified king of Brobdingnag, who represents the moral norm. But Hume must rely on his reader to react with outrage, for in the story of the Gunpowder Plot this speech of vengeance charms the bigoted co-conspirator. Indeed, Hume twice describes the conspirators as "charmed" by the prospect of mass murder; in another place, their plot is a "religiously kept" secret—a word choice of mordant irony. Surprisingly, those who were capable of planning this horrible massacre were by reputation honorable, esteemed citizens, not outlaws, rebels, or madmen. That religion was responsible for their crime is all the more telling: "It was bigotted zeal alone, the most absurd of prejudices masqued with reason, the most criminal of passions covered with the appearance of duty, which seduced them into measures, that were fatal to themselves, and had so nearly proved fatal to their country" (*H*, 5:31).

To be sure, the opposition between religion and morality is a favorite theme in Hume's more philosophical works. In part 12 of the *Dialogues,* the debate between Cleanthes and Philo focuses on the problem. At one point Philo would seem to have been reading Hume's *History:* "If the religious Spirit be ever mention'd in any historical Narration, we are sure to meet afterwards with a Detail of the Miseries, which attend it. And no Period of time can be happier or more prosperous, than those in which it is never regarded, or heard of" (*D*, 251). When Cleanthes objects that religion ideally operates by quietly softening our temper, indirectly enforcing "the Motives of Morality and Justice," consequently "in danger of being overlooked," Philo responds in a lengthy rebuttal, reflecting Hume's own views (D, 251–57). Philo argues that moral inclination, rooted in the heart, operates constantly, and like gravity always prevails over any other force, which is exerted only by fits and starts. Men are often moral in spite of religious promptings in a contrary direction, and all experience leads us to conclude that religious professions or their absence are no reliable indicator of conduct (except of course that fervent professions might well put us on guard against cheating and deception!) Therefore religion, not being needed for the existence of morality or justice, raises up "a new and frivolous Species of Merit" that weakens our "Attachment to the natural Motives of Justice and Humanity" (D, 251–54).

The *Dialogues* were probably being drafted while Hume was researching and writing the *History of England*.[35] The *Natural History of Religion*, appearing in 1757, was coeval with the *History*. Like the *Dialogues* but at greather length *NHR* explains psychologically how religion and morality are opposed. This opposition is the principal theme of *NHR*. In the penultimate section 14, the theme bluntly appears in the title: "Bad influence of popular religions on morality." (Hume originally qualified the title by writing "most popular religions," but in his final version he struck the word "most.") Hume does not mince words here. Religion and morality are incompatible, and even when religion preaches morality, its votaries ignore such commonplace advice and seek to placate their god in other ways—"not by virtue and good morals, which alone can be acceptable to a perfect being, but either by frivolous observances, by intemperate zeal, by rapturous extasies, or by the belief of mysterious and absurd opinions" (*NHR*, 87). How curious, Hume muses, when anyone ought to "esteem virtue and honesty," and when virtuous conduct is actually easier and more pleasant and useful than most religious exercises, why do people prefer one to the other? Precisely because these exercises serve no other purpose, Hume answers, a religionist imagines that they serve God: "In restoring a loan, or paying a debt, his divinity is noway beholden to him; because these acts of justice are what he was bound to perform, and what many would have performed, were there no god in the universe. But if he fast a day, or give himself a sound whipping; this has a direct reference, in his opinion, to the service of God" (*NHR*, 88–90). Consequently religious conduct often strays away from moral obligation: "Hence it is justly regarded as unsafe to draw any certain inference in favour of a man's morals, from the fervor or strictness of his religious exercises, even tho' he himself believe them sincere" (*NHR*, 90).

This self-deception makes religious mania insidious, and on this point Hume's analysis is subtle and trenchant. Considering his hostility to religion, we expect him to view the pious hypocrite as a calculating rascal fully aware of his knavery, hiding behind a mask of sanctity for no other reason than selfish advantage. We might take, for instance, the following hypothetical encounter with a hypocrite modeled somewhat after Molière's Tartuffe:

> *Disciple.* Oh, if I could but follow my master, Hypocrite, in his blessed piety and humility. Ah, here comes the dear saint now.
> *Hypocrite.* (*Aside.* And here comes that fool who believes in my pious face. I shall drown him in holy nonsense.) Blessings on you, my good friend, Disciple. Will you go with me on my errand to succor the helpless and comfort the poor and suffering? Would there were more gold to use in this holy endeavor!
> *Disciple.* I cannot go myself, dear master, but I can at least give you gold to use in your pious work. Here, take this (handing Hypocrite a large sack of gold).
> *Hypocrite.* May Heaven reward you, good Disciple. (*Aside.* This dupe will *bless me richly*, ha ha!)

On the contrary, however, whatever else Hume may say to asperse religion, he never claims that the religious hypocrite is insincere and calculating.

In Hume's analysis, religion sets up spurious standards of conduct that draw people away from moral inclinations that are more natural and pleasant. These new standards are difficult to maintain, demanding conduct quite different from that of ordinary life. A face of piety and a demeanor of holy fervor seem requisite, yet most people cannot be pious and fervent without continued effort and care. They forget; other, more natural concerns take hold. But to the world and to themselves they must pretend, at least, that all is as it should be. As Philo puts it in the *Dialogues*, "Many religious Exercises are enter'd into with seeming Fervor, where the Heart, at the time, feels cold and languid: A habit of Dissimulation is by degrees contracted" (*D*, 254). According to Hume, hypocrisy evolves in a pattern: people warmly embrace religious devotion as an answer to their problems and fears; at certain moments, devotion is fervent, and zeal is genuine and affecting; but common life, though lacking the emotional sublimity of inspiration, always and finally makes its demands, and dissimulation must follow. In a footnote added to the *History*, Hume analyzes the hypocrisy of the Puritan enthusiasts, explaining why fanaticism is almost always accompanied by self-deception:

> So congenial to the human mind are religious sentiments, that it is impossible to counterfeit long these holy fervours, without feeling some share of the assumed warmth. And, on the other hand, so precarious and temporary, from the frailty of human nature, is the operation of these spiritual views, that the religious ecstasies, if constantly employed, must often be counterfeit, and must be warped by those more familiar motives of interest and ambition, which insensibly gain upon the mind. This indeed seems the key to most of the celebrated characters of that age. Equally full of fraud and of ardour, these pious patriots talked perpetually of seeking the Lord, yet still pursued their own purposes; and have left a memorable lesson to posterity, how delusive, how destructive, that principle is by which they were animated. (*H*, 5:572)

The very sincerity of "these pious patriots" made them all the more dangerous.

In Hume's analysis, we note two important aspects of religious hypocrisy. Elsewhere in the *History* he puts it this way: "The religious hypocrisy . . . is of a peculiar nature; and being generally unknown to the person himself, though more dangerous, it implies less falsehood than any other species of insincerity" (*H*, 6:142). Other hypocrites are insincere: they know that they are playing a part. Hume's ascription of sincerity to the religious hypocrite may seem contradictory, for the etymological meaning of *hypocrisy* is playing a part, hence dissembling. But Hume is arguing that the religious hypocrite is playing a part without being fully aware that he is. This complete self-deception, then, leads to the other aspect of religious hypocrisy: that it is "more dangerous." The religionist starts off sincerely believing in his professions—in his sanctity—but he has the ordinary passions and selfish desires of any man. Now he must hide these worldly human motives from others, and from himself. He becomes convinced of his own sanctity, so much so that he is blind to everything else, even his own violations of common justice and humanity. Perhaps he may believe that his piety makes immoral conduct impossible, or that the holy end justifies any means. To any objective observer, of course, he is an arrant hypocrite. His behavior does not accord with his religious pretensions. He professes compassion and is cruel. He professes humility and altruism and is vainglorious and selfish. But despite his immorality, he is sincere: he believes himself to be good; he has been taken in by his own acting. We must remember Hume's assessment of Cromwell's most atrocious deed: "it is not impossible, but he might believe it, as many others did, the most meritorious action, that he could perform" (*H*, 6:110). It is this peculiar self-deception that makes religious hypocrisy more dangerous than any other kind, for it is not checked by normal motives of practical self-interest. The swindler will likely be content to cheat us of our money, but the fanatic may feel a call to shake the state.

The final prognosis for a society strongly infected with religious disease is the deterioration of civil stability, perhaps the eradication of all civil authority. The priest or pastor, along with his devoted flock, imagines nothing equal in importance to spiritual ideals—certainly not the mere exigencies of law and justice. Those doing God's work are either immune to civil authority or indeed superior to it, manifesting "that spiritual pride, to which a mistaken piety is so subject" (*H*, 5:494). Hume makes plain that although medieval bishops, more educated and civilized than the savage barons and kings, were best qualified for the civil offices they often held, they were unsuitable for more important reasons: they held themselves aloof from civil authority, regarding even treason as no canonical offense; likewise they swore fealty to a foreign potentate in Rome and considered ecclesiastical interests, including their own, preeminent to any other. Henry II's confrontation with Thomas à Becket is a striking instance. Thus priestcraft and clerical ambition had made the Church of Rome a salient example of religion's threat to human society: "few ecclesiastical establishments . . . have been attended with circumstances more hurtful to the peace and happiness of mankind" (*H*, 3:136). Yet as sweeping a condemnation as this is, Hume's view of Puritan rule is even less tolerant. Describing the last throes of the Protectorate, with government falling into anarchy, Hume speaks with vehement hatred of the Puritan army's malign power, noting, too, that "every signal violence, which they committed," was preceded by "a solemn fast":

> Throughout the three kingdoms there prevailed nothing but the melancholy fears, to the nobility and gentry, of a bloody massacre and extermination; to the rest of the people, of perpetual servitude, beneath those sanctified robbers, whose union and whose divisions would be equally destructive, and who, under pretence of superior illuminations, would soon extirpate, if possible, all private morality, as they had already done all public law and justice, from the British dominions. (*H*, 6:120)

But for Hume, no matter what form religion takes, the excesses to which it is subject desperately require the treatment of a philosophic physician.

Treatment of the Disease

What can be done? To the privileged few Hume offers the salvation of being like him, enjoying "a manly, steddy virtue, . . . the calm sunshine of the mind," before which "these spectres of false divinity never make their appearance" (NHR, 91). But what about "the ignorant multitude" (NHR, 27, 33), that is, the "vulgar, indeed, all mankind, a few excepted"? (NHR, 57) Philosophy hath neither light nor charms for them, and, as Hume makes abundantly clear in NHR and the History of England, their delusions born of spiritual mania threaten the stability of a society that the fit, though few, might otherwise enjoy to the fullest. Hume has no program as such, no ready answer, but implicit in NHR and other works published later in his career is a growing appreciation of the power of religious rites and images to control or even to neutralize the dangerous caprices of pious zeal. And why Hume came to regard extreme Protestantism as the most pernicious form of religion will become apparent.[36]

Central to the problem of pious zeal is the human attempt to understand the nature of God, indeed to make the deity concrete. Throughout NHR Hume tends to regard this effort to render the incomprehensible familiar to our feeble intellect as manifestly absurd. Still, if absurd, it is for all that a penchant of human nature:

> And thus, however strong men's propensity to believe invisible, intelligent power in nature, their propensity is equally strong to rest their attention on sensible, visible objects; and in order to reconcile these opposite inclinations, they are led to unite the invisible power with some visible object. . . . And as an invisible spiritual intelligence is an object too refined for vulgar apprehension, men naturally affix it to some sensible representation; such as either the more conspicuous parts of nature, or the statues, images, and pictures, which a more refined age forms of its divinities. (NHR, 46, 49)

It is important to remember that even though Hume's ridicule of idolatry is more often directed against primitive polytheism, his thesis in NHR is that polytheism and the more sophisticated forms of monotheism are not essentially different, except that, for reasons we shall soon explore, polytheism is actually preferable because by promoting sociability and materialism it is less immoral than monotheism. Men are idolaters by nature; the answer for Hume is to ensure that idolatry will be useful and constructive, instead of exerting that malign influence often observed in human history:

> The universal propensity to believe in invisible, intelligent power, if not an original instinct, being at least a general attendant of human nature, may be considered as a kind of mark or stamp, which the divine workman has set upon his work; and nothing surely can more dignify mankind, than to be thus selected from all the other parts of the creation, and to bear the image or impression of the universal Creator. But consult this image, as it commonly appears in the popular religions of the world. How is the deity disfigured in our representations of him! What caprice, absurdity, and immorality are attributed to him! (*NHR*, 93–94)

In this passage, even allowing for a degree of ironical overstatement, we see Hume ready to countenance the human desire to image the deity—"nothing surely can more dignify mankind"— except that people have invariably disgraced themselves in their actual efforts to fashion that image. Further, Hume regards the disfiguring of the deity as a moral problem. The way a believer images his god and all his ceremonial means of communing with that god will determine the moral complexion of his religion and hence the degree to which he will be a useful or destructive member of his society.

By 1757, the date of *NHR*, the question was not whether the worshiper should attempt to make his god concrete, but rather how and to what extent. By contrast, the early Hume regarded the use of icons, vestments, liturgy, and sacred rites of all kinds to be misguided and foolish but of little consequence to society. In the *Treatise* (Bk. 3; 1740) he had dismissed in passing religious ceremonies and symbols. They might be compared to certain legal ceremonies and practices, like those involving promises and contracts, but there is a fundamental difference: such forms do serve a purpose in the law because justice is necessary to society; they serve no purpose in religion except to bedazzle the masses (*T*, 515–16, 523–25). In the second *Enquiry* (1751) Hume developed this idea more fully.[37] After admitting that "those, who ridicule vulgar superstitions, and expose the folly of particular regards to meats, days, places, postures, apparel, have an easy task. . . ." Hume takes up that easy task by ridiculing these superstitions: "A fowl on Thursday is lawful food; on Friday abominable: Eggs in this house and in this diocese, are permitted during Lent; a hundred paces further, to eat them is a damnable sin. This earth or building, yesterday was profane; to-day, by the muttering of certain words, it has become holy and sacred" (*EPM*, 198). Then, after suggesting that legal rites are often just as silly, he makes this striking distinction between legal and religious forms:

> But there is this material difference between *superstition* and *justice*, that the former is frivolous, useless, and burdensome; the latter is absolutely requisite to the well-being of mankind and existence of society. . . . Were the interests of society nowise concerned, it is as unintelligible why another's articulating certain sounds implying consent, should change the nature of my actions with regard to a particular object, as why the reciting of a liturgy by a priest, in a certain habit and posture, should dedicate a heap of brick and timber, and render it, thenceforth and for ever, sacred. (*EPM*, 199)

Two points stand out that are of significance in our discussion: (1) as late as 1751 Hume considered religious forms "nowise concerned" in "the interests of society"; and (2) his language reveals an undisguised contempt for this useless mummery. This attitude, however, later underwent a marked change.[38]

Another important source for Hume's early opinions of religious forms is a letter written in 1743 to William Mure of Caldwell. In a part of that letter, Hume first divides "every thing we commonly call Religion" into (1) "Devotion & Prayer" and (2) "the Practice of Morality, & the assent of the Understanding to the Proposition *that God exists*" (*L*, 1:50). It is a division Hume would characteristically make throughout his writings on religion, and we sense that even that early he was formulating the argument that devotion and prayer could become the bane of the "Practice of Morality." The remainder of the letter concerns the abuses of worship, and it is revealing that Hume identifies the conjunction of invisible spirit and concrete object (to which I shall apply the general term "incarnation") as the germ of the problem. Consider these observations:

> I assert [the Deity] is not the natural Object of any Passion or Affection. He is no Object either of the Senses or Imagination, & very little of the Understanding, without which it is impossible to excite any Affection. A remote Ancestor, who has left us Estates & Honours, acquir'd with Virtue, is a great Benefactor, & yet 'tis impossible to bear him any Affection, because unknown to us; tho in general we know

him to be a Man or a human Creature, which brings him vastly nearer our Comprehension than an invisible infinite Spirit. (*L*, 1:51)

Then, after raising several objections to the use of prayer, Hume concludes: "Thus all wise Men have excluded the Use of Images & Pictures in Prayer, tho they certainly enliven Devotion; because 'tis found by Experience, that with the vulgar these visible Representations draw too much towards them, & become the only Objects of Devotion" (*L*, 1:52).

We note in these passages that Hume categorically opposes worship on the grounds that it is impossible even to conceptualize the Deity to any meaningful extent; thus it is certainly futile to attempt to bring God nearer by means of images or anthropomorphic analogies; worship accordingly degenerates into idolatry, which Hume dismisses with peremptory scorn. At that early stage in his philosophy, Hume found such worship empty and useless.

However, Hume's attitude toward idolatry and incarnation underwent a modification evident by 1757 in *NHR*. The evolution of this change of mind is to be found in the first volumes of the *History of England* (1754). As I trace that evolution, the reason for the change will begin to suggest itself.

In the early part of these volumes, Hume treats religious ceremonies and forms in that reductive fashion so prominent in the second *Enquiry*, where he said that a priest's muttering a liturgy made "a heap of brick and timber . . . thenceforth and for ever sacred." An excellent example is Hume's satirical description of (then) Bishop William Laud's consecration of St. Catherine's Church (*H*, 5:223–26). Having emphasized that the Puritans regarded any ceremonial practices that were even faintly popish with "the greatest horror and detestation," Hume then portrays Laud as imposing such rituals on them almost out of spite, as if determined to rub their noses in abominations. The humorless Puritans could not understand "that the very insignificancy of these ceremonies recommended them to the superstitious prelate, and made them appear the more peculiarly sacred and religious, as they could serve to no other purpose." These empty forms were apparently in the same class as those useless whippings and fasts imagined as a special service to God; for Hume, their only value was to vex Roundheads.

Hume describes the consecration at great length, indeed in sufficient detail to serve as a guidebook for priests. Laud went about the consecration with exaggerated formality, bowing and

kneeling, pronouncing blessings and imprecations with punc-
tilious regularity and strained solemnity. Hume presents every
symbolic nuance:

> As he approached the communion table, he made many lowly rever-
> ences: And coming up to that part of the table where the bread and
> wine lay, he bowed seven times. After the reading of many prayers,
> he approached the sacramental elements, and gently lifted up the
> corner of the napkin, in which the bread was placed. When he beheld
> the bread, he suddenly let fall the napkin, flew back a step or two,
> bowed three several times towards the bread; then he drew nigh
> again, opened the napkin, and bowed as before.
>   Next, he laid his hand on the cup, which had a cover upon it, and
> was filled with wine. He let go the cup, fell back, and bowed thrice
> towards it. He approached again; and lifting up the cover, peeped into
> the cup. Seeing the wine, he let fall the cover, started back, and bowed
> as before. Then he received the sacrament, and gave it to others. And
> many prayers being said, the solemnity of the consecration ended.
> The walls and floor and roof of the fabric were then supposed to be
> sufficiently holy. (H, V, 225–26)[39]

The whole description, particularly the final comment, which is
not in Hume's source but is rather all his own, exemplifies the
ideas of the second *Enquiry*. Clearly in this passage Hume regards
such forms as nothing but mummery. Their principal function, as
far as he is concerned, was to scandalize the Puritans, a bit of
torment he apparently thought they deserved.

The general comments about Laud's innovations also reveal
Hume's scorn for this pointless ceremony, consonant with his
remarks in the letter to Mure:

> All kinds of ornament, especially pictures, were necessary for sup-
> porting that mechanical devotion, which was purposed to be raised in
> this model of religion: But as these had been so much employed by the
> church of Rome, and had given rise to so much superstition, or what
> the puritans called idolatry; it was impossible to introduce them into
> English churches, without exciting general murmurs and com-
> plaints. . . . The crucifix, too, that eternal consolation of all pious
> catholics, and terror to all sound protestants, was not forgotten on this
> occasion. (H, 5:226)

Hume reminds us that ceremonial worship depends upon pictures or icons, and Hume may even agree with the Puritans that
such worship might well be called idolatry. Once again Hume is
simply contemptuous of this "mechanical devotion."

This gleeful debunking of sacred rites is characteristic of Hume, and yet in the *History* we also notice a somewhat less derisive attitude toward these ceremonies beginning to develop. Hume enjoyed mocking superstitious practice, without doubt, but he had to consider the implications of the other extreme, the amorphous simplicity of Puritan religion. What was the capacity of human beings for a spiritual communion liberated from the dross of material ornaments and liturgy? What would happen when these apparently meaningless forms were discarded? Writing of James I's efforts to introduce traditional ceremonies into the Kirk, Hume speculated on these problems in a long passage that deserves complete quotation:

The fire of devotion, excited by novelty, and inflamed by opposition, had so possessed the minds of the Scottish reformers, that all rites and ornaments, and even order of worship, were disdainfully rejected as useless burdens; retarding the imagination in its rapturous ecstasies, and cramping the operations of that divine spirit, by which they supposed themselves to be animated. A mode of worship was established, the most naked and most simple imaginable; one that borrowed nothing from the senses; but reposed itself entirely on the contemplation of that divine Essence, which discovers itself to the understanding only. This species of devotion, so worthy of the supreme Being, but so little suitable to human frailty, was observed to occasion great disturbances in the breast, and in many respects to confound all rational principles of conduct and behaviour. The mind, straining for these extraordinary raptures, reaching them by short glances, sinking again under its own weakness, rejecting all exterior aid of pomp and ceremony, was so occupied in this inward life, that it fled from every intercourse of society, and from every chearful amusement, which could soften or humanize the character. It was obvious to all discerning eyes, and had not escaped the king's, that, by the prevalence of fanaticism, a gloomy and sullen disposition established itself among the people; a spirit, obstinate and dangerous; independent and disorderly; animated equally with a contempt of authority, and a hatred to every other mode of religion, particularly to the catholic. In order to mellow these humours, James endeavoured to infuse a small tincture of ceremony into the national worship, and to introduce such rites as might, in some degree, occupy the mind, and please the senses, without departing too far from that simplicity, by which the reformation was distinguished. The finer arts too, though still rude in these northern kingdoms, were employed to adorn the churches; and the king's chapel, in which an organ was erected, and some pictures and statues displayed, was proposed as a model to the rest of the nation. But music was grating to the prejudiced ears of the Scottish clergy; sculpture and painting appeared instruments of idolatry; the surplice was a rag of popery; and every motion or gesture, prescribed by the liturgy, was a step towards that spiritual Babylon, so much the object of their horror and aversion. Every thing was deemed impious, but their own mystical comments on the Scriptures, which they idolized, and whose eastern prophetic style they employed in every common occurrence. (*H*, 5:68–69)

Here we see a rather different treatment of sacred rites. Faced with the other extreme—worship stripped of any ceremony at all—Hume is no longer as inclined simply to dismiss "mechanical devotion" as idolatry or superstition, pointless and absurd. In fact he seems close to recommending these ceremonies, and certainly he is quite sympathetic to James's efforts toward reform. In any case, writing the history of this troubled age made him sensitive to a new problem, one much more far-reaching in its implications than the mere nonsense of idolatry. He still maintains that a mode of worship dependent on a rational contemplation of the Supreme Being is perhaps the most appropriate to a spiritual idea, but such a rarefied conception is far beyond the capacity of most worshipers, if not indeed of all mankind. And what happens to these worshipers instead? They withdraw from the world of the senses, from an awareness of this life, and retreat into a state of uncontrollable, self-deceiving rapture.

This passage reveals Hume's essential objection to religion, as he expounded it later in *NHR*, particularly to the religion of the enthusiastic Puritans. In its peak of fervor, enthusiasm is the least tolerant form of religion, and, of even greater but related significance, it is the most destructive of civilization. Rational behavior, sociability and politeness, concern for one's fellow creatures, and an enterprising, courageous spirit, are all displaced by the whimsies of solitary man; a chaos of inner passions, and those the most sullen and bitter, threatens to tear apart the outward fabric of society, established by centuries of tradition and gradual progress. A final irony is that their rage against idolatry notwithstanding, these extremists were themselves idolaters— bibliolaters—worshiping in the Old Testament a text whose style and subject were least likely, in Hume's eyes, to make them rational or humane. The religion of the fanatics posed a threat to all that Hume regarded as sacred, to use a word that in any other Humean context would be unthinkable.

So large did this threat bulk that later in the *History* Hume moves from ridicule of liturgy to an endorsement of ritual as a means of insulating worshipers from the consequences of unchecked spiritual zeal. Hume had earlier made Laud's liturgical excesses into an example of that prelate's own zeal and of the patent folly of superstition itself. When he came to evaluate Laud's place in history, Hume had changed his mind. We are surprised to learn that however sectarian were his motives or misguided his means, it is regrettable that Laud did not succeed in his liturgical reforms. Indeed, Hume's first sentence quite plainly reflects his own changing view:

> Whatever ridicule, to a philosophical mind, may be thrown on pious ceremonies, it must be confessed, that, during a very religious age, no institutions can be more advantageous to the rude multitude, and tend more to mollify that fierce and gloomy spirit of devotion, to which they are subject. Even the English church, though it had retained a share of popish ceremonies, may justly be thought too naked and unadorned, and still to approach too near the abstract and spiritual religion of the puritans. Laud and his associates, by reviving a few primitive institutions of this nature, corrected the error of the first reformers, and presented to the affrighted and astonished mind, some sensible, exterior observance, which might occupy it during its religious exercises, and abate the violence of its disappointed efforts. The thought, no longer bent on that divine and mysterious essence, so superior to the narrow capacities of mankind, was able, by means of the new model of devotion, to relax itself in the contemplation of pictures, postures, vestments, buildings; and all the fine arts, which minister to religion, thereby received additional encouragement. The primate, it is true, conducted this scheme, not with the enlarged sentiments and cool reflection of a legislator, but with the intemperate zeal of a sectary; and by overlooking the circumstances of the times, served rather to inflame that religious fury, which he meant to repress. But this blemish is more to be regarded as a general imputation on the whole age, than any particular failing of Laud's; and it is sufficient for his vindication to observe, that his errors were the most excusable of all those, which prevailed during that zealous period (*H*, 5:460).[40]

This final assessment of Laud reflects a considerable degree of new sympathy with practices formerly regarded as useles idolatry. For Hume it is a matter of accommodation, of making the best of human weaknesses. As long as mankind is religious—and that seems a disposition well-nigh universal—anything serving as an antidote to the poison of fanaticism is to be promoted. Such an antidote is found in religious ceremony and images, which have the additional advantage of readily engrafting themselves on the high culture of a society. Anything drawing people out of themselves and into contact with their fellows or with the objects of this world is beneficial, and curiously for Hume sacred rites came to have that function.[41]

What is important to bear in mind when we consider Hume's astonishing endorsement of idolatry is that the image or ritual must always serve as a distraction from theogeny, from faith in divine afflatus. Such a conception of ritualism is, of course, something of a paradox. Despite his claim that people never in fact believe in a spiritual reality, so powerful are the "impressions, made by common sense and by experience" (NHR, 74), Hume seems to fear the possibility that religious preoccupations could supplant the reality of nature, unless people are constantly succored by contact with the external world. His obsessive concern with belief in the real presence, a concern appearing even in the History (H, 3:365), is an example. He does not mind the worship of an idol, as long as the idol remains more of a thing or object than an incarnation. If, to use Hume's phrasing, "profane reason" is to have any chance of defeating "sacred mystery" (NHR, 66), reason has to employ the weapon implied by the epithet "profane"; it has to commit sacrilege upon the sacred object, divesting the icon of its mysterious association and reaffirming instead its material reality. This is the intention behind much of Hume's rather crude raillery. The Egyptians worship cats—but only grown cats: they "drown the holy spawn or little sucking gods, without any scruple or remorse" because common sense dictates that "a couple of cats, in fifty years, would stock a whole kingdom" and "entirely starve the men" (NHR, 72). So much for feline incarnation. Even the more specious doctrine of transubstantiation, supported by all the learning of the Church of Rome, receives a similar jolt from everyday reality. In one of the "pleasant stories" mocking the real presence, Hume tells of a counter falling by accident among the holy wafers. The unfortunate communicant receiving this hard object exclaims at last to the priest: "I wish . . . you have not committed some mistake: I wish you have not given me God the Father: He is so hard and tough there is no swallowing him" (NHR, 67).[42] Confronted with such a real presence, there is indeed no swallowing any religious doctrine. Such is the effect of the numerous anecdotes interwoven into Hume's text.

Thus subtly Hume fights religion on its own ground. His treatment of holy objects tends to reverse the sacramental precedence of invisible and spiritual over visible and material. Sensation is first, and the order of reality it suggests displaces the nebulous witchings of theogeny. Is the image just an object, or rather an incarnation of the spirit? With Hume the spiritual dimension is a threat, and it can never gain an ascendent over the imagination when one focuses on the physical properties of the object: it is a shape fashioned from oak; it is made of cold, white, heavy marble.[43] Hume tolerates paganism because its gods are so palpably real, objects of human contrivance first and foremost, incapable of suggesting any large and mysterious spirit; and when they represent anything beyond themselves, it is usually something familiar—the sun or the moon, or deities with enough human frailty and passion to make them our distant relatives. To be sure, Hume finds the ethics of paganism congenial, but that happy influence on the believer is, after all, a result of mythology's palpable incarnations.

In many respects, of course, whether religious practice takes the form Hume recommends is beyond the power of anyone to predict or control. The efforts of James I to introduce decent forms and ceremonies into the Kirk, though commendable in theory, were so repugnant to the Scottish fanatics that his reforms were worse than no efforts at all. Moreover, those recommendations in the *History of England* and *NHR* for the control of religious zeal derive from centuries of human experience. From Hume's philosophical perspective, we can observe the pleasant mythology of the ancients, the suffocating superstition of the Middle Ages, the frightening enthusiasm of the Reformation. At best, we observe and conclude. Still, Hume's history teaches that the civil magistrate can do much to ensure that religion takes the form most likely to support, rather than destroy, human happiness and civilization. Let us consider these feasible policies.

In the great Tudor monarchs Henry VIII and Elizabeth we see examples of how the magistrate can hold ecclesiastical encroachment and mischief in check. By making himself head of the church, Henry effectively ensured the supremacy of civil authority. His daughter Elizabeth maintained this policy, conferring just enough dignity and pelf on the established church while frustrating efforts of both Puritan and Catholic extremists to exert power. Henry made civil authority supreme by the force of his own personality; Elizabeth, by political shrewdness and aloofness from doctrinal polemics. In their Stuart successors James and Charles, however, we see examples of what monarchs ought to avoid. Although head of the church, James became too involved in theological disputes and thereby lost that neutrality that alone could guarantee the magistrate's superiority:

he had not perceived, that, in the same proportion as this practical knowledge of theology is requisite, the speculative refinements in it are mean, and even dangerous in a monarch. By entering zealously into frivolous disputes, James gave them an air of importance and dignity, which they could not otherwise have acquired; and being himself inlisted in the quarrel, he could no longer have recourse to contempt and ridicule, the only proper method of appeasing it. (H, 5:11–12)

In the case of Charles, though his misfortunes were complicated by one imprudence after another and by a host of fateful circumstances seemingly beyond his control, he precipitated his downfall by granting the established church too much authority, all under the delusion of opposing Puritan sedition: "nor did he foresee, that the ecclesiastical power, which he exalted, not admitting of any precise boundary, might in time become more dangerous to public peace, and no less fatal to royal prerogative than the other" (H, 5:228). We note in both passages that a mistaken policy toward religion became "dangerous" to civil power. Stepping back in the *Dialogues,* Hume poses, "Is there any Maxim in Politics more certain and infallible, than that both the Number and Authority of Priests shou'd be confin'd within very narrow Limits, and that the civil Magistrate ought, for ever, to keep his *Fasces* and *Axes* from such dangerous Hands?" (D, 255)[44]

The warning is clear: the magistrate must at all costs stay aloof and superior; he must allow the religious spirit some freedom of expression—for Hume has posited that religious worship is a nearly universal human need—but the magistrate must keep that spirit from usurping civil authority. How can this end be attained? A three-page digression at the beginning of chapter 29 in the *History* explains what the magistrate must do.

Hume divides the "arts and professions" into two groups: (1) those providing profit, advantage, or pleasure to their practitioners and hence needing no encouragement by the state; and (2) those, such as civil service and the military, that require public support. Into which group do ecclesiastics fall? They may appear to be examples of the first kind, for surely assiduous ministry will win them adulation and income. Perhaps they should be allowed to prosper in a laissez-faire economy.

But if we consider the matter more closely, we shall find, that this interested diligence of the clergy is what every wise legislator will study to prevent. . . . Each ghostly practitioner, in order to render himself more precious and sacred in the eyes of his retainers, will inspire them with the most violent abhorrence of all other sects, and continually endeavour, by some novelty to excite the languid devotion of his audience. No regard will be paid to truth, morals, or decency in the doctrines inculcated. Every tenet will be adopted that best suits the disorderly affections of the human frame. Customers will be drawn to each conventicle by new industry and address in practising on the passions and credulity of the populace. And in the end, the civil magistrate will find, that he has dearly paid for his pretended frugality, in saving a fixed establishment for the priests; and that in reality the most decent and advantageous composition, which he can make with the spiritual guides, is to bribe their indolence, by assigning stated salaries to their profession, and rendering it superfluous for them to be farther active, than merely to prevent their flock from straying in quest of new pastures. And in this manner ecclesiastical establishments . . . prove in the end advantageous to the political interests of society. (*H*, 3:135–36)

Here is the passage that fully explicates that brief remark in the *Dialogues*, namely, that "the utmost a wise Magistrate can propose with regard to popular Religions, is, as far as possible, to make a saving Game of it" (*D*, 255). In both instances Hume's language is cynical: the "saving Game" becomes a "composition," an arrangement or deal by which the magistrate bribes the priest not to be overzealous in his spiritual duties! An established church becomes an ineffectual church, and thereby it serves the state. The citizens can worship God, but nothing religious will ever assume much place or sway in their lives. Ecclesiastics, meanwhile, will have sufficient reward to make it unnecessary for them to exercise spiritual power. Hume's recommendation is a travesty of religion, but on his terms it is an ideal. In respect to the metaphor used earlier, the establishment of a state church can be regarded as an inoculation against the religious disease.

This policy of ecclesiastical establishment might imply that the magistrate will permit no other religion but the official one, but Hume is adamant that only complete toleration will assure the tranquillity of society. We saw in the long passage just quoted that the indolent ecclesiastic is presumed to have just enough industry to prevent the straying of his flock. Exactly how he might herd them without some effort is not very clear. One imagines that some degree of zeal and intolerance might be required. However, Hume implies that most of these ovine human beings will be satisfied by being part of an official, albeit tepid, religion. For the others—apparently the black sheep—provision must be allowed for the exercise of their whimsies. "Like madmen, . . . [they must be] soothed, and flattered, and deceived into tranquillity" (*H*, 6:322). Under no circumstances, however, must the magistrate augment their zeal by attempting to extinguish it. Even more important than establishing a church, a policy of toleration is history's great lesson in the control of religious malady.

In case after case, attempts to suppress an unwanted sect by persecution have succeeded only in strengthening it. Hume is never amazed that a heretic braves horrible tortures and goes eagerly to the flames. The reason is not the miraculous intervention of divine power. During the reign of Edward VI, one Dutchman accused of heresy "suffered with so much satisfaction, that he hugged and caressed the faggots, that were consuming him; a species of frenzy, of which there is more than one instance among the martyrs of that age" (*H*, 3:367). Clearly, the reward of martyrs is the admiration and sympathy of mankind—not to mention a heavenly glory—and no man can be a martyr if there is no one to persecute him. Hume tells the story of one James Naylor, a Quaker who went mad in the conviction that he was Christ. The foolish Parliament took the matter seriously and

> condemned him to be pilloried, whipped, burned in the face, and to have his tongue bored through with a red hot iron. All these severities he bore with the usual patience. So far his delusion supported him. But the sequel spoiled all. He was sent to Bridewell, confined to hard labour, fed on bread and water, and debarred from all his disciples, male and female. His illusion dissipated; and after some time, he was contented to come out an ordinary man, and return to his usual occupations. (*H*, 6:146)

The incarceration of this holy lunatic may not seem an instance of toleration, but it was far more lenient and effective than the former torture and notoriety. The cure for Naylor illustrates the paradoxical maxim that the strength of religious zeal is proportional to the harshness of its attempted suppression.[45] And in this particular case the second treatment was ideal: what better way to snuff out the frenzy than to remove its fuel—the adulation of disciples, especially, as Hume cannot help noting, Naylor's female attendants?

Hume's longest and most important treatment of this subject occurs in the Tudor volumes (*H*, 3:430–35). Hume summarizes the arguments pro and contra toleration as if the two great spokesmen for these positions, Cardinal Pole and Lord Chancellor Gardiner respectively, were presenting their cases before Queen Mary and her consort Philip.[46] The passage is a brilliant piece of sustained irony. The case for toleration that Cardinal Pole "might have supported" rests on the assumption that any certitude concerning matters religious is hopeless anyway, whereas the case that Gardiner "might have supported" accepts that assumption by maintaining that therefore only one official religion should be permitted in order to create an illusion of certitude. Both positions—carefully fashioned by Hume—dismiss any possibility of truth or importance in religious questions; they differ mainly in their degree of enlightenment and humanity. And while both views claim to have civil tranquillity in mind, only Pole's—or more appositely, Hume's—would ensure such stability.[47]

Pole's arguments are as follows: (1) "persecution . . . is the scandal of all religion"; (2) those who are sure of their beliefs never feel threatened by those who disagree, and so zeal and acrimony in religious polemics prove only that the subject is one that "men . . . neither clearly comprehend, nor entirely believe," and thus is "least subjected to the criterion of human reason"; (3) persecution encourages a paranoid closemindedness, introducing "the abject terrors of superstition" and "the endless encroachments of ecclesiastics"; (4) it is barbarous to persecute "multitudes . . . of every rank and station"; (5) such persecution fails in any case because it "serves only to make men more obstinate in their persuasion, and to encrease . . . their proselytes"; (6) the solution is therefore obvious:

Open the door to toleration, mutual hatred relaxes among the sectaries; their attachment to their particular modes of religion decays; the common occupations and pleasures of life succeed to the acrimony of disputation; and the same man, who, in other circumstances, would have braved flames and tortures, is induced to change his sect from the smallest prospect of favour and advancement, or even from the frivolous hope of becoming more fashionable in his principles. (*H,* 3:433)

Essentially, then, toleration allows the common interests of life to take their rightful precedence over the pursuit of spiritual chimeras. In a parting shot Hume has the sly effrontery to make his enlightened cardinal observe that the only exception to "this maxim of toleration" would be a situation in which the magistrate quickly excised a completely new and alien religion before it had any chance of spreading. "But as this exception would imply some apology for the ancient pagan persecutions, or for the extirpation of Christianity in China and Japan; it ought surely on account of this detested consequence, to be rather buried in eternal silence and oblivion" (H, 3:433). Might it not seem that the ultimate solution to the problem of persecution would have been the total destruction of Christianity in the beginning, had that only been possible?

In any case, Hume regards the arguments put in the mouth of Pole as "entirely satisfactory, yet such is the subtilty of human wit, that Gardiner, and other enemies to toleration, were not reduced to silence. . . ." Gardiner supposedly argued as follows: (1) toleration implies "an indifference among all religions, such an obscurity in theological doctrines" as would suggest that "the dictates of Heaven . . . [are] the mere fictions of human imagination" [what else, we hear Hume ask]; (2) "persecution may . . . seem better calculated to make hypocrites than converts," but hypocrisy sometimes fosters belief and at least makes the children of hypocrites orthodox; (3) "the temporal and frivolous interests of civil society" are nothing in comparison with the spiritual; (4) even so, persecution will "restore, at least for a time, the public tranquillity"; (5) "if persecution of any kind be admitted, the most bloody and violent will surely be allowed the most justifiable, as the most effectual" because it will eradicate or at least intimidate the opposition (H, 3:433–34).

Surely no reader of the History would remain undecided for one moment. The narrow and sanguinary arguments of the persecutors stand in striking contrast to those advanced for toleration—mild, enlightened, plausible. It is telling, however, that the arguments against toleration in fact carried the day—"agreeable," as they were, "to the cruel bigotry of Mary and Philip." And thus ensued "the scenes of horror" in one of history's worst ages of persecution, earning for Mary the opprobrious epithet "Bloody."

Unfortunately, history provides more lessons of mistaken policy regarding religion than of success. However, in the example of what the Church of England had finally become in the eighteenth century after the policies of both ecclesiastical establishment and toleration had gradually been hammered out in the Restoration and Glorious Revolution, Hume found a desirable model. As John B. Stewart notes, Hume's attitude toward the Anglican Church went from suspicion in 1741 to approval by the time of the writing of the History and after.[48] It is not difficult to understand why. The church retained just enough ritual and liturgy—idolatry, if you will—to distract the worshiper from theogenic reverie and rivet his attention on the things of the world—but not to such a degree that he would be overwhelmed with superstitious fear. Therein it resembled ancient paganism. The clergy were by and large learned and worldly, little inclined to foment zeal or discord. They enjoyed sufficient advantage from the state. The magistrate sat at the head of the church, supporting it but at the same time controlling its power and enforcing toleration.

In many respects, then, the Church of England proved the validity of Hume's prescription for treating the religious malady. As a model, it doubtless suggested the answer to him even as he wrote. But we should not assume too much. We should not imagine that Hume's endorsement of the English church was unqualified. Like other communions, it could still be intolerant. Happily, civil power had been able to restrain that intolerance; as Hume notes with acerbity: "if, amongst *Christians*, the *English* and *Dutch* have embraced the principles of toleration, this singularity has proceeded from the steddy resolution of the civil magistrate, in opposition to the continued efforts of priests and bigots" (*NHR*, 60–61). Even the revolution that established the English magistrate, Henry VIII, over the church was hardly the triumph of human reason. Rather, its "many beneficial consequences" were "perhaps neither foreseen nor intended by the persons who had the chief hand in conducting [that revolution]" (*H*, 3:207). Hume may hold up Anglicanism as a model of popular religion, but its principal recommendation remains its subservience to civil authority, a subservience accidental and precarious.

The Historian's "Profane Reason against Sacred Mystery"

Gibbon called Hume "our philosophical historian."[49] Such a title describes quite well the attitude Hume takes toward his material and the relationship he cultivates with his readers in his history just as much as in his philosophy. The philosophical historian speaks to an elite readership as if to a close friend— indeed, as if to himself. His is the carefully modulated voice of superior vantage, registering both human folly and achievement. This attitude is what Hume himself describes at the end of *NHR*. He says to his enlightened reader that the only hope for objectivity and balance is to "enlarge our view, and opposing one species of superstition to another, set them a quarreling; while we ourselves, during their fury and contention, happily make our escape, into the calm, tho' obscure, regions of philosophy" (*NHR*,

95). This suggestion may appear smug and cynical; in some ways it signals Hume's exasperated flight from an entangling and by now wearisome subject. Yet the suggestion does underscore Hume's customary tone in almost all his writings—that almost Olympian detachment and superiority that must insulate the philosopher or philosophical historian from the contagion of human folly. Hume suggests that it is often a good idea to keep one's distance.

Hume is showing the ideal reader how to regard *homo religiosus*. Sometimes Hume seems almost unable to contain himself, so outrageously ludicrous is the matter before him—like the convoluted logic of the medieval church: "Such were the reasonings prevalent in that age; reasonings, which, though they cannot be passed over in silence, without omitting the most curious and, perhaps, not the least instructive part of history, can scarcely be delivered with the requisite decency and gravity" (*H*, 1:244). Perhaps the historian manages to keep a straight face, but the reader not infrequently laughs aloud: whether at the quixotic efforts of churchmen to proscribe long pointed shoes and long curly hair (*H*, 1:241–42); or at an English Parliament solemnly debating the problem of free will, a question "to which the greatest philosophers, in the tranquillity of retreat, had never hitherto been able to find any satisfactory solution" [until the *Treatise*, we wonder?] (*H*, 5:212); or at the absurdity and scandal, apparently lost on every contemporary churchman, that the altar of Thomas à Becket had eclipsed the altars of both God and the Virgin:

> The devotion towards him had quite effaced in that place the adoration of the Deity: nay, even that of the Virgin. At God's altar, for instance, there were offered in one year three pounds two shillings and six pence; at the Virgin's, sixty-three pounds five shillings and six pence; at St. Thomas's, eight hundred and thirty-two pounds twelve shillings and three pence. But next year, the disproportion was still greater: There was not a penny offered at God's altar; the Virgin's gained only four pounds one shilling and eight pence; but St. Thomas had got for his share nine hundred and fifty-four pounds six shillings and three pence. (*H*, 3:254)

The inclusion of monetary figures is here not beneath the notice of history—a history in any case that wishes to turn religious matters to ridicule, to employ "profane reason against sacred mystery" (*NHR*, 66).

It is instructive to compare Hume's phrasing with that of his source, Gilbert Burnet's *History of the Reformation of the Church of*

England[50]—not exactly an unbiased history, we might note, but no matter if the purpose is to discredit beatification. Burnet writes,

> So that for 300 Years, he was accounted one of the greatest Saints in Heaven, as may appear from the accounts in the Leger-Books, of the Offerings made to the three greatest Altars in Christ's Church in *Canterbury.* The one was to Christ, the other to the Virgin, and the third to *St. Thomas.* In one Year there was offered at Christ's Altar, *3 l. 2 s. 6 d.* To the Virgins Altar, *63 l. 5 s. 6 d.* But to *St. Thomas's* Altar *832 l. 12 s. 3 d.* But the next Year the Odds grew greater; for there was not a penny offered at Christ's Altar, and at the Virgins, only *4 l. 1 s. 8 d.* But at *St. Thomas's 954 l. 6 s. 3 d.*

Hume is entirely faithful to Burnet, but by interpolation and changes of phrasing he magnifies the scandal. Hume prefaces his ledger-book details with the pointed summary that devotion toward Becket "had quite effaced . . . the adoration of the Deity," with the afterthought of withering irony—"nay, even that of the Virgin"—as if we might expect in the illogical worship of the medieval church that a saint might well displace God, but the Virgin Mary, too? Hume also calls Christ's altar, God's, as though to make Becket's usurpation even more outrageous and absurd. And the alteration of Burnet's last sentence is effective. By making "St. Thomas" the subject of an active verb, Hume insinuates that the saint himself was competing with the Virgin for pennies— God being already out of the contest—and easily outbegging her: "but St. Thomas had got for his share. . . ."

The literary technique Hume uses in the foregoing narrative is known as low burlesque—that is, the ridicule of something supposedly elevated by means of undignified language and detail— such as counting pence at the holy altar. The most famous example in English is Samuel Butler's *Hudibras,* a work usually credited with discountenancing Puritanism once and for all. Hume says of *Hudibras,* "No composition abounds so much . . . in strokes of just and unimitable wit. . . . The advantage which the royal cause received from this poem, in exposing the fanaticism and false pretences of the former parliamentary party, was prodigious" (*H,* 6:544–45). Hume recognizes the power of ridicule against religion and he is not above using even low burlesque, in addition to his more customary verbal irony.[51]

Hume's portraits of three religious heroes—Thomas à Becket, Joan of Arc, and Sir Thomas More—illustrate how he examines the effects of religious zeal in certain great individuals, making full use of reason and ridicule. Hume's purpose, of course, is to break the spell of sanctity, to decanonize the saint, to guide the reader in seeing what lies behind the miraculous story, to know what the relic is in fact made of. Hume's portraits might be called profane exempla, or skeptical hagiography.

First, Thomas à Becket, whose life according to Hume we turn back to after already having witnessed the later scandal of his Canterbury shrine. To tell of Becket is to tell also of Henry II and of that famous friendship that turned to bitter enmity. It is a story of mitre against crown, an object lesson of the danger to civil authority posed by religion. It is also a metaphor of the Dark Ages, when only universal ignorance and superstition could have made the story possible.

There are qualities in Becket that Hume admires. He had abilities, enterprise, and courage, and Hume can only deplore that such admirable traits became successful weapons against civil authority. Essential to Hume's decanonization of Becket is to emphasize these qualities of the man. As natural concomitants to his abilities, enterprise, and courage were his inflexibility, pride, vaingloriousness. To be proud, to love glory, is for Hume no fault in a man of great abilities, but such a bent is more than a fault when it hides behind the cloak of the humble man of God and when that cloak becomes a means to power and glory. Such is the case of Thomas à Becket, according to Hume.

There were two phases in Becket's life. The first was as the trusted favorite and chancellor of Henry. This phase was all power and magnificence. Becket was not only chancellor, but also one of the greatest lords in England:

> As his way of life was splendid and opulent, his amusements and occupations were gay, and partook of the cavalier spirit, which, as he had only taken deacon's orders, he did not think unbefitting his character. He employed himself at leisure hours in hunting, hawking, gaming, and horsemanship; he exposed his person in several military actions; he carried over, at his own charge, seven hundred knights to attend the king in his wars at Toulouse; . . . and in an embassy to France, with which he was entrusted, he astonished that court by the number and magnificence of his retinue. (H, 1:308)

How could Henry have suspected that the same delight in service and show, manifest in the secular world, could be expressed even better in the religious?

Hoping to have a perfect accomplice in suppressing the church's power, Henry made Becket archbishop of Canterbury.

When Hume refers to the primate as "the second person in the kingdom, with some pretensions of aspiring to be the first" (*H*, 1:309), he not only foreshadows the conflict between these two strong figures, but also points to the ruling passion of Becket— ambition, that most dangerous aspect of the ecclesiastical character. And from that point on every action seems calculated to satisfy that ambition. Becket struck all by the sudden transformation of his character: no longer a magnificent epicurean, he became the most magnificently austere ascetic. Note, however, the explanation Hume offers:

> He maintained, in his retinue and attendants alone, his ancient pomp and lustre, which was useful to strike the vulgar: In his own person he affected the greatest austerity, and most rigid mortification, which, he was sensible, would have an equal or a greater tendency to the same end. He wore sack-cloth next to his skin, which, by his affected care to conceal it, was necessarily the more remarked by all the world: He changed it so seldom, that it was filled with dirt and vermin: His usual diet was bread; his drink water, which he even rendered farther unpalatable by the mixture of unsavoury herbs: He tore his back with the frequent discipline which he inflicted on it: He daily on his knees washed, in imitation of Christ, the feet of thirteen beggars, whom he afterwards dismissed with presents: He gained the affections of the monks by his frequent charities to the convents and hospitals: Every one, who made profession of sanctity, was admitted to his conversation, and returned full of panegyrics on the humility, as well as on the piety and mortification, of the holy primate: He seemed to be perpetually employed in reciting prayers and pious lectures, or in perusing religious discourses: His aspect wore the appearance of seriousness and mental recollection, and secret devotion. (*H*, 1:309– 10)

The details are true to the historical sources, but the emplotment stressing Becket's vainglorious piety and humility, and his conversion as a marvelous show, is Hume's own. The profane historian is fashioning his moral; he is guiding the reader to see through the saint's pretensions. Without question "all men of penetration plainly saw, that [Becket] was meditating some great design, and that the ambition and ostentation of his character had turned itself towards a new and more dangerous object" (*H*, 1:310). Hume's interpretation of the archbishop's character admits no other conclusion.

Then follows the well-known story of the increasing tension and conflict between king and archbishop—with Henry, a "sovereign of the greatest abilities," exerting all his considerable power to weaken the church and crush the primate, and with Becket, a "prelate of the most inflexible and intrepid character" (*H*, 1:312), opposing the king at every step. Even though Hume sides with Henry's goal of limiting the church's usurpation of civil power, he actually appears more sympathetic with Becket as Henry's measures become more and more tyrannical. Only after Becket's flight to France and the clear swing of fortune in his favor does Hume again sound the warning that Becket was not finally deserving of sympathy: "The violent and unjust prosecution of Becket, had a natural tendency to turn the public favour on his side, and to make men overlook his former ingratitude towards the king, and his departure from all oaths and engagements, as well as the enormity of those ecclesiastical privileges, of which he affected to be the champion" (*H*, 1:322). The reason for Hume's antipathy is that Becket, taking "it for granted, as a point incontestible, that his cause was the cause of God" (*H*, 1:324), was able to wield a power superior even to that of a great king. "Instigated by revenge, and animated by the present glory attending his situation . . . [Becket] suspended the spiritual thunder over Henry himself" (*H*, 1:325). Hume seems to share the abasement of the king when, "on one occasion [Henry] humiliated himself so far as to hold the stirrup of that haughty prelate, while he mounted" (*H*, 1:329). The symbolism of ecclesiastical power over civil could not be more graphic.

All of Henry's efforts to appease the archbishop were for naught. The "dangerous contest between the civil and spiritual powers" (*H*, 1:332), initiated by Henry, had now begun to augur well for Becket. The archbishop was now in control, dictating his will to the king, proceeding "with the more courage to dart his spiritual thunders" (*H*, 1:331). A despairing Henry cried out in frustration, and four of his knights hastened to serve him by carrying out the notorious assassination of the archbishop. If the murder were not Henry's wish, as of course he vehemently protested, it was mainly because of the probable retaliation by the church, only narrowly averted by his humiliation and penance. Otherwise the elimination of so powerful a champion for the church would seem the only solution to Henry's dilemma.

Hume's most damaging volley at Becket is his highly troped analysis of the martyr's character, set against the background of the age:

> This was the tragical end of Thomas à Becket, a prelate of the most lofty, intrepid, and inflexible spirit, who was able to cover, to the world and probably to himself, the enterprizes of pride and ambition,

under the disguise of sanctity and of zeal for the interests of religion: An extraordinary personage, surely, had he been allowed to remain in his first station, and had directed the vehemence of his character to the support of law and justice; instead of being engaged, by the prejudices of the times, to sacrifice all private duties and public con-nexions to tyes, which he imagined, or represented, as superior to every civil and political consideration. But no man, who enters into the genius of that age, can reasonably doubt of this prelate's sincerity. The spirit of superstition was so prevalent, that it infallibly caught every careless reasoner, much more every one whose interest, and honour, and ambition, were engaged to support it. All the wretched literature of the times was inlisted on that side: Some faint glimmer-ings of common sense might sometimes pierce through the thick cloud of ignorance, or what was worse, the illusions of perverted science, which had blotted out the sun, and enveloped the face of nature: But those who preserved themselves untainted by the general contagion, proceeded on no principles which they could pretend to justify: They were more indebted to their total want of instruction, than to their knowledge, if they still retained some share of under-standing: Folly was possessed of all the schools as well as all the churches; and her votaries assumed the garb of philosophers together with the ensigns of spiritual dignities. Throughout that large collec-tion of letters, which bears the name of St. Thomas, we find, in all the retainers of that aspiring prelate, no less than in himself, a most entire and absolute conviction of the reason and piety of their own party, and a disdain of their antagonists: Nor is there less cant and grimace in their stile, when they address each other, than when they compose manifestos for the perusal of the public. The spirit of revenge, vio-lence, and ambition, which accompanied their conduct, instead of forming a presumption of hypocrisy, are the surest pledges of their sincere attachment to a cause, which so much flattered these domi-neering passions. (*H*, 1:333–34)

It is a brilliant, if tendentious, character study, arguing forcefully that in the example of Becket we see how far holy zeal can lead a man from his private and public duties, how far it can deceive the world, and even the individual. Becket was a man whose great talent was perverted by religion and whose oppor-tunities to serve mankind were rejected in favor of what is to Hume a wretched, useless idealism. It is interesting also that Hume sees Becket as a perfect type of the religious hypocrite—sincere in all he did, more unaware than anyone else of the true motive for his saintliness: personal glory and power. We see in this passage evidence of Hume the close reader, capable of per-ceiving in the tone of Becket's correspondence those verbal man-nerisms and signs characteristic of delusion. It is a paradox, he observes, that those very pretensions suggesting arrant hypocrisy in fact prove Becket sincere—and self-deceived.

Hume shows himself personally involved in this passage as well. The case of Thomas à Becket is of extreme significance to him, and here his language becomes more figurative, passionate, hyperbolical. "Illusions of perverted science . . . blotted out the sun"; "votaries [of Folly] assumed the garb of philosophers." A reader might well imagine himself in the world of Pope's *Dunciad*, with the forces of Mother Dulness threatening the extinction of all light, the ultimate *fiat nox*. There can be little question that for Hume religious power in the hands of a devotee like Becket could ultimately threaten civilization itself.

In the case of Joan of Arc, Hume must deal with the miraculous, a subject the author of the first *Enquiry*, section 10, "Of Miracles," was well prepared for. Certainly the story of Joan was suited for inspiring the popular imagination, giving credence to the possibility of divine intervention in the affairs of mankind.[52] In this narrative Hume lays bare the whole miraculous imposture. He telescopes the argument in "Of Miracles" to the bald hypothesis that there can be no miracles in human history—presumably the only history worth studying—because there are always more reasonable explanations of supposedly miraculous events: "It is the business of history to distinguish between the *miraculous* and the *marvellous*; to reject the first in all narrations merely profane and human; to doubt the second; and when obliged by unquestionable testimony, as in the present case, to admit of something extraordinary, to receive as little of it as is consistent with the known facts and circumstances" (*H*, 2:398). Such is not a predisposition to believe much of this wondrous legend. Though most people eagerly attend the marvelous, Hume and his readers will not be so credulous. Yet Hume's account of the Maid of Orleans will show exactly why human credulity abounds.

Hume may be rigorously skeptical of Joan's miraculous power, but throughout his story he is quite sympathetic to her as an individual. Even her original inspiration of divine mission was owing to her "generous" and "tender" response to the pathetic misfortune of her king. She desperately wanted to assist him, and "an uncommon intrepidity of temper made her overlook all the dangers, which might attend her in such a path" (*H*, 2:398). She was but an unusually talented and brave girl who longed to be part of a noble enterprise to the extent that she at last believed herself divinely appointed to carry it out.

This insidious conjunction of desire, or interest, with belief is the thread running through the story, explaining why Joan was able to accomplish deeds that do appear extraordinary—if finally neither miraculous nor even marvelous. Hume offers a psychological explanation. She—and many of the French people likewise—believed because she needed to believe. Her role as savior was a manifestation of wish-fulfillment. Other Frenchmen, more cautious and rational, perceived the advantage of so powerful a weapon as this enthusiastic belief, which was thrust into their hands. In any event, the French soldiers regarded themselves as invincible and conducted themselves as if they were. The English soldiers, on the other hand, were paralyzed with superstitious fear: "their wonted courage and confidence was wholly gone, and had given place to amazement and despair" (*H*, 2:402). Mass hysteria took hold, and the tables were turned: "every circumstance was now reversed in the opinions of men, on which all depends" (*H*, 2:401). In a warfare of hand-to-hand combat, everything indeed depends upon self-confidence and morale. It is not surprising that the French won battle after battle. There was hardly a miracle in that. And Joan of Arc may have fought with great valor, but there is nothing miraculous in that. In this dangerous pass the English tried to ascribe Joan's power to the devil rather than to God, but, as Hume observes with dry understatement, what difference does it make who is one's supernatural enemy? Satan is surely as terrifying as God. Thus the English "derived not much consolation from the enforcing of this opinion" (*H*, 2:402).

Hume does not necessarily doubt what Joan accomplished nor even deny that it all was admittedly extraordinary. Ignoring the miraculous possibility, he simply looks for other answers. Repeatedly he asks, as in "Of Miracles," what is the more probable explanation?

> In the account of all these successes, the French writers, to magnify the wonder, represent the maid . . . as not only active in combat, but as performing the office of general; directing the troops, conducting the military operations, and swaying the deliberations in all councils of war. It is certain, that the policy of the French court endeavoured to maintain this appearance with the public: but it is much more probable, that Dunois and the wiser commanders prompted her in all her measures, than that a country girl, without experience or education, could, on a sudden, become expert in a profession, which requires more genius and capacity, than any other active scene of life. It is sufficient praise, that she could distinguish the persons on whose

judgment she might rely; that she could seize their hints and suggestions, and, on a sudden, deliver their opinions as her own; and that
she could curb, on occasion, that visionary and enthusiastic spirit,
with which she was actuated, and could temper it with prudence and
discretion. (*H*, 2:403–04)

To be sure, by a miracle a country girl could suddenly have the
ability of a great general, but Hume does not even entertain that
possibility: he looks only for the probable. He does praise this
wonderful girl, but not as a "celestial deliverer" or "prophetess"
(*H*, 2:400, 404). And at the end of this passage, in a strain of
amused irony, he seems to value her most for being able to
temper her enthusiastic fantasies with reason whenever it was to
her advantage.

Joan's capture and execution round off the story and drive
home the lesson. Captured in battle and guiltless of any crime,
she deserved honorable treatment as a prisoner of war. Yet the
English regent, the duke of Bedford, praised earlier for prudence
and capacity, now took mean revenge on her by using religion as
a pretext, covering "under that cloak his violation of justice and
humanity" (*H*, 2:408). Convicted of heresy and condemned to be
burned at the stake, Joan "felt her spirit at last subdued; and those
visionary dreams of inspiration, in which she had been buoyed
up by the triumphs of success and the applauses of her own party,
gave way to the terrors of that punishment to which she was
sentenced. She publicly declared herself willing to recant; she
acknowledged the illusion of those revelations . . . and she promised never more to maintain them" (*H*, 2:409). Despite the ac-
knowledgment that the miracles were without foundation, "the
barbarous vengeance of Joan's enemies was not satisfied." She was
tempted into putting on the male clothing that had formerly
brought her such success, this fault supposedly indicating "a
relapse into heresy" (*H*, 2:409). And "this admirable heroine, to
whom the more generous superstition of the ancients would have
erected altars, was, on pretence of heresy and magic, delivered
over alive to the flames" (*H*, 2:410).

In the story of Joan of Arc we see the pernicious uses of
religion. Though this power saved France for a time from the
oppression of the English, the source of that salvation was surely
an illusion; it became a means to deceive the masses and a means
finally to gain an ignoble revenge on a woman who was courageous, talented, and virtuous. Remarkably, Hume suggests that a

kind of idolatry might be suitable for this heroine, but the altar that he imagines for Joan would belong to "the more generous superstition of the ancients," whose worldly polytheism, as shown before, was tolerant, optimistic, and life-affirming. His whimsical suggestion is a censure of the magical, dark superstition of medieval Christianity and of the treachery and ignominy that superstition bred.

Writing of Sir Thomas More, everyone's type of the Renaissance man and the staunch hero of principle, posed problems for Hume, because this one individual exemplified qualities he most admired and others he most despised. In this respect, Sir, or Saint, Thomas may resemble Becket, but Sir Thomas is clearly more of an enigma—and a decidedly less vulnerable target. More was liberally educated in the classics, capable of philosophical detachment and of bold intellectual creativity, serene and cheerful in temper, successful in public service, acknowledged by all as a man of unimpeachable moral character. But for Hume there was the troubling fact of More's rigid adherence to Catholic orthodoxy and his role as martyr to the cause of Rome. True, Hume could find More's vigorous opposition to Henry VIII's trampling over civil rights and freedom as very sympathetic, even noble, but there was still the fact that to Hume More was a religious bigot. How was he to treat this paradoxical man?[53]

Hume does not make any attempt to deny More's greatness. When created Lord Chancellor, More is described as "a man, who, besides the ornaments of an elegant literature, possessed the highest virtue, integrity, and capacity" (*H,* 3:184). When deposed, More is praised for his cheerful fortitude and strong character:

> The austerity of this man's virtue, and the sanctity of his manners, had no wise encroached on the gentleness of his temper, or even diminished that frolic and gaiety, to which he was naturally inclined. He sported with all the varieties of fortune into which he was thrown; and neither the pride, naturally attending a high station, nor the melancholy incident to poverty and retreat, could ever lay hold of his serene and equal spirit. (*H,* 3:197)

In his continued refusal to bend his principles in deference to Henry's entreaties and threats, More appears admirably temperate but firm (*H,* 3:205ff., 221). In his death More exhibits that courage and superiority befitting the hero:

Not only his constancy, but even his cheerfulness, nay, his usual facetiousness, never forsook him; and he made a sacrifice of his life to his integrity with the same indifference that he maintained in any ordinary occurrence. When he was mounting the scaffold, he said to one, "Friend, help me up, and when I come down again, let me shift for myself." The executioner asking him forgiveness, he granted the request, but told him, "You will never get credit by beheading me, my neck is so short." Then laying his head on the block, he bade the executioner stay till he put aside his beard: "For," said he, "it never committed treason." (H, 3:222)

There is but one fact compromising this apotheosis: "Nothing was wanting to the glory of this end, except a better cause, more free from weakness and superstition. But as the man followed his principles and sense of duty, however misguided, his constancy and integrity are not the less the objects of our admiration." One might accuse Hume of niggling objections, of a doctrinaire refusal to accord More the full measure of admiration that he deserves simply because More finally represents a genuine religious hero whose stature is difficult to assail. More, unquestionably an enlightened and virtuous man, died for his Catholic ideals, and Hume cannot accept that reality gracefully.

But there is more to Hume's wish for "a better cause, more free from weakness and superstition." Earlier in a digressionary account of the Reformation, Hume had put his finger directly on why More's cause was so vitiated. In More we have one of the most amazing examples of religious zeal altering a man's virtue, both congenital and acquired. It so happens that while he was chancellor, he was a more intolerant persecutor of heretics than his predecessor Cardinal Wolsey, "who, though himself a clergyman, bore too small a regard to the ecclesiastical order, to serve as an instrument of their tyranny." More thus becomes another striking lesson in the corrupting power of religion:

Sir Thomas More . . . is at once an object deserving our compassion, and an instance of the usual progress of men's sentiments during that age. This man, whose elegant genius and familiar acquaintance with the noble spirit of antiquity, had given him very enlarged sentiments, and who had in his early years advanced principles, which even at present would be deemed somewhat too free, had, in the course of events, been so irritated by polemics, and thrown into such a superstitious attachment to the ancient faith, that few inquisitors have been guilty of greater violence in their prosecution of heresy. Though adorned with the gentlest manners, as well as the purest integrity, he carried to the utmost height his aversion to heterodoxy; and James

Bainham, in particular, a gentleman of the Temple, experienced from him the greatest severity. Bainham, accused of favouring the new opinions, was carried to More's house; and having refused to discover his accomplices, the chancellor ordered him to be whipped in his presence, and afterwards sent him to the Tower, where he himself saw him put to the torture. (*H*, 3:215–16)

Given the mania in this age for religious persecution and its depressing frequency of horrible examples, Hume hardly appears objective in calling More one of the most violent inquisitors in history. The particular example of Bainham does not begin to compare in detail or scope with many others in Hume's own presentation of the Reformation and Counter-Reformation.[54] The exaggeration reveals instead Hume's determination to show that religion can exert its influence on the most unlikely of human beings. There is something discordant in Hume's More. This paragon of enlightened views, humanity, and equanimity can also act the cruel persecutor and then invite a needless martyrdom. He would seem something of a frightening Dr. Jekyll–Mr. Hyde personality. Hume recognizes More's greatness, but his reservation concerning the cause for which More lived and died considerably tarnishes More's glory, undercutting the reader's admiration for this widely celebrated hero. Finally, the higher Hume's praise of the good Sir Thomas, the greater the impression is made of religion's power to corrupt that goodness.

The Trivial Becomes Momentous

Most studies of Hume and religion have examined the philosopher's rejection of popular worship in light of his own accommodation with a quasi-religious position, a rational religion—if there could be such a thing—or what J. C. A. Gaskin has termed an "attenuated deism."[55] These studies ask, what religion, if any, did Hume recommend for the enlightened? It is of course quite reasonable to consider such a question, for we must presume that Hume was writing to a reader somewhat like himself and not to the masses. However, there is another dimension to Hume's attitude toward religion: what remains for "the ignorant multitude" (*NHR*, 27, 33)—subjected to pathological examination in *NHR*, massed ominously in the background of the *Dialogues*, but running amok through the chapters of the *History of England*? Philosophers may fortunately be immune to the spiritual neuroses of the ignorant vulgar, but they cannot live happily insulated from that same mass of nonphilosophers who are very much agitated by these fears and demands. Hume's shaping of history clearly shows that religious extremists can make life miserable for others, even for philosophers. This chapter has offered substantial evidence of why the historian Hume was so concerned.

In the abstract, many of the religious questions that have plagued humankind are not in themselves significant—or, one might think, very difficult to settle reasonably and amicably. In reality, however, disagreement over minor issues has again and again had great consequences. Hume makes this particular point on three different occasions in the *History of England*. Although the passages essentially agree that trivial concerns in religion can sometimes become momentous, in each statement there is an increasing emphasis on this point.

The first occurs in the Stuart volumes of the *History* (1756; imprint, 1757) and concerns a post-Restoration conference between Anglican bishops and Presbyterian ministers:

> The surplice, the cross in baptism, the kneeling at the sacrament, the bowing at the name of Jesus, were anew canvassed; and the ignorant multitude were in hopes, that so many men of gravity and learning could not fail, after deliberate argumentation, to agree in all points of controversy: They were surprized to see them separate more inflamed than ever, and more confirmed in their several prejudices. To enter into particulars would be superfluous. Disputes concerning religious forms are, in themselves, the most frivolous of any; and merit attention only so far as they have influence on the peace and order of civil society. (*H*, 6:170–71)

The tone is ironical and aloof. Hume regards such frivolous questions as beneath the notice of philosophical history, however much they may concern the "ignorant multitude"—or theologians. These issues become important only if and when they affect society. The conditional possibility is granted, but here it does not seem especially threatening.

The second statement appears in the Tudor volumes, published in 1759. It is part of a long discussion about the merits of ritualism as an innocent distraction to the ignorant multitude. Hume commends Queen Elizabeth for recognizing the advantage to the magistrate that "these inoffensive observances" ideally give, but unfortunately the zealots, not daring to oppose the whole episcopal order and liturgy openly, seized on these apparently minor forms as objects of their hatred. Hume throws up his hands in despair:

> So fruitless is it for sovereigns to watch with a rigid care over ortho-
> doxy, and to employ the sword in religious controversy, that the work,
> perpetually renewed, is perpetually to begin; and a garb, a gesture,
> nay, a metaphysical or grammatical distinction, when rendered im-
> portant by the disputes of theologians and the zeal of the magistrate,
> is sufficient to destroy the unity of the church, and even the peace of
> society. (*H*, 4:121–23)

In this case religious controversy is no longer a matter to be dismissed as frivolous unless it threatens civil order. We see that such trivialities easily become momentous, often threatening the "peace of society." The advice here is that the magistrate would do well to steer clear of these controversies and so avoid giving them an importance they would otherwise lack. As I have shown ear-lier, particularly in the discussion of toleration or in the treatment of James I's immersion in religious polemics (*H*, 5:11–12), this advice bears the mark of Hume's mature reflection on the prob-lem. If possible, the magistrate should remain somewhat re-moved, determined not to exacerbate petty wounds and inflame silly squabbles. The implication, however, is that these religious questions are ultimately inconsequential and that the magistrate can remain indifferent. But is this always so?

Hume's last considered comment on the subject was made very late in his career, appearing in a footnote added to the 1770 edition of the *History* and written with certainty no earlier than 1768:[56]

> In a letter of the king [Charles I] to the queen, . . . he says, that unless
> religion was preserved, the militia (being not as in France a formed
> powerful strength) would be of little use to the crown; and that if the
> pulpits had not obedience, which would never be, if presbyterian
> government was absolutely established, the king would have but
> small comfort of the militia. This reasoning shows the king's good
> sense, and proves, that his attachment to episcopacy, though partly
> founded on religious principles, was also, in his situation, derived
> from the soundest views of civil policy. In reality, it was easy for the
> king to perceive, by the necessary connexion between trifles and
> important matters, and by the connexion maintained at that time
> between religion and politics, that, when he was contending for the
> surplice, he was, in effect, fighting for his crown and even for his
> head. (*H*, 5:575)

One might question whether the king's letter implies so much or proves him an astute political philosopher, one remarkably resembling David Hume. For our purposes, though, what Hume reads into the letter indicates how his thinking had developed. In the last statement Hume regards the religiously trivial as necessarily connected with important matters, that preserving the surplice, could Charles have done it, would ultimately have preserved his crown and head and ensured civil stability. This opinion does not exactly square with the other policy advising the magistrate not to meddle, nor with the view stated in the 1756 volumes deploring Charles's granting the bishops too much power (*H*, 5:228), but this opinion seems to represent a more realistic and comprehensive view that the little things in religion cannot finally be ignored out of existence. It should not be so, perhaps, but those frivolous and trivial matters do become prominent in the affairs of mankind. No philosopher or magistrate can afford to remain indifferent to this fact.

Exactly what type of religion Hume would have prescribed for *homo religiosus* cannot be reduced to articles and creed. And one must admit to an apparent contradiction in Hume's prescription, for while on the one hand Hume recognizes the strong human need for religion and the large place it usually assumes in human affairs, he then recommends a popular religion that is not likely to have much importance in life—one that would certainly not minister to the spirit, since nothing spiritual is recognized to exist in any event. His popular religion would seem a kind of hoax in which people are made to believe that they have the spiritual comfort they seek when in fact they have very little, if anything: at best a few (or perhaps many?) harmless incantations and idols and an entertaining mythology that fosters their art and secular culture. But granting that Hume's religious philosophy does not allow for that spiritual reality that most believers regard as a sine qua non, we can understand what prompts his recommendations for a popular religion. In his historical writings Hume does convincingly describe the ills religion brings on society, and he shows what weakness in human nature makes these ills so prevalent. He also suggests from an historical perspective that some forms of popular religion are much less pernicious than others.

All in all, Hume finds that a religion permitting believers to remain citizens of the world will contribute to their happiness and to the peace of society. They will not be gloomy eremites, suspicious of their sinful neighbors and under the dominion of an imaginary voice; nor will they be the cowed following of a demagogical priest or prophet, who has taught them that nothing matters more than the interests of religion. Such misled and exploited flocks were common in Hume's experience, and they are not uncommon even today. Instead, Hume would have believers of another complexion, people whose religious observances do not override the goodness of their nature or devalue the practical interests of society; their observances, on the contrary, would reinforce a faith in the goodness and reality of the world outside, whether in ignorance we call it Nature, the Universe, or God's Creation. Theirs is not a religion of *contemptus mundi* but rather *amor mundi*. Some will object that such "devotion" is no less than a travesty of genuine belief, but others may concede that this worldly faith might produce more happiness and peace than have many religions—certainly most that were familiar to Hume. If the "ignorant multitude" cannot all be philosophers—nor can even philosophers, Hume would add, be always philosophers—then Hume at least provides a way for all people to enjoy what he perceives as philosophy's greatest blessing: that is, some degree of superiority to the inherent fear and malaise of the human condition.

3

The Things of This World

A prince, that is possess'd of a stately palace, commands the esteem of the people upon that account.

—*T*(1739)

A machine, a piece of furniture, a vestment, a house well contrived for use and conveniency, is so far beautiful, and is contemplated with pleasure and approbation.

—*EPM* (1751)

I am engagd in the building a house, which is the second great Operation of human Life: For the taking a Wife is the first, which I hope will come in time.

—*L* (1770)

I suppose, if Cicero were now alive, it would be difficult to fetter his moral sentiments by narrow systems; or persuade him, that no qualities were to be admitted as *virtues,* or acknowledged to be a part of *personal merit,* but what were recommended by *The Whole Duty of Man.*

—*EPM* (1770)

Virtues of the Flesh; *Pecunia, Radix Bonorum*

MANY readers of the *Treatise* are probably surprised when they come to Hume's moral theories, enunciated in Books 2 and especially 3, for these readers discover an ethics that is essentially worldly and materialistic. When one hangs an ethical system on an opposition between pride and humility (what we think of ourselves) and love and contempt (what we think of others), completely ignoring any spiritual and otherworldy dimensions, then one's inclination is to appreciate only intelligence and wit, bodily strength and beauty, houses, clothes, food, wine, and other such mental or physical possessions.[1] And when Hume asks his readers what is useful or in their best interests, he does not even imagine that they will think of their immortal souls. That "men are always more concern'd about the present life than the future . . ." (*T,* 525) is not said with regret but with approval.

This emphasis is not peculiar to the *Treatise.* Even in the recast version of the second *Enquiry*—for Hume the most successful statement of his moral principles—Hume ends up admiring the worldly while condemning those supposedly "monkish" virtues that many moral works, including the New Testament, regard as the only virtues. There is surely truth in the observation of Paschal Larkin that "the gloomy faith, the austere morals, and the perverted view of the passions for which Scottish Puritanism stood in the seventeenth century, helped to produce that philosophical reaction in the eighteenth century of which Hume was the embodiment."[2] As Gaskin reminds us, Hume's "morality is social, utilitarian and secular. The will of god and the rewards and punishments of an afterlife play no part in Hume's scheme of morals."[3]

That is not to say that Hume would ever forget that signal virtue of benevolence or sympathy—that quality of humanity that must ultimately make the man—but as we saw in chapter 1, even the sentimental in Hume becomes no expression of meek altruism but instead something rather aristocratic and grand. Moreover, sometimes when Hume recommends benevolence he must concede that other qualities of personal merit often count for more, and justifiably so.

> Give me my choice, and I would rather, for my own happiness and self-enjoyment, have a friendly, humane heart, than possess all the other virtues of Demosthenes and Philip united: but I would rather pass with the world for one endowed with extensive genius and intrepid courage, and should thence expect stronger instances of general applause and admiration. . . . Had a man the best intentions in the world, and were the farthest removed from all injustice and violence, he would never be able to make himself be much regarded, without a moderate share, at least, of parts and understanding. (*EPM,* 315–16)

How a person appears to the world, how he makes his way in the world, is important, too, and as Hume enlarges the definition of virtue, his goal is to include many worldly qualities that an orthodox moralist schooled in *The Whole Duty of Man* would not much recommend. That late in his life Hume would add a long passage on Cicero's cosmopolitan ethics and comment petulantly on the superiority of Cicero's beliefs to modern-day opinions (*EPM,* 319n.) demonstrates how important to him these secular virtues were. Although Hume would grant that to avoid verbal disputes "personal merits" might be more satisfactory a term than "virtues," he insists that such merits as abilities and understanding are virtues nonetheless.

In any list of virtues in the second *Enquiry* and in the *Treatise*, those productive of worldly success or regard predominate. Consider these terms of praise in the second *Enquiry*: capacity, industry, ingenuity, courage, good-nature, honesty, discretion, frugality, secrecy, order, perseverance, forethought, judgment, honour, wit, good manners, cheerfulness, serenity, greatness of mind—besides benevolence and humanity.[4] These are the traits of the self-controlled, contented individual, successful in the world. Benjamin Franklin's "Project of arriving at moral Perfection," described in his *Autobiography,* illustrates quite well how an ethics based on these traits can be put into action—"5. FRUGALITY. Make no Expence but to do good to others or yourself: i.e, Waste nothing. 6. INDUSTRY. Lose no Time. Be always employ'd in something useful. . . . 11. TRANQUILITY. Be not disturbed at Trifles. . . . 12. CHASTITY. Rarely use Venery but for Health or Offspring; Never to Dulness, Weakness, or the Injury of your own or another's Peace or Reputation"[5]—and it is a good example of what kind of man this ethics produces: in Franklin himself, a man remarkably close to the Humean ideal. So blessed, one can lead a full and joyful life. What else is there, Hume seems to say? Certainly in his *Autobiography* Franklin says exactly that.

According to Hume, indeed, being moral ought to be easy because it is so much in our interest—not that it saves us from damnation but rather that it makes us happy and feels so good. Hume must show Virtue as the pretty charmer she is, no longer made ugly and forbidding by wrongheaded moralists:

> The dismall dress falls off, with which many divines, and some philosophers have covered her; and nothing appears but gentleness, humanity, beneficence, affability; nay even, at proper intervals, play, frolic, and gaiety. She talks not of useless austerities and rigours, suffering and self-denial. She declares, that her sole purpose is to make her votaries and all mankind, during every instant of their existence, if possible, cheerful and happy; nor does she ever willingly part with any pleasure but in hopes of ample compensation in some other period of their lives. The sole trouble which she demands, is that of just calculation, and a steady preference of the greater happiness. And if any austere pretenders approach her, enemies to joy and pleasure, she either rejects them as hypocrites and deceivers; or,

if she admit them in her train, they are ranked, however, among the least favoured of her votaries. (*EPM*, 279–80)

Hume's Virtue is more *fille de joie* than prioress or schoolmarm. And if this moralist does not sing *carpe diem*, it is only that the calculating hedonism recommended makes many days of pleasure the eventual reward of a virtuous life! If not eating, drinking, and being merry today, then tomorrow these joys in abundance—and all the while as the lover of Virtue.

When, on the other hand, life for some reason becomes insufferable, Hume calmly recommends killing oneself as the logical way out. The primary assumption behind his notorious essay "Of Suicide" is that the life that cannot be enjoyed is not worth living: "no one can question . . . that age, sickness, or misfortune may render life a burthen, and make it worse even than annihilation. I believe that no man ever threw away life, while it was worth keeping. For such is our natural horror of death, that small motives will never be able to reconcile us to it" (*E*, 588). Certainly it is reasonable to object that by this argument individuals may take their lives too hastily, making a mistake that cannot be retracted. The person's life may have been worth keeping after all, even though for a critical moment existence may have seemed hopeless. Hume's only attempt to anticipate this objection is to say "that any one, who, without apparent reason, has had recourse to [suicide], was curst with such an incurable depravity or gloominess of temper, as must poison all enjoyment, and render him equally miserable as if he had been loaded with the most grievous misfortunes" (*E*, 588). In other words, to be under the delusion of misfortunes is for all practical purposes the same as having them. Clinical depression itself would appear a justification for suicide. By any modern norms such reasoning is unacceptable, but it does reveal something about Hume. Life ought to be happy. Anything else is not life. Hume peremptorily concludes that without real misfortunes only a person with some congenital gloominess of temper would ever voluntarily depart this life. Any such person is better off dead!

There can be little doubt that Hume not only believed but lived these views. And fortunately he never appeared to have the least reason to commit suicide. He was a man who enjoyed life and valued the things of the world. Even his massive frame, for example, attests to his love of the table. "Diderot was amazed at the tremendous bulk of the Scottish philosopher, acknowledging that he would have mistaken him for a fat well-fed Bernardine monk—*un gros Bernardin bien nourri*"6—a double irony that Hume would have much appreciated. According to Lord Charlemont, "The corpulence of his whole person was far better fitted to communicate the idea of a turtle-eating alderman than of a refined philosopher."7 And in his letters and autobiography it is apparent that this refined philosopher is inordinately concerned about his progress in the world—about his clothing, his growing fortune, his new house, his reputation, his status as a "Citizen of the World" (*L*, 1:470).8 He writes to his brother about his "500 Pounds" profit at "Stockjobbing" (*L*, 2:7), mentions his "Equipage, and 300 Ounces of Plate for [his] Table," and dreams of securing "an Office of between 2 & 4000 a Year . . . [that] stands next in Dignity to all the great Offices of the State" (*L*, 1:510–11). Indeed, Jerome Christensen argues that Hume manipulated his own literary career to become "a versatile middleman: the eighteenth-century man of letters as gentleman gone to trade."9

Hume's constant mention of money in his letters indicates its value to him. In the *History*, when discussing the formal manners that once distinguished aristocrats, he notes that this elaborate degree of ceremony was necessary to set the higher ranks off from the lower because material wealth was too scarce to serve that purpose. But nothing does so well as money: "The advantages, which result from opulence, are so solid and real, that those who are possessed of them need not dread the near approaches of their inferiors. The distinctions of birth and title, being more empty and imaginary, soon vanish upon familiar access and acquaintance" (*H*, 5:132). Hume does not usually undervalue "the distinctions of birth and title," but in this case note how much more "solid and real" are the advantages of opulence. If, according to the *Treatise*, "we can never pretend to know body otherwise than by those external properties, which discover themselves to the senses" (*T*, 64), then money has that solidity, extension, figure, motion or rest, and number that fully satisfy the senses as to its "reality." In that respect, it is suggestive that in his discussions of commerce Hume would reject paper money as being in no way equivalent to gold and silver (*E*, 316–17), and it is similarly revealing that when defining the idea of substance, his primary example would be gold, a collection of simple ideas of "yellow colour, weight, malleableness, fusibility" (*T*, 16). In any case, one can touch gold; one can see what it will buy. Perhaps money is the preeminent thing of this world.10

It may seem that I am making Hume into little more than a crass materialist, but as will become apparent, "things of this world" include far more than mechanistic or physical reality or the possession of silver and gold. Nonetheless, in this chapter I will question Peter Jones's view that the Scottish philosopher's humanism essentially precludes materialism. On the other hand, Robert Fendal Anderson has argued that Hume's epistemology logically depends upon a theory of the reality or primacy of matter: "In saying that the true and secret causes of all events lie in the fabric and structure of minute parts, Hume has made matter the sole true power in the universe, and hence the ultimate source of all causal explanation. It appears to be fundamental in Hume's metaphysics, therefore, that matter is the actual cause of all events." Donald Livingston admits that there is good reason for viewing Hume as a materialist, although he sees Hume as finally rejecting materialism in favor of a "genuine, or philosophical, theism." But John P. Wright has maintained that "Hume believed that our mental processes and contents have mechanical causes. . . . Hume attempted to put forward a mechanistic conception of human nature and . . . his principles of human nature are, at bottom, psychophysiological." Revising Kemp Smith's emphasis, Wright says, "Reason is the slave of the passions; but Hume clearly also believes that the passions are themselves the servant of the imagination."[11] Wright's concern with epistemology and ontology takes him far beyond our purview, but what is very suggestive is Wright's point that imagination itself in Hume, much as in Descartes and Malebranche, is mechanistic, being therefore thoroughly grounded in physical reality.

Worldly Traveler

We have seen that prosperity, status, indeed materiality itself are benchmarks of Hume's everyday values. An epistolary travelogue or journal, written to his brother, provides an interesting elaboration.[12] The journal records Hume's experiences in 1748 while traveling with General James St. Clair on a diplomatic mission to Vienna and Turin, an excursion that would take Hume through Holland, Germany, Austria, down through the Alps to the plains of Lombardy, and into northwestern Italy.[13] The journal, written ostensibly both to inform and to entertain his brother, gives Hume a vehicle for philosophical observation and reflection on the lives of people in other lands, much after the vogue of Enlightenment travel books and perhaps even after the genre of the citizen-of-the-world letter. There is a wealth of commentary on subjects ranging from current affairs, the conduct of the War of the Austrian Succession, the famous personages he encountered, and the landscapes and scenery. Hume makes acerbic gibes at the Court of Chastity instituted by Maria Theresa, and he gives a farcical account of how the British party was fortunately absolved from doing the customary obeissance to the empress:

> So that after we had had a little Conversation with her Imperial Majesty, we were to walk backwards, thro a very long Room, curtsying all the way: And there was very great Danger of our falling foul of each other, as well as to tumbling topsy-turvy. She saw the Difficulty we were in: And immediately calld to us: Allez, Allez, Messieurs, sans ceremonie. . . . We esteemd ourselves very much oblig'd to her for this Attention, especially my Companions, who were desperately afraid of my Falling on them & crushing them. (*L*, 1:127)

Likewise Hume smiles at himself for kissing the "Classic Ground [of Mantua] . . . that produc'd Virgil." But amongst all the news, the descriptions of strange scenes and customs, the gossip, and the badinage, one particular interest is dominant. What are the physical or material conditions of mankind in other places? What are the standards of living? Are the inhabitants well-fed, well-clothed, well-housed? Are they attractive? How well have they adapted to their environment? In material terms, are they happy?

Wherever he goes, Hume always has his eye out for evidence of prosperity and success—for buildings, bridges, roads, commerce, and the cultivation of the land. Contrivances to circumvent some natural obstruction always catch his eye. In Holland he spends a paragraph explaining the operation of an ice-boat, "an extraordinary Boat except only that it runs upon two Keels, shod with Iron." As Hume describes it, there is something comical in the alternation between sliding along on the ice and then plopping suddenly down into the water for a more conventional boat ride, but the invention does facilitate travel. The ice-boat is successful, at least after a fashion (*L*, 1:117). Hume is even more pleased with the "flying Bridge" seen on his trip down the Rhine. There is no question but that this contrivance works wonderfully:

> a flying Bridge . . . is a boat, fixt by a Chain: This chain is fixt by an Anchor to the bottom of the middle of the River far above, & is supported by seven little Boats placd at Intervals that keep it along the surface of the Water. By means of the rudder, they turn the head of the large Boat to the opposite Bank & the Current of the River carries it

over of itself. It goes over in about 4 Minutes, and will carry four or five hundred People. It stays about five or six Minutes, and then returns: Two Men are sufficient to guide it; And it is certainly a very pretty Machine. (*L* 1:121)

Hume is obviously pleased. What better indication of human ingenuity and adaptability could he find than this "very pretty Machine"?

Hume sends his own picture postcard, but consider how he sketches the scene:

Rotterdam is . . . a handsome Town. The Mixture of Houses, Trees, & Ships, has a fine Effect, & unites Town, Country, & Sea in one Prospect. Every person & every house has the Appearance of Plenty & Sobriety, of Industry & Ease. I own, however, that the Outside of their Houses are the best: They are too slight: Full of bad Windows, & not very well contriv'd. (*L*, 1:115)

If the picture is pretty, it is because Hume can see the worldly success of the Dutch, but he is disappointed that the picture is somewhat misleading: the houses are not really as comfortable as they appear. Near Cologne he is pleased to see "the Beauty of the Roads," in a "Province [that] is not fertile but is well cultivated," and that "the Country is all very populous, the Houses good, & the Inhabitants well cloth'd & well fed." But in Cologne itself, the initial appearance of a large city with sizable houses is deceptive:

You wou'd expect it must be very populous. But it is not so. It is extremely decay'd, & is even falling to ruin. Nothing can strike one with more melancholy than its Appearance where there are Marks of past Opulence & Grandeur, but such present Waste & Decay, as if it had lately escap'd a Pestilence or Famine. (*L*, 1:119–20)

Ruins, even if they had to be created, filled many an eighteenth-century aesthete with pleasurable melancholy, but for Hume there is not even sweet-sadness in contemplating the decay of "past Opulence & Grandeur."

Overall, however, Germany struck Hume as surprisingly populous, with well-built towns and cultivated fields, and his experiences there elicited this reflection:

Germany is undoubtedly a very fine Country, full of industrious honest People, & were it united it woud be the greatest Power that ever was in the World. The common People are here, almost every where, much better treated & more at their Ease, than in France; and are not very much inferior to the English, notwithstanding all the Airs the latter give themselves. There are great Advantages, in travelling, & nothing serves more to remove Prejudices: For I confess I had entertain'd no such advantageous Idea of Germany: And it gives a Man of Humanity Pleasure to see that so considerable a Part of Mankind as the Germans are in so tolerable a Condition. (L, 1:126)

Hume may appear caught up in a pose here, enjoying the role of a philosophical traveler and man of feeling, but reading the entire journal leaves us in little doubt that Hume's response to the human condition—that is to say the human material condition—is sincere. Nothing pleases him more than seeing mankind successful in this world.

But what of rugged nature—of woods, rivers, mountains, valleys—of those wild prospects that inspired the rhapsodies of eighteenth-century travelers like Thomas Gray and Horace Walpole? Hume can rise to the occasion as he winds through the Alps: "The way of travelling thro' a mountainous Country is generally very agreeable. We are oblig'd to trace the Course of the Rivers; and are always in a pretty Valley surrounded by high Hills, & have a constant & very quick Succession of wild agreeable Prospects every quarter of a Mile" (L, 1:130). But those passages have a perfunctory air about them, as if they are a necessary part of the trip and must be included. The traveler does not seem exactly overwhelmed by these scenes, as they agreeably pass by at very regular quarter-mile intervals. And Hume is soon descanting on the "fertile & finely cultivated" valleys and on the snow, not so much for its pristine beauty but rather because of how the "industrious Inhabitants" use melted snow to irrigate their fields—and later he writes about their "many Iron mines."

In fact, Hume never appreciates the natural scene very long before he notices how it affects human comfort, or discomfort, or what people have done to alter it. On the Rhine he exclaims, "Surely there never was such an Assemblage of the wild & cultivated Beauties in one Scene." And immediately we see whether it is wild or cultivated beauty that he values most: "There are . . . several magnificent Convents & Palaces to embellish the Prospects" (L, 1:121). Then he is off describing "a very thriving well built Town," "a handsome Stone Bridge," and the "flying Bridge" noted earlier. Likewise, "the first Part of the Road from Coblentz to Weis-Baden is very mountainous & woody: But populous & well cultivated" (L, 1:122). The boat trip down the Danube surely offered breathtaking scenery. Hume tames the experience into "a Variety of Scenes continually presented to us, & immediately shifted, as it were in an Opera." Among those shifting stage sets—in an opera, no less, that ultimate genre of artificiality—is the great river itself, with its banks "very wild & savage" and its "Water . . . so straitend betwixt these Mountains, that this immense River is often not 60 foot Broad." But Hume is more interested in creature comforts: "We have lain in and seen several very good Towns, in Bavaria & Austria such as Strauberg, Passau, Lintz: But what is most remarkable is the great Magnificence of some Convents, particularly Moelk, where a set of lazy Rascals of Monks live in the most splendid Misery of the World" (*L*, 1:125). Hume may not have looked with much approbation on this particular example of worldly success, but it is astonishing that he would find magnificent convents the "most remarkable" sight on the Danube.

In his observations on what humankind has built, Hume appreciates both beauty and utility. To be sure, what is useful generally strikes Hume as aesthetically pleasing as well. The useful and the beautiful are normally one and the same for him. However, in his surveys of grand buildings, for example, Hume seems more discriminating. Not every great and solid structure—no matter how well it affords shelter—is ipso facto beautiful: gothic architecture is to him less pleasing than classic. Is this judgment simply a reflection of a pronounced eighteenth-century preference—a taste or fashion, if you will—for orderly, symmetrical design over the clutter and chaos that his age perceived in the gothic? Or would Hume argue more specifically that the whole purpose of a building is in fact better served in the superior economy, simplicity, and logic of classic styles than in the superfluity and apparent illogic of the gothic? Hume never explicitly answers these questions, but in his writings he consistently displays a preference for a beauty defined by that clarity and simplicity that might seem a sine qua non of utility.[14]

Certainly this travelogue confirms that Hume's discrimination of the beautiful is connected with his predilection for the useful. We see that the gentleman of taste will not praise just any magnificent building: "Prince Eugene's Palace in the Suburbs is an expensive stately Building; but of a very barbarous Gothic Taste. He was *more skilld in battering Walls than building;* as was said of his Friend, the Duke of Marlborough" (*L*, 1:129). In the context of Hume's journal the allusion to popular witticisms about Marlborough's elephantine pile, Blenheim Palace, takes on a new edge. It is doubly an insult to consider that a man who could not build well could destroy, and from Hume's vantage what is more to be censured than the warrior who breaks down structures and causes human misery? The barbarous excess of Prince Eugene's gothic palace, like the excess of Marlborough's own baroque monstrosity, becomes a fitting emblem of the militarist's role in civilization—the emblem of waste on a large scale. The house, like the man, represents the negation of utility.

Nonetheless, a magnificent, if classic and hence beautiful, building, is a thing of joy to Hume, even if erected by a warrior, or perhaps worse, by a churchman: the appropriate symbolic equation of house and man is not always the rule. Thus Wurzburg, itself a "very well built Town" with "a very handsome Bridge," is "chiefly remarkable" because of

> a prodigious magnificent Palace of the Bishop, who is the Sovereign. Tis all of hewn Stone and of the richest Architecture. I do think the King of France has not such a House. If it be less than Versailles, tis more compleat & finish'd. What a surprizing thing it is, that these petty Princes can build such Palaces? But it has been fifty Years a rearing; & tis the chief Expence of Eclesiastics. (L, 1:124)

Manifestly Hume appreciates the grandeur and elegance of great buildings like this one. Of all the objects that have caught his attention during his travels, they are the most salient works of human art. Beauty, in a thing—an object of contrivance, of "art," in Hume's parlance—is its own excuse for being. Yet throughout the journal grandeur and elegance are seldom valued apart from utility. Of the archbishop of Cologne's grandiose palace, elegant entertainments, luxurious appointments and style of living—all, to be sure, viewed approvingly—Hume remarks wryly in closing, "However we cou'd wish, that he took a little more care of his high Ways [i.e., highways], even tho his Furniture, Pictures & Building were a little less elegant" (L, 1:120).

Hume the traveler bears a striking resemblance to Hume the moral philosopher. As philosopher Hume contends that the value of anything derives from its usefulness to ourselves or to society, and of course by this reasoning he can argue that "personal merits," or worldly attributes, are rightly classed as virtues. But this argument is grounded in the inherently greater utility of some things over others, or of some prospects over others. If a good citizen—charming, affable, enlightened, and enterprising—is superior to a monk—by Hume's reckoning, sour, rude, narrow-minded, and lazy—it is because the citizen is more useful to himself and society. Hume bases this argument on the analogy with things. A pear is more useful than a crabapple, and cultivated vineyards are certainly preferable to rugged mountainsides, in spite of the mountains' appeal to an eighteenth-century taste, whetted by Salvator Rosa.

This kind of reasoning, indeed this whole turn of mind, easily accounts for the responses noted in Hume's journal. No wonder his eye passed quickly from wild prospects to cultivated fields, from mighty rivers to flying bridges, from gothic excrescences to structures of classic harmony. The journal is in many respects a confirmation from actual experience of certain more theoretical passages in both the *Treatise* and the second *Enquiry*. Consider these two:

> I know not but a plain, overgrown with furze and broom, may be, in itself, as beautiful as a hill cover'd with vines or olive-trees; tho' it will never appear so to one, who is acquainted with the value of each. But this is a beauty merely of imagination, and has no foundation in what appears to the senses. Fertility and value have a plain reference to use; and that to riches, joy, and plenty; in which tho' we have no hope of partaking, yet we enter into them by the vivacity of the fancy, and share them, in some measure, with the proprietor. (*T,* 364)

> The eye is pleased with the prospect of corn-fields and loaded vine-yards; horses grazing, and flocks pasturing: but flies the view of briars and brambles, affording shelter to wolves and serpents.
>
> A machine, a piece of furniture, a vestment, a house well contrived for use and conveniency, is so far beautiful, and is contemplated with pleasure and approbation. . . .
>
> Can anything stronger be said in praise of a profession, such as merchandize or manufacture, than to observe the advantages which it procures to society; and is not a monk or inquisitor enraged when we treat his order as useless or pernicious to mankind? (*EPM,* 179)

It is interesting that in the first passage Hume limits imagination to a perception of utility. Once the senses have done their part, then fancy (which I am assuming here is equivalent to imagination) appears to take flight, allowing the perceiver to share in the ownership of useful and hence rich goods, apparently the highest sort of bliss! According to Hume's thinking, intense imaginative experience essentially becomes a conviction that one possesses something valuable—or at least has a sympathetic identification with someone else who owns expensive things.[15] Hume's response to a Grecian urn is worlds apart from that of Keats. In the second passage, Hume equates utility with beauty: a well-built, useful machine is beautiful (a sentiment that should strike the bosom of our own age). And even though he also mentions objects more customarily styled beautiful—furniture, clothes, houses—his inclusion of a machine and his later pointing to merchandise and manufacture as good examples of advantageous professions suggest how high a value he placed on the very ordinary things of this world.[16] Although Hume may have admired stately palaces and fine silverware, he also prized bridges and woolen goods. In fact, the ordinary precedes the elegant, just as arts and manufacturing become the bedrock of high culture and even morality.

The Moral Benefits of Luxury

Hume's most extended treatment of the relationship between the things of this world on the one hand and culture and morality on the other is to be found in the essays, in particular the *Political Discourses* of 1752. Yet this subject occupied him throughout his career, and ten years before the *Political Discourses* he had published the long and rambling discussion "Of the Rise and Progress of the Arts and Sciences" as part of his *Essays, Moral and Political*.

What is most interesting to us in this early paper is the contrast he sets up between the cultural milieu of a modern republic and that of a modern civilized monarchy. He argues that the sciences flourish most in a republic, whereas polite manners and the liberal arts are more noticeable in a monarchy. The reasons are these:

> in a republic, the candidates for office must look downwards, to gain the suffrages of the people; in a monarchy, they must turn their attention upwards, to court the good graces and favour of the great. To be successful in the former way, it is necessary for a man to make himself *useful*, by his industry, capacity, or knowledge: To be prosperous in the latter way, it is requisite for him to render himself *agreeable*, by his wit, complaisance, or civility. A strong genius succeeds best in republics: A refined taste in monarchies. . . .
>
> Not to mention, that monarchies, receiving their chief stability from a superstitious reverence to priests and princes, have commonly abridged the liberty of reasoning, with regard to religion, and politics, and consequently metaphysics and morals. (*E*, 126)

A contrast such as this is hardly balanced, for who would not conclude that the republic fosters more considerable values? Even to one unfamiliar with Hume's emphasis on utility, the useful clearly outweighs the merely agreeable; the genius, the connoisseur. Furthermore, the monarchy is tainted with an atmosphere of superstitious timidity: free inquiry cannot be pursued there.

Thus in 1742 the liberal arts and elegance appear to be inferior to the mechanical arts and science—that is, to utilitarian knowledge. And the liberal is antithetical to the mechanical and scientific. But even in this discussion, as Hume elaborates his contrast, one senses that those fine manners may have more value—more usefulness—than was first apparent. The ancients, for example, despite their primitive strength, simplicity, and nobility were rude, scurrilous, and even obscene. And modern republicans are notably rustic, impolite, and unpleasant. Late in the essay Hume is more inclined to strike a balance (see *E*, 126–35). And in his remarks on modern gallantry, Hume recognizes that artificial manners make men less brutal; indeed they help to temper vices.

> But gallantry is as *generous* and it is *natural*. To correct such gross vices, as lead us to commit real injury on others, is the part of morals. . . . Where *that* is not attended to, in some degree, no human society can subsist. . . . Wherever nature has given the mind a propensity to any vice, or to any passion disagreeable to others, refined breeding has taught men to throw the biass on the opposite side, and to preserve, in all their behaviour, the appearance of sentiments different from those to which they naturally incline. (*E*, 132)

This begins to sound more like the Hume who lauded Parisian society, and it points toward his later thinking. The mechanical and the liberal are not antithetical; both are the foundations of morality.

Of the twelve essays published in 1752 as the *Political Discourses*, seven deal with questions of economics, called "commerce" in Hume's day. The titles themselves emphasize both the breadth and detail of Hume's interest in monetary subjects: "Of Commerce," "Of Luxury," "Of Money," "Of Interest," "Of the Balance of Trade," "Of Taxes," and "Of Public Credit." Two other essays, "Of the Populousness of Ancient Nations" and "Of the Balance of Power," also deal in economic assumptions, and in 1758 he added to his canon another purely economic essay, "Of the Jealousy of Trade." Anticipating Adam Smith's theory of capitalism, Hume engages those basic questions that still form the core of economic study. Concerning Hume's economic opinions, Gay puts his finger precisely on their importance:

> What is remarkable about these views is not merely their largeness and benevolence, but their shrewdness, their fund of good sense,

their delight in civility, their clearsighted effort to tie economics to psychology, and, perhaps most important of all for the future of the science, their attempt to get beyond mere words to actual transactions, to the realities that lie concealed behind appearances. Adam Smith paid tribute to these qualities in his masterpiece when he hailed Hume as "by far the most illustrious philosopher and historian of the present age."[17]

Although the details of Hume's economic theories fall beyond our purview, it is of significance that Hume did devote so much of his energy to this subject. It substantiates the argument that for him, money and all that money can buy are primarily involved in the happiness of mankind. Indeed, Larkin states somewhat disapprovingly that in Hume we see "the best illustration of a social philosophy shorn of all enthusiasm save that for wealth production."[18] These excerpts from the leading essay "Of Commerce" make that point unequivocal:

> The greatness of a state, and the happiness of its subjects, . . . are . . . inseparable with regard to commerce. . . . (E, 255)

> If . . . superfluous hands apply themselves to the finer arts, which are commonly denominated the arts of *luxury*, they add to the happiness of the state. . . . (E, 256)

> Every thing in the world is purchased by labor [in turn, by money]; and our passions are the only causes of labour. (E, 261)

> Thus the greatness of the sovereign and the happiness of the state are, in a great measure, united with regard to trade and manufactures. (E, 262)

> . . . it is requisite to govern . . . and animate [men] with a spirit of avarice and industry, art and luxury. (E, 264)

> [By means of world trade and competition] steel and iron . . . become equal to the gold and rubies of the INDIES. (E, 264)

In such pronouncements one gets the drift of Hume's economics. The second essay, "Of Luxury," deserves more careful attention.

After 1758 Hume retitled this essay "Of Refinement in the Arts." The change of title reminds us of how controversial a topic luxury was in the eighteenth century.[19] Of the varying connotations of "luxury," Hume must have wished to avoid the commonly unfavorable one of sybaritic indulgence and moral degeneration, an association familiar in ancient diatribes against luxury—or even in Hume himself, when, carried along by the peroration of the second *Enquiry*, he contrasts the "worthless toys and gewgaws . . . of luxury" with such pleasures as friendship and peace of mind (*EPM*, 283–84).

On the contrary, "luxury" to Hume normally spells something far different, something inaccurately conveyed by his new title "Of Refinement in the Arts."[20] By "luxury" he means "great refinement in the gratification of the senses" (*E*, 268), but more extensively he means what we call a high standard of living, combined with a highly sophisticated, cultured enjoyment of that prosperity. In any case Hume's views on luxury are part of a lively discussion involving such figures as Bernard Mandeville, Shaftesbury, Montesquieu, Rousseau, the contributors to the *Encyclopédie*, Gibbon, and even Boswell's Johnson.[21] And of all the positions taken, one could argue that Hume's is the most radical and extreme. In a general sense he agrees with Mandeville that luxury benefits society, but he rejects Mandeville's ostensibly prudish but actually devious construction that luxury is innately vicious, if nonetheless the sine qua non of civilization: private vices, public benefits. Even Saint-Lambert in the *Encyclopédie*, though referring to Hume by name and taking his cue from Hume's argument, nonetheless points a warning finger at vicious luxury and then goes on to argue that luxury does not by itself either benefit or corrupt a state; rather, government, good or bad, is the great determinant.[22] More boldly, Hume contends "*first,* that the ages of refinement are both the happiest and most virtuous; *secondly,* that wherever luxury ceases to be innocent, it also ceases to be beneficial; and when carried a degree too far, is a quality pernicious, though perhaps not the most pernicious, to political society" (*E*, 269).

Of the two contentions, Hume's second point is the more conventional, but it is not completely so. Naturally, he cannot put himself in the position of recommending selfish overindulgence— of looking with satisfaction at wicked lords debauching milkmaids, at obese courtiers feasting on pheasant and turtle while emaciated peasants dine on breadcrusts, or at brutal fathers squandering all on drink while their families are reduced to beggary. Mandeville may have said slyly that this selfishness does stimulate the economy and is thus ultimately beneficial to society, but Hume will have none of that argument. Vice is still vice, "and indeed it seems upon any system of morality, little less than a contradiction in terms, to talk of a vice, which is in general beneficial to society" (*E*, 280). What is noteworthy about his treatment of this issue is that he minimizes the viciousness of overindulgence. Yes, it must be granted that overindulgence is reprehensible, but there are many worse vices: "Luxury, when excessive, is the source of many ills; but is in general preferable to sloth and idleness, which would commonly succeed in its place, and are more hurtful both to private persons and to the public" (*E*, 280). In a sense Hume is having Mandeville's cake and eating it, too. He can agree that overindulgence does promote trade without being caught in the paradox that vice is virtue.[23]

But as he downplays the evils of excessive luxury, Hume makes another, rather bolder, claim. Those who cultivate sensual pleasure are not likely to carry it to excess, and the pleasures they cultivate are not as objectionable as those of savages:

> One may safely affirm, that the TARTARS are oftener guilty of beastly gluttony, when they feast on their dead horses, than EUROPEAN courtiers with all their refinement of cookery. And if libertine love, or even infidelity to the marriage-bed, be more frequent in polite ages, when it is often regarded only as a piece of gallantry; drunkenness, on the other hand, is much less common: A vice more odious, and more pernicious both to mind and body. (*E*, 271–72)

Regardless of how convincing the argument may be, it does tell us something of Hume's mind. Despite the obligatory censure of excessive luxury, Hume does not really find sophisticated pleasures, even if excessive, very objectionable. Anything that characterizes elegant life is to be at least condoned. Indeed, there is good reason behind his apparent infatuation with elegant pleasure. We fancy his courtiers enjoying witty conversation between their delicate bites of ortolans, while the Tartars devour their horses with speechless snarls and grunts; we imagine his guilty lovers carrying out their assignations with billets-doux, gifts, and other polite attentions, while the solitary drunkard belches loudly before collapsing under the table. The one is a social, thus not an entirely selfish indulgence, and, depending on one's values, a refined pleasure; the other is antisocial, entirely selfish, brutal, and revolting. In these views we are reminded of Hume's appreciation of the social, this-worldly advantages of rites and ceremonies in religion.

This-worldliness and sociability brought about by luxury explain how "ages of refinement are both the happiest and most virtuous," Hume's principal thesis in the essay. In several rapturous passages Hume paints scenes of human felicity, of great ages of intellectual and artistic ferment, of freedom, of beneficial competition, of wealth increasing and passing from hand to hand,

of people coming together and becoming more gentle and humane:

> The spirit of the age affects all the arts; and the minds of men, being
> once roused from their lethargy, and put into a fermentation, turn
> themselves on all sides, and carry improvements into every art and
> science. Profound ignorance is totally banished, and men enjoy the
> privilege of rational creatures, to think as well as to act, to cultivate the
> pleasures of the mind as well as those of the body.
>
> The more these refined arts advance, the more sociable men be-
> come. . . . They flock into cities; love to receive and communicate
> knowledge; to show their wit or their breeding; their taste in con-
> versation or living, in clothes or furniture. Curiosity allures the wise;
> vanity the foolish; and pleasure both. Particular clubs and societies are
> everywhere formed: Both sexes meet in an easy and sociable manner:
> and the tempers of men, as well as their behaviour, refine apace. So
> that, beside the improvements which they receive from knowledge
> and the liberal arts, it is impossible but they must feel an encrease of
> humanity, from the very habit of conversing together, and contribut-
> ing to each other's pleasure and entertainment. Thus *industry, knowl-
> edge,* and *humanity,* are linked together by an indissoluble chain, and
> are found, from experience as well as reason, to be peculiar to the
> more polished, and, what are commonly denominated, the more
> luxurious ages. (*E*, 271)

Perhaps the solid benefits of luxurious worldliness have never,
before or since, been so warmly extolled. Indeed, Duncan Forbes
observes that "this is Hume at his least sceptical: he had none of
the doubts and misgivings which Adam Smith and the other
leading thinkers of the Scottish Enlightenment had about the all-
around benefits of commercial civilization."[24] But on the other
hand, Hume is at his most skeptical here in another sense, skeptical of the prevailing often hypocritical spiritualism and otherworldliness of orthodoxy.

It is helpful to look more closely at Hume's indissoluble linkage
of industry, knowledge, and humanity. By "industry" he means
labor, but he specifically means the labor of the mechanical arts—
trades, crafts, manufacturing. Earlier he makes it very clear that
these supposedly lower occupations and the higher sciences are
interconnected,

> nor can one be carried to perfection, without being accompanied, in
> some degree, with the other. The same age, which produces great
> philosophers and politicians, renowned generals and poets, usually

abounds with skilful weavers, and ship-carpenters. We cannot reasonably expect, that a piece of woollen cloth will be wrought to perfection
in a nation which is ignorant of astronomy, or where ethics are
neglected. (E, 270–71)

Later he asks, "Can we expect, that a government will be well
modelled by a people, who know not how to make a spinning-
wheel, or to employ a loom to advantage?" (E, 273). One might
expect the lower to be prerequisite to the higher, but in Hume's
scheme the two—industry and knowlege—are interdependent
and equally desirable. The distinction between higher and lower
blurs. Weaving and carpentry are just as essential to civilization as
medicine and philosophy. And the opposition noted in the earlier
essay between the mechanical and liberal arts has disappeared.

The final link in the triad is humanity, the moral connection,
and the ultimate benefit of luxury. To propose, of course, that
luxury promotes morality instead of corrupting it is the most
heterodox and boldest claim of the entire essay, and it sets Hume
apart from other eighteenth-century participants in the discussion of luxury, who, when they favored luxury, did so mainly on
political, economic, or at best humanitarian grounds. To be sure,
Hume resembles Shaftesbury, whose insistence that virtue is a
manifestation of politeness or polished life made him the defender of luxury, not rusticity,[25] but Hume is more radical than
Shaftesbury. The remarks on the refined pleasures of courtiers
and adulterers and on the softening effect of social intercourse in
the city suggest the direction of Hume's argument: when people
intermingle in polite society, they defer their own wants to others;
hence they temper the selfishness inherent in human nature. It is
admittedly not Hume's most optimistic moral theory. Social man
is still an animal at heart, but he has learned to disguise his
nature. If, however, he is a wolf in sheep's clothing, in wishing to
appear a sheep he not only hides his fangs and talons, but he also
refuses to use them. In a sense this is the essential argument
presented in Hume's essay "Of the Dignity or Meanness of
Human Nature." Despite the imperfections of our nature, it is
better for the cause of virtue that we think well of human nature,
for then we will try to be worthy of our flattering self-image.[26]
After all, even though Hume believes that many people are naturally gentle and benevolent, others lack this disposition, and if a
mechanism of social interaction will make these boors act at least
more like men of feeling, then so much the better.

Morality is the child that worldly luxury begot on human

nature, even if a bastard child. Regardless, luxury makes men less savage and brutal. By distributing goods and wealth, luxury breaks down stagnant feudal systems, creating a "middling rank of men, who are the best and firmest basis of public liberty" (*E*, 277). These gentlemen respect those laws that secure their prosperity, and they are perforce the most virtuous types of mankind. As must be obvious by now, primitivism is one fashionable eighteenth-century theory that Hume had little use for: "An ancient FRANK or SAXON may be highly extolled: But I believe every man would think his life or fortune much less secure in the hands of a MOOR or TARTAR, than in those of a FRENCH or ENGLISH gentleman, the rank of men the most civilized in the most civilized nations" (*E*, 278). We may smile at Hume's provincialism, or indeed at his self-worship, as Hume looks in the mirror for his model of perfect virtue.[27] Still, the point remains that from luxury come gentle politeness and in turn morality itself. In this respect Hume is in close agreement with Cicero's *De Officiis* (2.4), that guide to pagan ethics he preferred to contemporary Christian manuals. Even that ultimate immorality, human violence, is mollified in ages of civilized luxury:

> When the tempers of men are softened as well as their knowledge improved, this humanity appears still more conspicuous, and is the chief characteristic which distinguishes a civilized age from times of barbarity and ignorance. Factions are then less inveterate, revolutions less tragical, authority less severe, and seditions less frequent. Even foreign wars abate of their cruelty; and after the field of battle, where honour and interest steel men against compassion as well as fear, the combatants divest themselves of the brute, and resume the man. (*E*, 274)

Mundane History

Hume's *History* often appears monumental and stately. Great personages, caught up in great events, cross the stage. The historian as dramatist accentuates their heroism or their iniquity. He frequently views their actions with the superior detachment of a philosopher, but sometimes he is overwhelmed by the magnanimity or baseness of his *dramatis personae*. He is concerned with what human nature is capable of and with the past and future of civilization. He deals in the momentous, not the trivial. Standing in the full regalia of the historian, Hume pronounces, "History charges herself willingly with a relation of the great crimes, and still more with that of the great virtues of mankind; but she appears to fall from her dignity, when necessitated to dwell on . . . frivolous events and ignoble personages" (H, 5:53).

Evidently, Hume did have this impression of history. After all, thinking of history as "the great mistress of wisdom" (H, 5:545), he surely viewed himself as discharging a weighty trust. When he talks of history falling from her dignity when dwelling on "frivolous events and ignoble personages," he speaks defensively. For when we read the whole context of his statement, it becomes clear that the pronouncement does not apply very well to his historical methods. Unfortunately, however, the view persists that Hume the historian sought only the heights of grandeur and generality. Robert Folkenflik cites Hume's apologetic sentence to prove that "Hume . . . unwillingly described James I, rod in hand, instructing his ignorant favorite Robert Carr." Likewise Donald Livingston misses the mark when he speaks of

> Hume's conception of the dignity of history. Because history is the story of the progress of the human mind and the critical understanding of that progress, it is a high, solemn, and noble inquiry. . . . For this reason some events are excluded as falling beneath the dignity of history. Thus Hume refuses to explore in any detail James I's weakness for his favorites.[28]

But in fact Hume explores this weakness in great detail. This particular section of the *History* relates how handsome but undeserving young men caught the king's eye and left him infatuated. The details of the account are undignified, but they reveal something important about James—his weakness for superficial merit; his vanity, especially in his learning; his shallowness and instability; his capacity for folly. Later, when one of James's darling minions, Buckingham, had persuaded the king to send the crown prince to Spain to court a princess, Hume provides these frivolous details of the king's consultation with Sir Francis Cottington:

> James told Cottington, that he had always been an honest man, and therefore he was now to trust him in an affair of the highest importance, which he was not, upon his life, to disclose to any man whatever. "Cottington," added he, "here is baby Charles and Stenny," (these ridiculous appellations he usually gave to the prince and Buckingham), "who have a great mind to go post into Spain, and fetch home the Infanta: They will have but two more in their company, and have chosen you for one. What think you of the journey?" Sir Francis,

who was a prudent man, and had resided some years in Spain as the king's agent, was struck with all the obvious objections to such an enterprize, and scrupled not to declare them. The king threw himself upon his bed, and cried, *I told you this before;* and fell into a new passion and new lamentation, complaining that he was undone, and should lose baby Charles. (*H*, 5:105)

After further vacillation and histrionics, James lets Buckingham have his way. Hume's closing comment: "These circumstances, . . . though minute, are not undeserving a place in history." Indeed so. Perhaps it is regrettable that Hume feels that need to apologize, but in any case he is right: "Stenny" and "Baby Charles" have a genuine place in history; they tell us something that would never emerge from an elegant "Character of King James I." Likewise, when he analyzes the conflict between Mary, Queen of Scots, and John Knox, he shows how far apart their values were as they react to the same news about some young libertine nobles who broke into a whorehouse. After finishing the story, he writes: "We have related these incidents at greater length, than the necessity of our subject may seem to require: But even trivial circumstances, which show the manners of the age, are often more instructive, as well as entertaining, than the great transactions of wars and negociations, which are nearly similar in all periods and in all countries of the world" (*H*, 4:44).[29] Who says that history must always be dignified and general? In practice, at least, certainly not Hume.

If history is "the great mistress of wisdom" about human nature, then from what is history to draw her inferences but from the commonplace details of past life? This fact is obvious, but I wish to emphasize in this section just how much Hume concerns himself with ordinary details in his sources. His historical epistemology is very much drawn to, and dependent on, the mundane. He presents his history by means of traditional diachronic narration, but he also feels it necessary to include appendices to important periods that get at the truth of history differently. For in these sections he can wrest truth from the most ordinary things of this world. These appendices typically present individual discourses on such topics as Manners, Government, Sciences, Learning and Arts, but also on more mundane subjects like Finances and Commerce, Manufacture, Arms, and Navy. Hume justifies these surveys of fact at three different points in the *History:*

It may not be improper . . . to make a pause: and to take a survey of the state of the kingdom, with regard to government, manners, finances, arms, trade, learning. Where a just notion is not formed of these particulars, history can be little instructive, and often will not be intelligible. (1754) (*H*, 5:124)

The chief use of history is, that it affords materials for disquisitions of this nature; and it seems the duty of an historian to point out the proper inferences and conclusions. (1756) (*H*, 6:140)

The rise, progress, perfection, and decline of art and science, are curious objects of contemplation, and intimately connected with a narration of civil transactions. The events of no particular period can be fully accounted for, but by considering the degrees of advancement which men have reached in those particulars. (1762) (*H*, 2:519)

Again, Hume may seem defensive. Should the gowned historian really be telling his reader the price of grain during the Renaissance, or of Harvey's discovery of circulating blood? But to Hume these details are important. They are things of this world that daily affect human life much more than heroism on the battlefield or intrigues at court. From such a position he anticipates much twentieth-century, especially recent, work in the humanities and social sciences.

And so with great delight the historian lays aside his gown to examine the commonplace. Page after page is full of facts that would be tedious to quote in full but must at least be sampled. We learn that in Elizabeth's reign there were monopolies on currants, cards, calf-skins, ox-shin-bones, oil of blubber, and thirty-five other items mentioned by name (*H*, 4:344); that her revenue probably "fell much short of five hundred thousand pounds a year" and her fleet had 774 guns; that she "was presented with a pair of black silk knit stockings by her silkwoman, and never wore cloth hose any more"; that she had three thousand dresses in her wardrobe; that pocket watches, coaches, and post-houses came into use; that prices doubled and the first law for the relief of the poor was enacted (*H*, 4:372–83). In detail we learn what were the probable revenues of James I and why he was always in debt; that during his reign "all butcher's meat, as well as bread, was rather higher than at present," that "a turkey-cock [cost] four shillings and sixpence, a turkey-hen three shillings, a pheasant cock six, . . . a capon two and six-pence, . . . a rabbit eight-pence," and so on; that James did not have a single regiment at his command and that England could not find enough horses to mount even two thousand men; that London was then built of wood and was very ugly, but improved prodigiously in riches and beauty during the seventeenth century, quadrupling its population; that in the reign of James, English manufactures consisted only of ship-building and founding cannon, that nine-tenths of the commerce was in woolen goods, that the balance of trade fell from plus 346,284 pounds in 1613 to minus 298,879 in 1622; that "the first sedan chair, seen in England, was in this reign, and was used by the duke of Buckingham; to the great indignation of the people, who exclaimed, that he was employing his fellow-creatures to do the service of beasts" (*H*, 5:133–46).

Assortments like these may give the impression that Hume was simply intent on fact, regardless of what it might signify.[30] And indeed one must confess that sometimes Hume does seem to relish these details for no other reason than that they represent the things of the world: they are the stuff that life is made of. Nonetheless, more characteristically he uses these facts to substantiate history: James's straitened income, while his subjects' wealth was increasing, explains some of his imprudent measures and in particular his difficulties with an ever-stronger Parliament, and it foreshadows the fate of his son. Occasionally Hume extracts his conclusions from the apparently inscrutable jetsam of history with a flourish. In the "petition of the elder Spenser to parliament" during the reign of Edward II, "complaining of the devastation committed on his lands by the barons," Hume discovers "the manners of the age": that the Parliament had no true power or liberty and that each man was on his own to protect himself, his family, and his possessions from others. Hume also notes something very revealing in one particular detail. Spenser lost a larder containing salted meat—some "600 bacons, 80 carcasses of beef, 600 muttons." And yet it was after the third of May, in the temperate climate of southern England. And thus we learn "the wretched state of ancient husbandry" that could keep livestock alive only in summer and had to resort to salting mutton, "a miserable expedient, which has every where been long disused." Note how pleased Hume is to have blown away the dust from this ancient manuscript: "From this circumstance, however trivial in appearance, may be drawn important inferences, with regard to the domestic economy and manner of life in those ages" (*H*, 2:178–80). In a manner comparable to that of recent critical theory, Hume demonstrates that every text, however bare and unprepossessing, can reveal much of value to a percipient reader.

Similarly in this same discussion Hume considers other aspects of the primitive medieval economy gleaned from chronicles and manuscripts. Severe famines drove up prices, while Parliament shortsightedly tried to control prices, only compounding the problem.[31] From the individual prices fixed, Hume infers that "the raising of corn was a species of manufactory, which few in that age could practise with advantage: And there is reason to think, that other manufactures more refined, were sold even beyond their present prices." That great nobles settled their "velvet beds and silken robes" as they did their "estates and manors" proves that "all trade and manufactures indeed were then at a very low ebb," from which he infers that the country could not possibly have been very populous. Hume's final inference from the data on life during the unhappy reign of Edward II is amusingly apt: "I have seen a French manuscript, containing accounts of some private disbursements of this king. There is an article, among others, of a crown paid to one for making the king laugh. To judge by the events of the reign, this ought not to have been an easy undertaking" (H, 2:178–81).[32]

The motive behind this use of detail in the medieval period is to establish that life itself was then miserable and brutish, despite what primitivists or other romantics might fantasize. Even great lords lived much worse than the middling rank of the eighteenth century. Hume seizes on a household book of the fifth earl of Northumberland (1478–1527), recently made available to him, to prove his point in a long footnote added in 1773. In a letter to Thomas Percy, Hume explains his purpose for using the household book: "My Notion is, that the uncultivated Nations are not only inferior to civiliz'd in Government, Civil, military, and ecclesiastical; but also in Morals" (NL, 198). Hume introduces his extensive list of details with this comment: "it contains many curious particulars, which mark the manners and way of living in that rude, not to say barbarous age; . . . [and it gives] a true picture of ancient manners, and is one of the most singular monuments that English antiquity affords us" (H, 3:469). Hume then carefully examines the earl's budget, computing the equivalent in current money of what was spent for various items of daily life. The sum allotted per individual in the household, including even the earl's immediate family, would not suggest that anyone was well-off, except perhaps in drinking, and certainly not well-fed. Since salted meat was the diet for most of the year, Hume notes that 160 gallons of mustard was allowed to make it palatable. The diet was in general so "very bad and unhealthy . . . that there cannot be any thing more erroneous, than the magnificent ideas formed of the Roast Beef of Old England. . . . The drinking, however, was tolerable, namely, ten tuns and two hogsheads of Gascogny wine, at the rate of four pounds thirteen shillings and four pence a tun" (*H*, 3:470). Other figures indicate that no one in the household was very clean, comfortable, or in winter, very warm. That horses were used in milling suggests "that mills, either water or wind-mills, were then unknown, at least very rare: (*H*, 3:471). His lordship's furniture must have been sparse and crude, for he carried it all with him in seventeen carts and one wagon from one country seat to another.

Toward the end of this exposé of medieval living, Hume grows more caustic:

> One remarkable circumstance is, that he has eleven priests in his house, besides seventeen persons, chanters, musicians, &c. belonging to his chapel: Yet he has only two cooks for a family of 223 persons. . . . Their meals were certainly dressed in the slovenly manner of a ship's company. It is amusing to observe the pompous and even royal style assumed by this Tartar chief: He does not give any orders, though only for the right making of mustard; but it is introduced with this preamble, *It seemeth good to us and our council.* If we consider the magnificent and elegant manner in which the Venetian and other Italian noblemen then lived, with the progress made by the Italians in literature and the fine arts, we shall not wonder that they considered the ultramontaine nations as barbarous. (*H*, 3:471–72)

The picture is inescapably satirical: when the "Tartar chief" issues pompous orders for making mustard, we may be reminded of the tiny king of Lilliput styling himself the "Delight and Terror of the Universe."[33] Much more damning, in Humean terms, is the contrast between the retinue of ecclesiastics and the pair of cooks. What stronger indictment could there be than that Lord Northumberland would employ many to do the unnecessary—or in Hume's thinking, even the morally harmful—while he was content to have two prepare what had to be wretched food? Hume had little inclination to perceive any spiritual or metaphorical meaning in the "bread of life."

For Hume, good and happy existence consists of fine things in abundance. Only in the growth of manufacturing and commerce can one find the possibility of civilized and hence moral life. As Hume frequently emphasizes in the *History,* just as he had in "Of Luxury," this spread of manufacturing and commerce meant the end of feudalism, the distribution of wealth and power to the Commons, and hence, the beginning of liberty, justice, and morality. As Forbes concludes, "This is the unobtrusive central theme or frame of reference of the *History.*" Likewise, J. G. A. Pocock says that Hume "accepted commerce as, for the present era in history, a liberating force which enlarged men's minds through the nourishment of their appetites."[34] Taking issue with William Camden's complaint that the nobility's elegant luxury spoiled hospitality, Hume says, "It is . . . more reasonable to think, that this new turn of expence promoted arts and industry; while the ancient hospitality was the source of vice, disorder, sedition, and idleness" (*H*, 4:383). Hume goes on to explain his thinking:

> The habits of luxury dissipated the immense fortunes of the ancient barons; and as the new methods of expence gave subsistance to mechanics and merchants, who lived in an independant manner on the fruits of their own industry, a nobleman, instead of that unlimited ascendant, which he was wont to assume over those who were maintained at this board, . . . retained only that moderate influence, which customers have over tradesmen, and which can never be dangerous to civil government. The landed proprietors also, having a greater demand for money than for men, endeavoured to turn their lands to the best account with regard to profit, and either inclosing their fields, or joining many small farms into a few large ones, dismissed those useless hands, which formerly were always at their call in every attempt to subvert the government, or oppose a neighbouring baron. By all these means the cities encreased; the middle rank of men began to be rich and powerful; the prince, who, in effect, was the same with the law, was implicitly obeyed; and . . . the farther progress of the same causes begat a new plan of liberty, founded on the privileges of the commons. (*H*, 4:384)

Unlike the *Encyclopédie*, which views luxury as merely a probable accompaniment of good government, Hume's *History* makes arts and commerce, indeed all civilized luxury, "the necessary attendants of liberty and equality" (*H*, 2:109).

And of morality, too. Noting the rapidly diminishing number of executions from the reign of Henry VIII to that of Elizabeth and finally to his own age, Hume observes, "If these facts be just, there has been a great improvement in morals since the reign of Henry VIII. And this improvement has been chiefly owing to the encrease of industry and of the arts, which have given maintenance, and, what is almost of equal importance, occupation, to the lower classes" (*H*, 3:329). Hume's reasoning here is somewhat amusing, and questionable. A man who can buy bread is less tempted to steal it, but is not necessarily of higher morality, which by Hume's estimation here would seem reduced to nothing but the crime rate. And if a declining number of executions shows an improvement in morals, might one not think first that the ruling class has shown the improvement? But whatever our objections to statistical morality, his jumping to the conclusion shows how eager Hume is to equate commerce with morality. Having material goods, being occupied with material things, all represent salvation to fallen man. The wolf in sheep's clothing, seen earlier, begins to think of himself as a sheep, and acts like one. The peasant with a job and money sees no reason to commit violent crime. What if he is still not innately good? We nevertheless have the practical result and the appearance of morality, if not a state of grace.

A man possessed with things of this world has what he most wants. He is happy himself and not a threat to the happiness of others. He is ready to be a fast learner of those advantageous principles of justice taught in the *Treatise* and the second *Enquiry.* Or put another way, he has little reason to worry about ethics, for in a world of plenty, like the Golden Age, justice is as unnecessary as a system of social welfare or a police force. As Hume had theorized as early as the *Treatise:* "Encrease to a sufficient degree the benevolence of men, or the bounty of nature, and you render justice useless, by supplying its place with much nobler virtues, and more valuable blessings" (*T,* 494–95). Quite obviously, however, it is easier to make the world better by cultivating nature's bounty than by increasing benevolence. One is within the capacity of mankind; the other demands a divine new modeling of human nature.

In Hume's optimistic vision of civilized life, there is little possibility of crime or violence: "science and civility . . . has so close a connexion with virtue and humanity, and . . . as it is a sovereign antidote against superstition, is also the most effectual remedy against vice and disorders of every kind" (*H,* 2:519). And "science and civility" are to be found only in an age of flourishing trade and commerce—an age of busy spinning wheels and looms.

In *Spectator* No. 69 Joseph Addison indulges himself in a panegyric to the Royal Exchange, that great seat of English commerce that fills him with every kind of "secret [and not so secret] Satisfaction":

my Heart naturally overflows with Pleasure at the sight of a prosperous and happy Multitude, insomuch that . . . I cannot forbear expressing my Joy with Tears that have stoln down my Cheeks. For this Reason I am wonderfully delighted to see such a Body of Men thriving in their own private Fortunes, and at the same time promoting the Publick Stock; or in other Words, raising Estates for their own

> Families, by bringing into their Country whatever is wanting, and carrying out of it whatever is superfluous. . . . If we consider our own Country in its natural Prospect, without any of the Benefits and Advantages of Commerce, what a barren uncomfortable Spot of Earth falls to our Share! . . . For these Reasons there are not more useful Members in a Commonwealth than Merchants.

Hume's own comment on the Royal Exchange is somewhat more tempered—he calls it "the magnificent fabric of the Exchange" built magnanimously by Sir Thomas Gresham (*H*, 4:379)—but though he does not shed Whiggish tears of joy at the sight of thriving merchants, his own response to the progress and happiness brought about by worldly enterprise is much the same as Addison's. And in this respect his *History* is clearly Whiggish, not Tory, for suspicion of luxury was a common Tory theme.

We can imagine him, in an ebullient mood at least, writing Addison's paper, for he characteristically finds the evidence of any kind of successful worldliness as gratifying, sometimes inspiring. When he surveys the Renaissance ferment of Henry VII's reign, it is easy to sense his excitement. This is an age that saw the discovery of the New World and the passage to the East Indies, of Greek and Latin classics, of printing and other technology. With a certain Addisonian satisfaction Hume contemplates "these great events" marking that time where "commences the useful, as well as the more agreeable part of modern annals" (*H*, 3:82). In the reign of James I, he calls those efforts to discover the Northwest Passage "noble projects" in which "despair ought never to be admitted, till the absolute impossibility of success be fully ascertained"; and he extols the planting of English colonies in America, "established on the noblest footing that has been known in any age or nation" (*H*, 5:145–46).[35]

Even the introduction of artillery gives Hume reason to be pleased:

> this furious engine, . . . though it seemed contrived for the destruction of mankind, and the overthrow of empires, has in the issue rendered battles less bloody, and has given greater stability to civil societies. Nations, by its means, have been brought more to a level: Conquests have become less frequent and rapid: Success in war has been reduced nearly to be a matter of calculation: And any nation, overmatched by its enemies, either yields to their demands, or secures itself by alliances against their violence and invasion. (*H*, 2:230)

Once again, we may find Hume's reasoning debatable, but he does make a subtle point. Perhaps any factor that intrudes rationality into conflict has a tendency to palliate blind anger and ferocity. Calculating the cost of success or the likelihood of failure may compel a country to think twice before going to war. In our day it is of course difficult to rest comfortable in the belief that a parity of terrible armaments among the great powers is a surety of peace, though that argument has been made. In any event, however, Hume's observation concerning artillery is by no means absurd. For our purposes it establishes once again his marked propensity to find good in any advance of human knowledge, in mankind's growing control of the world.

As an historian, then, Hume is ready to give commerce, manufacture, agriculture and husbandry, technological discovery—indeed, all the arts and sciences of physical experience—their just importance in the shaping of civilization. As we have seen, even the lowly mechanical arts stand on a par with the liberal; artisans and merchants are no less worthy than poets and philosophers. To be good, life must first be physically easy; the world must be made comfortable.

In this thinking Hume was not alone in his century. We just saw it in Addison; we might see it in Benjamin Franklin; and that great *philosophe* Diderot certainly shared these ideas:

> Place on one side of the scales the actual advantages of the most sublime sciences and the most honored arts, and on the other the advantages of the mechanical arts, and you will find that esteem has not been accorded to the one and to the other in just proportion to the benefits they bring. You will discover that far more praise has been heaped on those men who spend their time making us believe that we are happy, than on those who actually bring us happiness. How strangely we judge! We expect everyone to pass his time in a useful manner, and we disdain useful men. . . . Let us finally render artists the justice that is their due. The liberal arts have sung their own praise long enough; they should now raise their voice in praise of the mechanical arts.[36]

Certainly in the *History of England* Hume raises his voice in praise of material progress, progress in the mechanical arts not the least. So strong is that praise that sometimes it would appear that these arts were themselves the indispensable catalyst of modern civilization and not just one of many concurrent ingredients of change. So it would seem from the following passage:

> The encrease of the arts, more effectively than all the severities of law, put an end to this pernicious practice [of the barons' use of retainers to

commit acts of violence and pervert justice itself]. The nobility, instead of vying with each other, in the number and boldness of their retainers, acquired by degrees a more civilized species of emulation, and endeavoured to excel in the splendour and elegance of their equipage, houses, and tables. The common people, no longer maintained in vicious idleness by their superiors, were obliged to learn some calling or industry, and became useful both to themselves and to others. And it must be acknowledged, in spite of those who declaim so violently against refinement in the arts, or what they are pleased to call luxury, that, as much as an industrious tradesman is both a better man and a better citizen than one of those idle retainers, who formerly depended on the great families; so much is the life of a modern nobleman more laudable than that of an ancient baron. (*H*, 3:76–77)

The arts of luxury transformed the warfare among savage barons into the polite and beneficial competition of elegant noblemen. The same arts transformed the "vicious idleness" of common people into rewarding industry. Both orders enjoyed life more and lived together in greater security, with mutual deference and humanity. Studied aright, history becomes the gospel of salvation by the things of this world.

Of Somewhat Higher Things

So much of Hume's important work in the productive years of the midcentury makes worldliness, whether physical or intellectual, the answer to human problems and the source of people's happiness, if they are to have it at all. The theme pervades the *History of England*, and also the *Four Dissertations* of 1757. As I showed in chapter 2, in perhaps the most important of the *Four Dissertations*, *The Natural History of Religion*, Hume argues that people can be basically moral if religion does not assume too much importance in their lives, and it never can when people are not seduced from believing in the primacy of mundane fact and experience. Hume recognizes that man needs to invest objects with significance, that he is a contriver of symbols, a Maker. Hume's many references to the poets—Homer, Hesiod, Sophocles, Euripides, Milton, to name only the most sublime—confirm this impression. The poets tell idle stories, it is true, but in so doing they can also demonstrate the extent of human capacity in this life, the resilience and resourcefulness of man the civilized animal. Thus in *NHR* and in two other of the *Four Dissertations*,

Hume calls for an art of this world to assist people in living successfully.[37]

Of Tragedy seeks to explain how a representation of human suffering can please. We need not follow the details of Hume's explanation,[38] but we should note that underlying Hume's reasoning is an assumption about art perfectly consonant with his ideas about the role of worldliness in civilization. Exactly as in Hume's own writing of history, great tragic art pleases because it demonstrates man's ability to shape his suffering and thereby to control it; he emerges a victor, not a victim. The emphasis is always to be on this life, not on an afterlife. For Hume tragic art must display mankind in an active role, wresting a kind of triumph from defeat, exhibiting "a noble courageous despair." The most pernicious art, on the other hand, panders to gloom and weakness, to other-worldly values, by showing only "passive suffering" in "such horrible subjects as crucifixions and martyrdoms" (*E*, 224). That religion should foster this corrupting art comes as no surprise to a student of Hume.

The last dissertation is *Of the Standard of Taste*. For Hume taste is not just a metaphor. We taste art or we taste morality just as we taste food. It is interesting and significant that Hume places so much emphasis on the objective reality of what taste discovers. In other words, this aesthetic and moral faculty does not rely on inspiration from without—or from within, as in the case of a fanatical imagination—but detects only the secondary qualities of objects. Hume tells the story of Sancho's two kinsmen in *Don Quixote* who respectively tasted leather and iron in their wine; though ridiculed by their companions, they had their good taste confirmed by the discovery of a key attached to a leather thong in the hogshead (*E*, 234–35).[39] It is a real presence, we are tempted to think, but the wine's essence is altered by a very sensible and ordinary phenomenon. Hume may be implying that taste would always belie the miracle of the consecrated wine. Regardless, taste depends upon a clear understanding, on experience, and on freedom from prejudice, but all these advantages derive from an accurate sensation of external reality, a true savoring of the things of this world. Few will have good taste, but those few will be capable of judging correctly, whether of wine, art, or morality.[40]

Nothing could be further from the truth than Gay's remark that Hume's essays on taste are mere amusements, "free from any conceivable utility except the important one of giving gratification to the writer and pleasure to the reader."[41] As we have noted again and again, virtue for Hume takes its origin in quotidian reality, in sensation, in the world of things. Sentient taste leads to moral taste, and moral taste can help create an ideal of beauty that reason alone can never perceive. As Hume says in the second *Enquiry*, this taste "has a productive faculty, and gilding or staining all natural objects with the colours, borrowed from internal sentiment, raises in a manner a new creation" (*EPM*, 294).

This is a conception of some moment. Unlike Pope's "true Expression," which "gilds all objects, but . . . alters none" (*Essay on Criticism*, 2. 11. 315–17), Hume's moral taste is surprisingly more akin to a Coleridgean creative imagination—or perhaps to neo-Platonic defenses of poetry over history, the poetry that re-creates *la belle nature*.[42] As early as the *Treatise* Hume had recognized a rather strange and mysterious way of knowing—a higher instinct or intuition: "But however philosophers may have been bewilder'd in those speculations [about a state of nature, or a golden age], poets have been guided more infallibly, by a certain taste or common instinct, which in most kinds of reasoning goes farther than any of that art and philosophy, with which we have been yet acquainted" (*T*, 494). Is Hume saying that the highest truth, moral truth, is the gift of some transcendental power? If so, he has almost ventured into the very unfamiliar, indeed for him heretofore unrecognized, region of the numinous and spiritual. I say "almost" with emphasis, because these intriguing hints are all we have of a romantic—dare I say mystical?—Hume. But at the very least we have been considering in Hume no kind of utilitarianism that Jeremy Bentham would have understood. Hume, however, does not belong with Bentham. His theories of materialism have a higher reach.

In this chapter I have emphasized Hume's treatment of physical things—bridges, furniture, cloth, gunpowder, salted meat, money—but we should not restrict our conception of physical things too much. That worldliness that Hume so prized includes artistic and intellectual endeavors of all kinds. His conception is of a highly sophisticated worldliness. Despite his praise of craftsmen and merchants, he most admires the intellectual hero. Thus Francis Bacon was the greatest figure in the English Renaissance, and even James I, otherwise pedantic and ineffectual, was lifted above the ordinary by his modest attainment in letters: "Such a superiority do the pursuits of literature possess above every other occupation, that even he, who attains but a mediocrity in them, merits the preeminence above those that excel the most in the common and vulgar professions" (*H*, 5:155). Civilized values derive finally from learning and taste, from an elegant appreciation of the things of this world. With great approval Hume quotes Ovid's reminder to the Thracian prince Cotys: *"Ingenuas didicisse fideliter artes,/ Emollit mores, nec sinit esse feros"* (E, 6). That is to say, to have learned the liberal arts well softens the manners and makes barbarity impossible. Or as Hume elsewhere paraphrased and enlarged this sentiment: "It is certain, that a serious attention to the sciences and liberal arts softens and humanizes the temper, and cherishes those fine emotions, in which true virtue and honor consists. It rarely, very rarely happens, that a man of taste and learning is not, at least, an honest man, whatever frailties may attend him" (E, 170).

4

Moral Skepticism

The empire of philosophy extends over a few; and with regard to these too, her authority is very weak and limited. Men may well be sensible of the value of virtue, and may desire to attain it; but it is not always certain, that they will be successful in their wishes.

—E (1742)

As to my Opinions, you know I defend none of them positively: I only propose my Doubts, where I am so unhappy as not to receive the same Conviction with the rest of Mankind.

—L (1757)

[In the *Dialogues on Natural Religion*] I . . . introduce a Sceptic, who is indeed refuted, and at last gives up the Argument, nay confesses that he was only amusing himself by all his Cavils; yet before he is silenced, he advances several Topics, which will give Umbrage, and will be deemed very bold and free, as well as much out of the Common Road.

—L (1776)

Strategies of Disengagement

ONE of the most whimsical passages in all of Hume's published writing occurs in that earliest and, to many, most important formulation of his philosophy, *A Treatise of Human Nature*. I am referring to the concluding section of Book 1. In this long passage Hume steps back and contemplates his achievement thus far, the significance of his work, his state of mind, and indeed his whole vocation as a philosopher. The rhetoric of this apologia reveals certain basic patterns that inform his thinking as a philosopher and a moralist. Let me examine the Conclusion in some detail.

A Treatise of Human Nature is a very personal work, perhaps more personal than anything else Hume ever published, even including his autobiography. One of the hallmarks of Hume's philosophical style is a certain detachment, a striving for control, and hence a frequent resorting to irony as a means of enforcing that distance—overall, an air of Olympian superiority.[1] The importance of detachment and self-possession is in fact what Humean philosophy teaches—certainly as a goal for the elite, if not of likely attainment by the masses. Without question this self-possession marks the *Treatise*, but from a deconstructive point of view there are two styles, one reflecting the idealized philosopher, calm and wise, and the other style, that of a more uncertain, more involved and emotional, even troubled young man. Hume's guard is not always up, and we can see a philosopher who is not quite as self-assured and composed as he might prefer, one not entirely at peace with the ultimate implications of his doctrines.[2]

The mention of a troubled Hume may seem ludicrous, especially to anyone familiar with Hume's autobiography. There Hume reviews his life and pronounces serenely that he has little to regret; his life was a success. But the Hume of the *Treatise* is not the elderly man of letters, carefully composing his last words. Although we need not think that during the gestation of the *Treatise* there occurred Hume's dark night of the soul, the notion is not as preposterous as it might at first appear. If we must look for autobiographical documents to understand Hume's personality, we would do well to turn back from *My own Life*, written at the close of his career, to another self-revelation composed while the *Treatise* was taking shape—Hume's long confessional letter, presumably to Dr. John Arbuthnot, the famous physician, scholar, and wit.[3]

It seems clear that Hume had experienced a nervous breakdown at about this time, and in the letter he describes his illness, with its apparent prognosis and cure. As Ernest Mossner remarks, "Although not written in modern technical terminology, Hume's case-history of his psychosomatic disorder is as clear as could possibly be penned by an highly intelligent person today, and, as such, is diagnosable by modern psychiatrists."[4] There is a significant resemblance between the letter and certain aspects of the *Treatise*, particularly the concluding section of Book 1, and the letter provides insight into Hume's highly wrought-up state of mind during the genesis of the *Treatise*. Hume tells his correspondent how he felt when the possibilities opened up by the *Treatise* became fully apparent. It is no serene philosopher who exclaims with pride:

Upon Examination of these [endless disputes of previous philoso-
phy], I found a certain Boldness of Temper, growing in me, which was
not enclin'd to submit to any Authority in these Subjects, but led me
to seek out some new Medium, by which Truth might be establisht.
After much Study, & Reflection of this, at last, when I was about 18
Years of Age, there seem'd to be open'd up to me a new Scene of
thought, which transported me beyond Measure, & made me, with
an Ardor natural to young men, throw up every other Pleasure or
Business to apply entirely to it. (L, 1:13)

The mood described here is that which Hume later associates with
the *Treatise*—that same "Ardor of Youth," that "Heat of Youth &
Invention" (L, 1:187, 158). Then comes a collapse, a transformation from excited activity to lethargy and indifference: "all my
Ardor seem'd in a moment to be extinguished, & I cou'd no longer
raise my Mind to that pitch, which formerly gave me such excessive Pleasure. . . . In this Condition I remain'd for nine Months."
Hume does not indicate the exact reason for his depression or any
explanation of how he freed himself from it. What is interesting is
that the pattern of Hume's movement from ecstatic discovery to
bewilderment and anxiety and then on to salvation through common life is reenacted in the *Treatise*, Book 1. The pattern is, as John
Sitter has termed it, "a phenomenology of doubt."[5]

When Hume wrote the conclusion to Book 1 of the *Treatise* a few
years after the letter to Arbuthnot, he had largely resolved his
doubts, and so his account is for the most part retrospective and
objective. That is, he is capable of looking back on his malaise and
describing it with self-humor and a certain exuberance. Yet we
still sense how close he is to that state of anxiety. Although John
Richetti sees the conclusion as a disingenuous pose—"[it] is the
broadest philosophical comedy, featuring a persona who begins
in clowning mock terror and isolation and passes gradually to a
paralyzing crisis"—there is good reason to think that Hume is not
completely detached from the "metaphysical agony" noted by
readers like James Noxon.[6] Hume's is the somewhat frenzied
jubilation of a man who has just narrowly escaped disaster and
has not quite regained his poise. Hume is relieved to be on firm
ground once more, yet he knows how terrifying are the dangers
he has passed. He declaims, half-amused, half still afraid of his
shadow:

Methinks I am like a man, who having struck on many shoals, and
having narrowly escap'd shipwreck in passing a small frith, has yet

the temerity to put out to sea in the same leaky weather-beaten vessel, and even carries his ambition so far as to think of compassing the globe under these disadvantageous circumstances. . . . [My difficulty] reduces me almost to despair, and makes me resolve to perish on the barren rock, on which I am at present, rather than venture myself upon that boundless ocean, which runs out into immensity. . . .

I am first affrighted and confounded with that forelorn solitude, in which I am plac'd in my philosophy, and fancy myself some strange uncouth monster, who not being able to mingle and unite in society, has been expell'd all human commerce, and left utterly abandon'd and disconsolate. Fain wou'd I run into the crowd for shelter and warmth; but cannot prevail with myself to mix with such deformity. I call upon others to join me, in order to make a company apart; but no one will hearken to me. Every one keeps at a distance, and dreads that storm, which beats upon me from every side. I have expos'd myself to the enmity of all metaphysicians, logicians, mathematicians, and even theologians; and can I wonder at the insults I must suffer? (*T*, 263–64)

And so on. This amazing departure from the style of the book is hardly a passage admirers of Hume fasten on and celebrate. However, viewed within the framework of his previous mental breakdown, Hume's rhetoric is understandable and meaningful. And this passage also helps to illuminate why Hume's later philosophical stance would be so different—meticulously controlled, never enthusiastic.

Finding himself in this woeful plight—"in the most deplorable condition imaginable, inviron'd with the deepest darkness, and utterly depriv'd of the use of every member and faculty" (*T*, 269)— what hope remains for the wretched Hume? The denouement of this eighteenth-century tragedy, complete with a happy ending, is almost bathetic, but it is faithful to Hume's own experience. It is likewise his intention to shock the reader with the primacy of nature. Windows must be flung open; light and air must be let in to drive away the fumes of philosophical enthusiasm:

Most fortunately it happens, that since reason is incapable of dispelling these clouds, nature herself suffices to that purpose, and cures me of this philosophical melancholy and delirium, either by relaxing this bent of mind, or by some avocation, and lively impression of my senses, which obliterate all these chimeras. I dine, I play a game of back-gammon, I converse, and am merry with my friends; and when after three or four hours' amusement, I wou'd return to these speculations, they appear so cold, and strain'd, and ridiculous, that I cannot find in my heart to enter into them any farther. (*T*, 269)

Has any other propounder of a system, ever before or since, so lightly dismissed his own arguments? With some justice, Sitter has even compared Hume in the Conclusion to the insane narrator of Swift's *Tale of a Tub*.[7] Understood rightly, however, Hume has been demonstrating the slippery purchase of the classical Pyrrhonian, whose wrongheaded attempts to suspend judgment can lead only to anxiety and even madness.[8]

To be sure, Hume is presenting us with a spectacle of his own despair, one apparently requiring miraculous deliverance, only to reassure us that the remedy is quite simple—and unavoidable in any case. That may be the purpose of Hume's drama, and it points the way toward his later definition of mitigated skepticism. However, his presentation is extremely personal and unrestrained. Hume wishes to illustrate the bankrupcy of Pyrrhonian (or, more properly, Cartesian) skepticism and its inevitable cure. To do so, he makes a confessional display of himself. He acts out the part of the Pyrrhonist and then metamorphoses before our eyes into a true skeptic—the mitigated skeptic—one chary of his own doubts. In the process, however, he has played the exhibitionist.

After the *Treatise* Hume continues to warn against Pyrrhonism, but it is never Hume himself who might be the victim of this malaise.[9] By 1748, in the first *Enquiry*, he speaks from a comfortable distance of the errors of Pyrrhonism; he pities the unfortunate extremist whose principles, unlike those of other philosophical sectarians, can have nothing to do with human life or conviction. Luckily, nature will rouse him from his dreams and cure him of his life-threatening paradoxes:

> were his principles universally and steadily to prevail[,] All discourse, all action would immediately cease; and men remain in total lethargy, till the necessities of nature, unsatisfied, put an end to their miserable existence. It is true; so fatal an event is very little to be dreaded. Nature is always too strong for principle. . . . When [the Pyrrhonist] awakes from his dream, he will be the first to join in the laugh against himself, and to confess, that all his objections are mere amusement, and can have no other tendency than to show the whimsical condition of mankind. (*EHU*, 160)

The description of the problem matches exactly that in the *Treatise*, but there are important changes in presentation. In this instance Hume describes the problem in the third person, not the first. Hume views the extreme skeptic objectively; it is not his experience but rather that of some hypothetical enthusiast. In the *Treatise* he laughs at himself, but here he watches the enthusiast laugh at himself. Hume has assumed control of his material; he has detached himself from metaphysical agony.

Similarly in the first *Enquiry* he personifies Reason—"so dazzled and confounded, that she scarcely can pronounce with certainty and assurance concerning any one object" (*EHU*, 157)—carefully separating himself from the bewilderment of Reason. In these strategies of disassociation we see the philosophical stance of the mature Hume being formed. From very personal, extravagant, hand-wringing rhetoric, he is moving toward that manner more characteristic of him—cautious, self-assured, distant, serene.

And is not that prized "mitigated scepticism" defined in the first *Enquiry* an indication of this direction? As one moves back and forth between the degree of belief that philosophy might allow and that belief characteristic of common life, one becomes very diffident. One is skeptical of common beliefs, but by the same token skeptical of these same corroding doubts. "In general, there is a degree of doubt, and caution, and modesty, which, in all kinds of scrutiny and decision, ought for ever to accompany a just reasoner" (*EHU*, 161–62). In the letter to Arbuthnot, we sense that Hume's overconfidence—his hubris, if you will—in thinking that he was on the brink of sighting a new world of philosophy brought about his fall into despair. At the very end of the first book of the *Treatise* we see him apologizing for being too positive and assured:

> I may have fallen into this fault after the example of others; but I here enter a *caveat* against any objections, which may be offer'd on that head; and declare that such expressions [as " 'tis certain," " 'tis undeniable"] were extorted from me by the present view of the object, and imply no dogmatical spirit, nor conceited idea of my own judgment, which are sentiments that I am sensible can become no body, and a sceptic still less than any other. (*T*, 274)

It is a clear admission that he had been betrayed into dogmatism, but never again. Henceforth he will be on guard against too positive a commitment to belief.[10]

The change from first person to third person is but one strategy of disengagement. A more prominent manifestation is Hume's preference for the dialogue as a method of exposition, for the dialogue form gives Hume the freedom he seeks.[11] For example, in section 11 of the first *Enquiry* there is the conversation between Hume and his "friend who loves skeptical paradoxes" (*EHU*, 132).

This invented friend is allowed much more license than would be seemly for Hume himself, and through most of the chapter this friend pretends to speak as if he were Epicurus defending his freethinking philosophy before the wise men of Athens. This character thinks boldly enough to begin with, but he becomes even bolder in his new guise as the notorious Epicurus. Hume has fashioned a voice that is two removes from his own. He is clearly enjoying the opportunity to play Epicurus, and yet there is absolutely no commitment implied by his strategy and no liability to censure. Likewise, in "A Dialogue" appended to the second *Enquiry*, which will be discussed later, Hume creates a similar iconoclastic voice, the extremely cosmopolitan friend "Palamedes, who is as great a rambler in his principles as in his person" (*EPM*, 324). This Palamedes tells shocking stories of a strange land, stories suggesting that there can be no absolute standard of morality.

The *Dialogues Concerning Natural Religion* are of course the most prominent and brilliant example of Hume's dialogue technique. From the date of their publication, readers have tried to decide whether Philo or Cleanthes best represents Hume, though Pamphilus and even Demea have been identified by some.[12] Perhaps no particular speaker should be taken exclusively as Hume, but Kemp Smith's appraisal is tempered and sensible: "Philo, from start to finish, represents Hume; . . . Cleanthes can be regarded as Hume's mouthpiece only in those passages in which he is explicitly agreeing with Philo, or in those other passages in which, while refuting Demea, he is also being used to prepare the way for one or other of Philo's independent conclusions."[14]

But whichever mask hides the real Hume, has he not done well in making us speculate? And of course he is hiding behind all the masks, even though he must have played Cleanthes and Philo with the most sympathy. Even if, as Gaskin suggests, an unbiased reader familiar with the first *Enquiry* will always pick Philo as the hero,[15] Hume has still gone some lengths to make that facile identification impossible. Has he not, disingenuously no doubt, had Pamphilus declare Cleanthes the soundest reasoner? (*D*, 261). Does he not in a letter name Cleanthes the hero? (*L*, 1:153). That there would be any controversy at all over who speaks for Hume proves the intention of his using the dialogue form. He obviously does not want to be inflexibly committed to any particular position or identified with one. Rather, does he not want to consider multiple points of view, and sometimes agree or not agree with Philo, Cleanthes, and even with the unimaginative and orthodox

Demea? Would he not have been pleased to read Gaskin's statement—"The answer which Hume appears to give . . . is . . ."—and to see Gaskin's admission—"I say 'appears' because the dialogue context of the discussion makes it particularly difficult in this instance to identify exactly Hume's personal conclusions"?[16] Surely that is the way Hume preferred it.[17]

The letter to Gilbert Elliot identifying Cleanthes as his hero contains an interesting elaboration:

> Whatever you can think of, to strengthen [Cleanthes'] side of the Argument, will be most acceptable to me. Any Propensity you imagine I have to [Philo's] Side, crept in upon me against my Will: And tis not long ago that I burn'd an old Manuscript Book, wrote before I was twenty; which contain'd, Page after Page, the gradual Progress of my Thoughts on that head. It begun with an anxious Search after Arguments, to confirm the common Opinion: Doubts stole in, dissipated, return'd, were again dissipated, return'd again; and it was a perpetual Struggle of a restless Imagination against Inclination, perhaps against Reason. (*L*, 1:153–54)

Reaching back to that perilous time of the nervous collapse, Hume remembers the origin of Philo's arguments. They were ones he wanted to refute, but it would seem that he could not entirely succeed. They emerge in the mouth of Philo, but Hume resists calling them his own. He even burns his own notes, destroying his connection with Philo. Cleanthes is his hero, he insists. But could his friend help him to make Cleanthes' arguments stronger? In spite of himself, as Hume seems to admit, Philo is carrying the day once again.

I do not wish to push this argument too far, as if to say that Philo was some demonic side of Hume that he sought vainly to control or exorcise. Indeed, I am mindful of Gay's reservation about making a rhetorical form into a psychological revelation: "It has become fashionable to see the dialogue as a prototype of modern man's dilemmas, to visualize each protagonist as merely one facet of the author, and the clash of opinion as symptomatic of some unresolved inner conflict."[18] In fact, Hume had no doubt a comfortable attachment to Philo, and his remarks to Elliot, like that final appraisal given to Pamphilus, have their share of irony. Rather, I am suggesting that Hume wanted to explore quite heterodox thinking without being too close to it. And he did not want to be tied to one viewpoint. He could oppose Cleanthes to Philo, or Demea to both, just as he could express reservations about the views of his paradoxical alter ego of *Enquiry* 11, or find a reassuring solution to the moral iconoclasm of Palamedes, another alter ego.

Occasionally Hume withdraws from commitment of any kind. So troubling are the possibilities that he renounces argumentation altogether, the ultimate act of disengagement. We see this strategy most prominently at the end of *NHR:*

> The whole is a riddle, an aenigma, an inexplicable mystery. Doubt, uncertainty, suspence of judgment appear the only result of our most accurate scrutiny, concerning this subject. But such is the frailty of human reason, and such the irresistible contagion of opinion, that even this deliberate doubt could scarce be upheld; did we not enlarge our view, and opposing one species of superstition to another, set them a quarreling; while we ourselves, during their fury and contention, happily make our escape, into the calm, tho' obscure, regions of philosophy. (*NHR*, 95)

Assuredly, the paragraph is partly a way of breaking off. Having said all he wishes, Hume says, like the letter writer, "I must go now." But if we look closely at the final section, we see that Hume has been considering some very troubling moral issues. I say "moral" because they concern the way we live, our choices of life:

> Good and ill are universally intermingled and confounded; happiness and misery, wisdom and folly, virtue and vice. Nothing is pure and entirely of a piece. All advantages are attended with disadvantages. . . . And it is scarce possible for us, by our most chimerical wishes, to form the idea of a station or situation altogether desirable. (*NHR*, 92–93)

Further, we are capable of believing in sublime principles, but we disgrace human nature by our actual beliefs—and by our lives. What absurdities and contradictions are everywhere to be seen among mankind, among the supposedly rational and cultivated just as much as among the brutal. It is away from these thoughts that Hume escorts his enlightened reader, as they make their "escape into the calm, though obscure regions of philosophy." Hume has vastly enjoyed the devastating scrutiny of *NHR*, but at this point the temptation to belief or commitment of some kind seems threateningly close. Even "men of the greatest and most cultivated understanding" have embraced absurdities. The impossibility of making an altogether satisfactory choice of life belongs also to the true philosopher. And it is no longer easy, as it was at the beginning of *NHR*, to separate those refined "principles of genuine Theism and Religion" from the repellent "origin of religion in human nature" (*NHR*, 25). Hence the strategy of withdrawal, a device for regaining composure and control. The strategy does not seem entirely successful, however, as the "calm sunshine of the mind," evoked earlier, clouds over into the "calm, though obscure regions of philosophy."

Hume uses other strategies of disengagement. Verbal irony is one other obvious way in which he can deal with controversial subjects without getting too close to them, without committing himself to a definite position. Perhaps the most notorious of Hume's ironies occurs in "Of Miracles," whose power Gay describes with acumen: "The essay . . . is pervaded by the attitude that marks all his work—his moderate skepticism, his confident philosophical modesty. This very modesty reinforces his strategic position: seeking to prove little, he disproves much."[19] But even as we become certain of Hume's meaning behind the veil of irony, there is room for doubt. Sitter remarks, "It is just possible that Hume's famous conclusion . . . —that Christianity not only must have been attended by miracles at its beginning but cannot be believed at present without one—is at some level less ironic than is usually supposed; for in Hume's psychology, *any* belief is virtually miraculous."[20] Noxon points out that in any case "this cryptic flourish of double talk" has contradictory implications that Hume himself may not have realized.[21]

But if Hume's habit of ironical discourse might sometimes have gotten him in over his head, it nonetheless served him well as an instrument both of self-protection and useful ambiguity. Lionel Gossman's brilliant analysis of this Enlightenment mode describes Hume's use of it precisely:

> Irony is preeminently an instrument of inclusion and exclusion, and its playful exterior disguises a certain repressiveness. As the Enlightened critic unmasks the religious enthusiast, the historical hero, the devoted spouse, the metaphysician, as he reveals what is "behind the back" of the other's noble discourse, he is careful not to expose his own back. It often happens that irony . . . does not point to a hidden sense which is the opposite of the manifest one—the traditional meaning of irony. It is infinitely receding, turning the reader back from every formulation of a position, so that the laws by which all others are judged—and condemned—are never enunciated. It both permits and requires the values, through which the initiated come together and recognize each other, to remain unspoken. These values are, indeed, what cannot and may not be openly said, for being said

they would in turn lie open to criticism and question. They must be insinuated in such a way that the reader hardly notices it happening, and they can, of course, never be systematized.[22]

As in the case of Hume's dialogues, irony functions to make us unsure of his exact position and readier to question our own.

Hume's penchant for disengagement may not seem directly related to his moral thought, but this turn of mind does make Hume a particular kind of moralist, a rather modern moralist who is highly open-minded and tolerant about ethical possibilities, one who believes that virtuous life is more a matter of cultivating an attitude than of conforming to a system. He is a moralist with a pronounced suspicion of certitude and dogmatism, who tests out unconventional ideas and broadens the definition of virtue. And yet there is a certain pessimism in his thinking, too, which makes it all the more necessary for him to ensure control and hence to maintain that disengaged attitude so essential to moral life. We shall see in the following sections how this disposition shapes his moral skepticism.

Testing Conventional Morality

One thing is clear about Hume the moralist. Although he often supports conventional positions—one should love one's family and help one's fellow creatures—he also advocates the heterodox: pride is normally good, adultery is no real vice, suicide is occasionally advisable, religious worship is too frequently an abomination. Hence the inclination of otherwise perceptive historians of ideas like Basil Willey to view Hume's morality as safely orthodox is difficult to account for.[23] Hume's whole disposition to build virtue on a foundation of hedonism and materialism must separate him from almost every other person—certainly in the eighteenth century but perhaps in most others—whom we might seriously denominate a moralist. If Hume said of Mandeville's theories that it is contradictory to talk of vice that is beneficial to society, then we might wonder whether it is contradictory to talk of a moralist who is a thoroughgoing iconoclast—or as the orthodox might say, an enemy to virtue. We remember his rodomontade to a friend: "I believe I shall write no more History; but proceed directly to attack the Lord's Prayer & the ten Commandments & the single Cat[echism]; and recommend Suicide & Adultery: And so persist, till it shall please the Lord to take me to himself" (*NL*, 43). Jesting words are not always intended entirely as jest.

The *Enquiry Concerning the Principles of Morals* provides Hume with a forum to develop his new definition of virtue, one deriving from values of worldly utilitarianism rather than from those of useless austerity or otherworldliness. However, this heterodoxy is fairly well balanced by two elements: (1) Hume's frequent perorations on classical examples of virtue, which, though they may illustrate his new morality, were nonetheless in his day safely part of the Western tradition; (2) his warm recommendation of benevolence, a sentimental tone that sweetens the strong new taste of worldly virtue. Hume speaks of this work as "incomparably the best" (*MOL*, 613) of his writings, and his pride may stem from the success with which he makes his new morality so palatable. The unveiling of True Virtue toward the end, as shown in chapter 3, climactically sweeps the reader away with admiration. At least that seems to be the intention.

Although Hume must have been pleased with his success of combining the painter and the anatomist, did he finally believe that an innate human propensity toward sympathy, allied with the human ability to create such artificial virtues as justice, would result in the control of moral evil? Was he really as optimistic as he seems to be throughout most of the second *Enquiry*? Was he satisfied with his own answers?

If we look at the conclusion to the second *Enquiry*, we may wonder. There his purpose is to argue in the best tradition of classical moralists that men naturally prefer the beauty of virtue to the deformity of vice. But he thinks of a possible exception—"in the case of justice, where a man, taking things in a certain light, may often seem to be a loser by his integrity." That is, "a sensible knave . . . may think that an act of iniquity or infidelity will make a considerable addition to his fortune, without causing any considerable breach in the social union and confederacy" (*EPM*, 282). It is true that justice is an artificial virtue and thus is based more on reason than on nature. Nevertheless, Hume has earlier implied in his discussion of artificial virtues that something like justice rests on a secure foundation. The sensible knave—"sensible" here meaning something like "perceptive," "alert," "savvy," but certainly not "morally sensitive"[24]—is indeed a problem to Hume's theory. It is revealing that in the *Treatise* this "sensible knave" is the first-person Hume, and he seems to understand all too well the thinking of the dishonest man: "Your example [of injustice] both pushes me forward . . . by imitation, and also affords me a new reason for any breach of equity, by shewing me, that I should be the cully of my integrity, if I alone shou'd impose on myself a severe restraint amidst the licentiousness of others" (*T*, 535). At least in the "improved" version of the *Enquiry*, Hume assumes more decorous control, looking with distaste at the sensible knave. Nonetheless, the fact still remains that many a scoundrel may think that "honesty is the best policy" is a good rule for others but not for him, profitably excepting himself from the general rule.

What is Hume's answer to this reasoning? He begins to "a-hem" and stammer: "I must confess that, if a man think that this reasoning much requires an answer, it will be a little difficult to find any which will to him appear satisfactory and convincing. If his heart rebel not against such pernicious maxims, if he feel no reluctance to the thoughts of villainy or baseness, he has indeed lost a considerable motive to virtue" (*EPM*, 283). This is no answer, however, and Hume ends weakly with two variations of the crime-does-not-pay truism. (1) An honest man has "the frequent satisfaction of seeing knaves, with all their pretended cunning and abilities, betrayed by their own maxims"—not too high-minded a satisfaction, one might think. (2) But even if knaves are successful, the honest man knows that they have duped themselves in acquiring "worthless toys and gewgaws" rather than the real pleasures of life, the greatest being "the peaceful reflection on one's own conduct" (*EPM*, 283–84). But these arguments are addressed to the man who is already honest; they do not answer the knave, who will either be caught in his web of deception or be highly successful, causing him to reflect very contentedly on his own conduct. Consequently, there are knaves in the world who will never be reached by heartfelt or any other kind of argument. And one might well ask why Hume feels the honest man needs so much exhortation when confronted with the thinking of the sensible knave.[25] Overall, this work may be optimistic, but there is a canker in the rose. Man's love of virtue is not universal by any means, and might the standards of morality be in all cases relative rather than absolute?

Hume explores this vexing question in "A Dialogue" he appended to the second *Enquiry*. That he chose the dialogue form itself suggests that he would here test answers that could prove upsetting to conventional morality. Hume happens upon his freethinking friend Palamedes, whom we met before, who tells him of a land called Fourli "whose inhabitants have ways of thinking, in many things, particularly in morals, diametrically opposite to ours," despite their being "extremely civilized and intelligent" (*EPM*, 324). Palamedes describes one Fourlian named Alcheic who is esteemed the most noble and virtuous Fourlian of all, even though, or perhaps because, he is a pederast, committer of incest, parricide, traitor, assassin, coward, railer and ill-mannered lout, liar, and, finally, suicide. After hearing of these facts and of other strange customs, the good Mr. Hume is so shocked that he exclaims, "Such barbarous and savage manners are not only incompatible with a civilized, intelligent people, such as you said these were; but are scarcely compatible with human nature" (*EPM*, 328). But he has fallen into the trap laid by Palamedes. He discovers that Palamedes has been telling him of the celebrated ancient Greeks and Romans under cover of these strange names.

The surprised Hume protests that such a tactic is unfair, and he proceeds to illustrate his point by describing modern-day France with similar distortions. What would the ancient Greek think of a people who practice adultery with incredible freedom and joy, who enslave themselves to their tyrannical king, who murder each other over trifles (their dueling), who suffer any disgrace or pain rather than kill themselves, who would send most of their children to the poorhouse so that one son can live voluptuously (primogeniture), and who would make women, their natural inferiors, "their masters and sovereigns" (chivalry)? The ancient Greek would hardly believe these people human. But of course here the pious Hume has been supporting, not opposing, his bold friend. Palamedes has no objection to Hume's turning the tables. It all goes to prove his basic point that there are no absolute standards of morality:

> I only meant to represent the uncertainty of all these judgments concerning characters; and to convince you, that fashion, vogue, custom, and law, were the chief foundation of all moral determinations. The Athenians surely, were a civilized, intelligent people, if ever there were one; and yet their man of merit might, in this age, be held in horror and execration. The French are also, without doubt, a very civilized, intelligent people; and yet their man of merit might, with the Athenians, be an object of the highest contempt and ridicule, and even hatred. . . . How shall we pretend to fix a standard for judgments of this nature? (*EPM*, 333)

Despite the difficulty he faces, Hume's answers to Palamedes have a certain plausibility. If we trace matters higher, he says, we shall find that "the principles upon which men reason in morals are always the same; though the conclusions which they draw are often very different" (*EPM*, 335–36). Besides, men agree more than they differ: both the Athenian and the Frenchman would admire "good sense, knowledge, wit, eloquence, humanity, fidelity, truth, justice, courage, temperance, constancy, dignity of mind" (*EPM*, 334). Perhaps so, we may concede, but they often differ greatly in their operational definitions of these abstractions.[26] Humanity for a Greek might include mercifully killing his children; for a Frenchman, favoring one child over all the others. So what difference does it make that they might agree on first principles if they draw such contrasting conclusions from those same principles? Surely Hume does not think that he has settled the matter, reassuring us that differences in morals are minor and inconsequential.

One of the few Hume scholars to consider "A Dialogue" in detail is Donald Livingston, who appears satisfied that the work's disquieting specter of moral relativism is finally laid to rest: "What Hume brilliantly shows in 'A Dialogue' is that any practice in any period, if described externally, may appear unintelligible and alien." Duncan Forbes likewise is satisfied that Hume adequately explains away "any kind of ethical relativism." I suggest, however, that one cannot escape the unsettling implications of "A Dialogue" so easily, for the meaning of a master ironist like Hume is not always on the surface. Livingston seems to view this work as a sparring match between the iconoclast Palamedes and the right-thinking Hume, as if the two viewpoints never mesh, and in the fashion of The Mummers' Play the wicked Turkish knight is defeated by St. George, or St. David. The trouble is, however, that the Turkish knight Palamedes is not defeated, nor is he a being apart from Hume.[27]

Hume compounds the problem of moral relativism by undertaking an explanation of these individual aberrations. Greek homosexuality derived, he claims, from their frequent gymnastic exercises and "were recommended, though absurdly, as the source of friendship, sympathy, mutual attachment, and fidelity; qualities esteemed in all nations and all ages." The marriage of near relations may be "contrary to reason and public utility," but where will reason draw the line?" (*EPM*, 334)[28] As to the French toleration of adultery, they "have resolved to sacrifice some of the domestic to the sociable pleasures; and to prefer ease, freedom, and an open commerce, to a strict fidelity and constancy. The ends are both good, and are somewhat difficult to reconcile; nor need we be surprised, if the customs of nations incline too much, sometimes to the one side, sometimes to the other" (*EPM*, 335).

But we may still be surprised that reasoning from the same principles, nations would differ so much. Then Hume continues to offer
reasons for different standards of morality among nations, reasons including types of government and political exigencies, degrees of refinement, customs, climate, accidents, and even varying judgments about "the usefulness of any habit or action" (*EPM*,
336–41).

When people begin to differ radically in what they consider
useful, we may question whether Hume has left much of anything that would give morality a solid foundation or even reg-
ularize ethics. There are so many factors making one man's
morality another's scandal that all Hume's fine talk about "first
principles" is largely meaningless. The defeat of Palamedes by
Hume's "I," much like the defeat of Philo in the *Dialogues*, is a
masterstroke of irony. The "I" and Palamedes have worked together to chip away the foundation of moral absolutism.

It is true that Hume's friend Gilbert Elliot read "A Dialogue,"
was confounded with "doubt and uncertainty," and then thanked
Hume for leading him out of the maze.[29] Perhaps Hume wel-
comed that reaction because it was his intention to answer these
doubts for himself and others. In any case, even if he has proven
an absolute foundation for morality, in the process he has certainly broadened that foundation to encompass a variety of moral
practices that many would find repugnant. His own anxious satisfaction with "A Dialogue" is evident in the letter by which he
introduces it to Elliot: "It is pretty usual for People to be pleas'd
with their own Performance, especially in the Heat of Composition; but I have scarcely wrote any thing more whimsical, or
whose Merit I am more diffident of" (*L*, 1:145). Hume knew how
extravagant his thinking was.

"A Dialogue" has a very interesting conclusion. Palamedes concedes that Hume's rationale "may have some foundation"—in the
language of politeness, damning it with faint praise—but Palamedes brings up the problem of *"artificial* lives and manners"—in
other words the ways in which theology or philosophy mold
behavior. In ancient times, philosophy had the ascendent; in
modern times, religion. And Palamedes holds up two men whose
lives were totally controlled respectively by philosophy and religion—Diogenes and Pascal. The opposition is diametrical, with
both extremes running to absurdity. Diogenes attempted to make
himself superior to fortune and to all other men; Pascal exulted in
his total helplessness and inferiority. "The philosopher indulged
himself in the most beastly pleasures, even in public: The saint

refused himself the most innocent, even in private." The former expressed his love by scolding and reproving his friends and turned his wit loose against all religious beliefs. The latter was indifferent to his friends and loved his enemies, "and an extreme contempt of this life, in comparison of the future, was the chief foundation of his conduct" (*EPM*, 341–43). Palamedes appears to condemn both equally, but the Humean preference for Diogenes' spirited iconoclasm and pride comes across unmistakably. In some ways once again the railing, abusive, self-indulgent, but vigorously magnanimous and honest Diogenes of the classical age is Hume's secret hero—so much more admirable than the Christian Pascal, with his self-effacement and relentless denial of this life.

Palamedes' ostensible purpose in bringing up this contrast is to present Hume with another objection to moral absolutism. Both Diogenes and Pascal "have been proposed as models of imitation. Where then is the universal standard of morals, which you talk of?" Hume's answer is that those acting under these artificial dictates have so completely departed from "maxims of common sense" that they cannot be judged like ordinary men (*EPM*, 343). How well that answer satisfies Palamedes' objection may be questioned—indeed it may not be intended to answer the objection entirely—but it does teach the lesson that dogmatic adherence to any code, philosophical or religious, in effect corrupts morality. And it is not surprising that religious dogmatism would be the most corrupting by far.

"A Dialogue," then, is an excellent example of both Hume's moral iconoclasm and his insistence on openness, flexibility, and toleration as the only reliable guidelines of moral thought. Hume does not advocate homosexuality and sexual permissiveness, to be sure, even though his attitude toward intrigues, gallantry, and what he calls "open commerce" (in our idiom, "free love") is extremely liberal: quoting La Fontaine on female infidelity, he writes, *"that if one knows it, it is but a small matter; if one knows it not, it is nothing"* (*EPM*, 339). Thus he is quite tolerant. It is more dangerous to morality, he implies, to restrict one's thinking too much, to view one's own particular preferences as the only morality. Indeed Hume was so suspicious of dogmatism that he resorted to dialogues and contrasting exempla as vehicles of these controversial ideas. Hume wanted the liberty of playing Palamedes and Diogenes—or Philo and Epicurus—without being rigidly committed to any one position. As he might himself have said, he was a highly whimsical moralist.

Four Choices of Life

The four essays Hume published in 1742 under the titles "The Epicurean," "The Stoic," "The Platonist," and "The Sceptic" form a tetralogy that deserves further attention, for these essays represent some of Hume's best and most interesting writing on the subject of practical morality. Hume's method here is similar to the dialogue.[30] Wearing separate masks, he makes a spirited defense of four distinct worldviews and ways of life. Hume explains in a note: "The intention of [these essays] is not so much to explain accurately the sentiments of the ancient sects of philosophy, as to deliver the sentiments of sects, that naturally form themselves in the world, and entertain different ideas of human life and happiness" (*E*, 138n.). Thus he considers them as four common but widely differing moral choices of life.

It might be expected that the first three would be ironical personae, and the last, the appearance of an unmasked Hume, finally revealing how his cherished mitigated skepticism is superior to the others. To a certain degree this interpretation is correct, because the last speech is the most faithful to Hume's sensibility. But there are complications. It might be more accurate to say that Hume enjoys trying on the identity of each speaker, and he is demonstrating that each choice of life may be right, given the disposition of the individual. Unlike Johnson's *Rasselas* (1759), where each choice of life proves defective, except perhaps the choice of eternity, Hume's tetralogy recognizes the multiplicity of good choices.[31]

"The Epicurean," or *"man of elegance and pleasure,"* leads off. From all that has been shown thus far of Hume's attention to elegance and worldly pleasure, we would not expect his Epicurean to emerge too unfavorably. And this hedonist is no vacuous playboy bent on good times, damn all else. He eschews "the barbarous dissonance of Bacchus" in his revels, preferring the "sprightly muses" and "peace, harmony, and concord" (*E*, 142). Indeed, he resembles Hume in a relaxed and carefree mood: "In our chearful discourses, better than in the formal reasonings of the schools, is true wisdom to be found" (*E*, 142). It is only slightly farfetched to imagine Hume in the arms of "the charming CAELIA," enjoying the real, though decorously phrased, pleasures of the flesh: "How amiable this solitude, this silence, this darkness! No objects now importune the ravished soul. The thought, the sense, all full of nothing but our mutual happiness, wholly possess the mind, and convey a pleasure, which deluded mortals vainly seek for in every other enjoyment—" (E, 144). Hume points his sentence with a final dash to suggest the ecstatic oblivion of his lovers. If carnality seems a bit out of place in the Works of David Hume, the justification for this life of pleasure accords with Hume's familiar assumptions. As many a *carpe diem* poet might tell us, "the image of our frail mortality" compels us to live for the moment, for there is no afterlife: "We shall be, as if we had never been." And this philosophy of pleasure has the additional advantage of removing "all the scruples of a vain superstition" (E, 145). Hume wears the Epicurean's silken robe rather well.

Nor does he look bad in the toga of the Stoic or "man of action and virtue," even though this identity requires him to become more stern and austere. Like the Epicurean, the Stoic sees happiness as the end of life, but he finds that happiness in hard work and in the exercise of reason and self-control, lifting man above the primitive existence of mere animals. This Stoic, like the Stoics of old, and like the Hume we often see in his writings, lives in a "temple of wisdom [that] is seated on a rock, above the rage of the fighting elements, and inaccessible to all the malice of man" (E, 150). But strangely unlike the ancient Stoics, who aspired to be indifferent to human suffering, whether their own or that of others, this Stoic is a man of feeling:

> But does the sage always preserve himself in this philosophical indif-ference, and rest contented with lamenting the miseries of mankind, without ever employing himself for their relief? . . . No; he knows that in this sullen *Apathy*, neither true wisdom nor happiness can be found. He feels too strongly the charm of the social affections ever to counteract so sweet, no natural, so virtuous a propensity. Even when, bathed in tears, he laments the miseries of the human race, of his country, of his friends, and unable to give succor, can only relieve them by compassion; he yet rejoices in the generous disposition, and feels a satisfaction superior to that of the most indulged sense. (E, 151).

It is remarkable that in his characterization of the Stoic, a figure usually criticized by sentimentalists precisely for his indifference to the suffering of others,[32] Hume would insert one of his most emotional recommendations of sentimentality. Regardless of their historical identity, Hume makes his philosophical characters as attractive as he can. Why render the Stoic as unemotional and indifferent? In a sense Hume's Stoic is his most dazzling and exaggerated philosophical portrait, somewhat in the manner of the hero of feeling seen in chapter 1. As he contemplates the "moral beauty" of his own life (*E*, 153), the Stoic realizes that whether or not there is an afterlife, the glory of having shown what human nature is capable of is reward enough. Since the character is hypothetical, any degree of heightening is allowable, and Hume seems determined to spare no pains in embellishing his man of action and virtue, two keywords that always inspire him, regardless of how in calmer moments he might be skeptical of these glorious possibilities.

The mask that Hume finds hardest to wear is that of the Platonist, or "man of contemplation and *philosophical* devotion" (*E*, 155).[33] In this case Hume sticks most closely to the tenets suggested by the name. He apparently feels little inspiration to take the part and play it to the hilt. That "The Platonist" is much shorter than either "The Epicurean" or "The Stoic"—indeed, not even half as long—tells us where Hume's sympathies lie. Nonetheless, Hume does not try to undercut this position by making it weak or ridiculous.

The Platonist points out that the pleasures of the voluptuary do not finally satisfy: they produce self-disgust and anguish. The Epicurean might not make such a concession, but at least to an idealist the pursuit of sensual pleasure must appear shortsighted. The Platonist then devotes the rest of his argument to discrediting the Stoic, whom he perceives as his chief rival. He points out with some justification that the Stoic in his "magnificent pretensions" is his "own idol" (*E*, 156–57); the Stoic ascribes a putative moral beauty to himself and overvalues the art of man. The Platonist urges us to adore divine beauty and wisdom instead. And rather than trying in vain to achieve perfection in this all too brief existence, we should begin working to make ourselves worthy of contemplating divinity: "it is our comfort, that, if we employ worthily the faculties here assigned us, they will be enlarged in another state of existence, so as to render us more suitable worshippers of our maker: And that the task, which can never be finished in time, will be the business of an eternity" (*E*, 158). Words such as these must have been difficult for Hume to say with a straight face—or to say at all. Yet he says them and says them rather well. His device of competing speakers demands that he play this part, too. The device forces him to dismiss human achievement in this world in favor of a longing for spiritual perfection in the next. After all, idealism, adoration of divine beauty, and spiritual values are "sentiments . . . that naturally form themselves in the world" (*E*, 138). A host of Platonists, neo-Platonists, and other assorted idealists have made these general ideas their guide to living well. It is to Hume's credit that he does his best to give this position a fair hearing, however little enthusiasm he brings to the task.

Having the final say, the Sceptic has the strategically best position. (Hume does not give the Sceptic an alternate title, apparently thinking any additional explanation superfluous.) The title tells us that here is the part Hume has been waiting for, one requiring little acting. And Hume's comfort with the role is seen in the style. He drops the fustian employed by the previous personae and speaks plainly in the manner of the *Treatise*, or better, the second *Enquiry*. The Sceptic has by far the most to say, another indication of Hume's readiness for the part. He does not have to struggle to invent arguments here. They come from the heart.

The Sceptic maintains that the other speakers commit the error of dogmatism: they and almost all proponents of one system "are led astray, not only by the narrowness of their understandings, but by that also of their passions"; they think their road "the only one that leads to happiness" (*E*, 160). In fact, however, "beauty and worth are merely of a relative nature" (*E*, 163); by constitution and temper we are inclined to seek quite different kinds of beauty and worth. "The catching of flies, like DOMITIAN, if it gives more pleasure, is preferable to the hunting of wild beasts, like WILLIAM RUFUS, or conquering of kingdoms, like ALEXANDER" (*E*, 171). We are in the position of concluding, as in "A Dialogue," that one man's morality is not another's, but here the explanation is not so much a difference in reasoning as a difference in passions—or indeed, in genetic make-up. We have very little ability to make ourselves pursue a virtue contrary to our inclinations. No amount of reasoning or exhortation will ever make us behave in a way that is not initiated by our passions. It is an argument familiar to readers of the *Treatise* and second *Enquiry*, although here it seems particularly dispiriting. In the second *Enquiry* we can at least find reassurance by thinking that these passions tend to make us benevolent and finally just, but here they tend willy-nilly toward many contrary choices of life, some of which are indeed contemptible.

To a degree, this essay is an attack on philosophy's pretensions to regulate conduct, to teach morality, or even to make men happy. The Sceptic spends considerable time demolishing the various consolations of philosophy, especially those of the Stoics. For example,

Let not the injuries or violence of men, say the philosophers, *ever discompose you by anger or hatred. Would you be angry at the ape for its malice, or the tyger for its ferocity?* This reflection leads us into a bad opinion of human nature, and must extinguish the social affections. It tends also to prevent all remorse for a man's own crimes, when he considers, that vice is as natural to mankind, as the particular instincts to brute-creatures. (*E*, 173)

Another consolation: "*Your sorrow is fruitless, and will not change the course of destiny.* Very true: And for that very reason I am sorry" (*E*, 174)—a paraphrase of Solon's reply to the pedant. Even the best of these consolations—that we can receive comfort from comparing our situation to that of others—is faulty. We tend to compare ourselves to our superiors, but even if we redirect our gaze downward, there can be little comfort: "to a very good-natured man, the view of human miseries should rather produce sorrow than comfort, and add, to his lamentations for his own misfortunes, a deep compassion for those of others" (*E*, 177).

At this point Hume interrupts himself by means of a footnote, protesting that "the Sceptic, perhaps, carries the matter too far" (*E*, 177n.). Hume offers twelve "philosophical reflections" that may at least fortify and nourish the temper, even though they are incapable of remaking human life. They are such platitudes as these:

(1.) Is it not certain, that every condition has concealed ills? Then why envy anybody?
(5.) How many other good things have I? Then why be vexed for one ill?

Hume's interruption is a gesture of open-mindedness: the Sceptic may himself have been growing too narrow in his pessimism, despite his own warning against dogmatism. In fact, however, the interruption serves more to reinforce the Sceptic's case than to qualify it. For how well do all these consolations work? They are

So convincing, that it is a wonder they persuade not every man. But perhaps they do occur to and persuade most men; when they consider human life, by a general and calm survey: But where any real, affecting incident happens; when passion is awakened, fancy agitated, example draws, and counsel urges; the philosopher is lost in the man, and he seeks in vain for that persuasion which before seemed so firm and unshaken.

Once again, what good is wisdom to a person afflicted with loss or disappointment? Thence what good, wisdom? In fact, Hume is agreeing with the Sceptic, even though he wants to leave the possibility open that moral instruction may offer some small degree of help: "Despise not these helps; but confide not too much in them neither; unless nature has been favourable in the temper, with which she has endowed you" (*E,* 179n).

Moral philosophy is impotent. It can do nothing for the knave who has no inclination of temper or passion to do good; it can do very little for the man of reflection and intelligence even if his studies have made him wish to acquire virtue, unless he is already predisposed to that end. And the virtuous man is naturally good and does not need it. This may indeed be Hume's most morally pessimistic work.[34] Hear the words of the Sceptic:

> The empire of philosophy extends over a few; and with regard to these too, her authority is very weak and limited. Men may well be sensible of the value of virtue, and may desire to attain it; but it is not always certain, that they will be successful in their wishes. (*E,.* 169)

> Here then is the chief triumph of art and philosophy: It insensibly refines the temper, and it points out to us those dispositions which we should endeavour to attain, by a constant *bent* of mind, and by repeated *habit.* Beyond this I cannot acknowledge it to have great influence; and I must entertain doubts concerning all those exhortations and consolations, which are in such vogue among speculative reasoners. (*E,* 171)

> It is certain, were a superior being thrust into a human body, that the whole of life would to him appear so mean, contemptible, and puerile, that he never could be induced to take part in any thing, and would scarcely give attention to what passes around him. (*E,* 175)

> In a word, human life is more governed by fortune than by reason; is to be regarded more as a dull pastime than as a serious occupation; and is more influenced by particular humour, than by general principles. Shall we engage ourselves in it with passion and anxiety? It is not worthy of so much concern. Shall we be indifferent about what happens? We lose all the pleasure of the game by our phlegm and carelessness. While we are reasoning concerning life, life is gone; and death, though *perhaps* they receive him differently, yet treats alike the fool and the philosopher. To reduce life to exact rule and method, is commonly a painful, oft a fruitless occupation: And is it not also a proof, that we overvalue the prize for which we contend? Even to reason so carefully concerning it, and to fix with accuracy its just idea, would be overvaluing it, were it not that, to some tempers, this

occupation is one of the most amusing, in which life could possibly be employed. (*E*, 180)

This is some of Hume's most eloquent writing—a philosopher's Ecclesiastes—and he surely says it from the heart. It is similar to his defense of vocation at the end of *Treatise* Book 1, though certainly less sanguine. Can the moral philosopher do very much to change mankind? Is philosophy itself but a harmless amusement like Domitian's catching of flies?

The Sceptic does not synthesize the other points of view, nor does he reject the other choices, except as choices. Each of the three other ways of life may be good for the individual and praiseworthy in many respects, but these philosophies are not really choices, after all. How we live is chosen for us. Moral philosophy has much to teach us, but unfortunately we are only classroom-learners. Outside we forget most of our lessons. Even the man with the greatest capacity to learn is not much better off: "He . . . is always a sublime philosopher, when he needs not; that is, as long as nothing disturbs him, or rouzes his affections" (*E*, 176). We take eclectically from moral philosophy what we think we can use, but in the sum total of life that gleaning of wisdom figures only a little.

However, the true brilliance of Hume's sobering look at the worth of moral philosophy is the manner in which he presents it. The Sceptic is not Hume, after all. If the preceding three speakers are ironical personae, then so is this one. Put the other way, if through the Sceptic Hume is speaking for himself, then to an extent so he is through the others. Surely he would like to be the Man of Action and Virtue, were such a being possible in human form. He pretends to be the Man of Elegance and Pleasure with a certain relish. He even tries on the unfamiliar identity of the Man of Contemplation and Philosophical Devotion with curiosity. When at last he appears as the Sceptic, that persona closest to his own nature, he does so simply to admit that neither he nor any other person can choose just any kind of wisdom. Each individual must tailor philosophy to fit himself and at the same time understand that philosophy will fit others differently. The Sceptic insists on a tolerant, open-ended morality. Still, the Sceptic is not Hume—witness the author's protest that the Sceptic goes too far, or the almost debilitating despair in the Sceptic's conclusions, a predicament not unlike the Pyrrhonian's in the *Treatise*, Book 1, and in the first *Enquiry*. When we hear the defeatist view that life seems scarcely worth the trouble, Hume is not talking *in propria persona*. Indeed, he is speaking from the heart at the same time that he is playing a role. Like the Epicurean, Stoic, and Platonist before him, the Sceptic finally has committed the fault of excess. Preferring a singular attitude toward life, he has done the very thing he initially warned against. Perhaps a person may very well learn more from philosophy than the Sceptic's jaded determinism would allow for. But whether anybody can, the moralist Hume has not committed himself to the answer. Juxtaposing the recommendations of four very different moralists, he has once again slipped through our fingers.

"The Calm Sunshine of the Mind"

Years ago, writing on a much broader topic than Hume's morality, but still from the perspective of Hume's worldliness, Paschal Larkin made this unfriendly observation: "Viewed in the most favourable light, his ethical system was a plea for a fuller recognition of the facts of life on the part of the moralist. Considered from another and more correct standpoint, it was an attempt to discredit objective standards and ultimate values." Certainly there is much to challenge in Larkin's assessment—in particular, his accusation that Hume had made "moral criteria a negligible force in actual life"[35]—still, Larkin's apparently damaging conclusion need not finally constitute a dismissal of Hume's position. Why is it undesirable for a moralist to subsume the bald facts of life in his system or to question rigid standards of ethics?

Admittedly, there are contradictions or at least difficulties in Hume's moral thinking. On the one hand, for the benefit of humankind he shapes and displays models of practical morality in works such as the second *Enquiry* and even more insistently in the *History of England*. And yet implicit in his theory of morality is the assumption that it is less by reason than by their passions that human beings will be moral, if they are at all. The man of feeling will be virtuous; the sensible knave will be profitably dishonest. Why then write a moral treatise to either? And that suspicion of dogmatism, that toleration of varying standards of morality, which characterize Hume the ethical theorist, sometimes seem to disappear when Hume becomes the practicing moralist: his own moral preferences, indeed those of the British or French gentleman, are the absolute standard. To be civilized is to be part of Hume's civilization. The outlandish customs of Moslems or aborigines are beneath contempt. As an historian Hume seems reluctant to begin his account of medieval England. From a position that is in this case quite antithetical to the assumptions of modern theory, he wonders what we could possibly learn from such a study: "the adventures of barbarous nations, even if they were recorded, could afford little or no entertainment to men born in a more cultivated age . . . and it is rather fortunate for letters that they are buried in silence and oblivion" (*H*, 1:3–4).

There may be no perfect answer to these difficulties. Human beings take the measure of morality from themselves and from their ambient culture; Hume recognizes this problem and employs devices of disengagement and flexibility to make himself as openminded as he can. Besides, those basic values of his such as sympathy, cheerfulness, and enterprise have great appeal. Hume gives us good reason to think that a person who is caught up in the things of this world will have the best opportunity possible to be happy, productive, and caring—states of mind conducive to Hume's preferred morality and indeed to that of many moralists, even though they may propose other ways of acquiring that virtue.

"The calm sunshine of the mind" by which Hume describes the temper of the genuinely moral individual is an ideal of cheerful equanimity. It is to that moral ideal that Hume aspired in his own life. Peter Gay believes that toward that end Hume achieved remarkable success:

> For David Hume was both courageous and modern; he understood the implications of his philosophy and did not shrink from them. He was so courageous that he did not have to insist on his courage; he followed his thinking where it led him. . . . He was willing to live with uncertainty, with no supernatural justifications, no complete explanations, no promise of permanent stability, with guides of merely probable validity; and what is more, he lived in his world without complaining, a cheerful Stoic. Hume, therefore, more decisively than many of his brethren in the Enlightenment, stands at the threshold of modernity and exhibits its risks and its possibilities. Without melodrama but with the sober eloquence one would expect from an accomplished classicist, Hume makes plain that since God is silent, man is his own master: he must live in a disenchanted world, submit everything to criticism, and make his own way.[36]

Hume does not so much teach morality as he advocates conditions under which morality can flourish, while he cautions against conditions that pervert morality—whether by morality we mean acquired ("artificial" in his terminology) honesty and sociability or even some kind of innate benevolence. In the pessimistic mode of "The Sceptic," Hume may appear to slight moral teaching, but that skepticism concerning exhortation does not preclude his use of moral conditioning. "Men's views of things are the result of their understanding alone: Their conduct is regulated by their understanding, their temper, and their passions" (H, 5:257), as the historian says, but temper and passions are in some measure the products of environment. Separate men from the world by means of religious fanaticism, for instance, and "all the ties of morality" (H, 5:494)—whether natural or artificial—are loosened. Give men something advantageous to do—ships to sail, goods to make and trade, fine clothes to wear—"and the tempers of men, as well as their behaviour, refine apace" (E, 271). For Hume, morality is the complex product of a fully realized existence in this world. One might term Hume, if not a moral teacher, then a moral behaviorist.

And one might also term Hume a moral skeptic. The label need not be invidious. If Hume's morality involves a rational enjoyment of the things of this world, then for him moral skepticism implies a hesitation about which things to recommend most or which to proscribe. A too narrow morality is no morality at all, and Hume takes great pains to keep himself disengaged enough to see that there are many paths to virtue. Hume was as unfriendly to religion as was Thomas Hobbes, yet this is his criticism of Hobbes: "Though an enemy to religion, he partakes nothing of the spirit of scepticism; but is as positive and dogmatical as if human reason, and his reason in particular, could attain a thorough conviction in these subjects" (H, 6:153). Given this remark, it is not surprising that Hume's most searching examination of "these subjects" would take the form of the dialogue, an insurance against dogmatism. However strongly he spoke out against the abuses of institutional religion, he still found the militant atheism of the *philosophes* repugnant,[37] and he never would declare his final word on the religious hypothesis. He regarded good humor, serenity, resilience and detachment—in a word, skepticism[38]—as a sure guide to philosophy and to virtuous life. As I shall demonstrate in the final chapter, his personal example may be his most compelling moral argument.

5

David Hume's Last Words

A genuine and hearty pride, or self-esteem, if well conceal'd
and well founded, is essential to the character of a man of
honour, and . . . there is no quality of mind, which is more
indispensably requisite to procure the esteem and approbation
of mankind.

—*T* (1740)

Before I left Edinburgh, I wrote a small piece (you may believe
it woud be but a small one) which I call the History of my own
life. . . . It will be thought curious and entertaining.

—*L* (1776)

Virtuous Pride

DAVID Hume's is a remarkable autobiography, even though it
may lack the usual attractions of that genre. Anyone in search of
startling revelations or amusing anecdotes had better look
elsewhere. Perhaps Hume, knowing exactly how his refractory
"pupil" Rousseau would display himself in lengthy *Confessions*,
wanted to make *My own Life* as different as possible: modest,
restrained, scrupulously factual, and brief, so brief indeed that
T. E. Jessop has called it "one of the shortest autobiographies
written by famous men."[1]

Yet if we expect the temperamentally unlike to treat themselves
differently, what about two figures much more closely resembling
Hume in character and philosophy, who were known and respected by Hume, and who also wrote autobiographies—namely,
Benjamin Franklin and Edward Gibbon? In these cases the sim-
ilarity among memoirs is intriguing, for in all three accounts we
can hardly fail to notice the same tone of self-satisfaction, almost
irritating in its resolute complacency. Is anything more amazing
than finding these three spokesmen of their times, not any one of
them an exemplar of piety and conventionality, reviewing their

own lives and pronouncing, "It was a great success"? There is no self-doubt or anguish, and yet no reliance on some extrapersonal source of strength and assurance; rather, a cheerful resignation to what is. But the resemblance stops there. The accounts of Franklin and Gibbon are candidly biographical. We see how they perceived themselvs as human beings, caught up in relationships with others, working out their beliefs in reaction to people and books. In both there is the wealth of ana, for which eighteenth-century literature is so known, a characteristic almost entirely lacking in Hume's account. Even in its smugness Hume's *Life* might seem more extreme. In Franklin's work we have the playful admission of printer's errors, his "errata"; these were only slips, to be sure, prominently listed for the reader's benefit but hardly affecting the meaning of the work; still, these errata do acknowledge some human weakness. Likewise, Gibbon is not very upset by any of his miscalculations, yet there is at least a tepid degree of humanity in confessing, "I sighed as a lover: I obeyed as a son."[2] There is none of this sort of thing in Hume.

Nevertheless, in spite of Hume's failure to admit mistakes and his pervasive self-assurance, *My own Life* is not an insufferably vain work. Like Franklin, Hume deals with the problem partially by getting it out in the open. The act of talking about oneself is itself vain. Franklin speaks of his struggle to vanquish his pride, achieving finally only the appearance of humility—which is often a prudential equivalent—and he rationalizes with playful ingenuity: "In reality there is perhaps no one of our natural Passions so hard to subdue as *Pride*. . . . You will see it perhaps often in this History. For even if I could conceive that I had compleatly overcome it, I should probably by [be] proud of my Humility."[3] Hume goes even further in anticipating the charge of vanity, for he begins and ends his *Life* with an open assertion that what he is doing will seem vain. Hume appears almost embarrassed by the topic and determined to show his sensitivity to the issue. Franklin is self-confident and even a bit coy; Hume is defensive in his final sentence: "I cannot say, there is no Vanity in making this funeral Oration of myself; but I hope it is not a misplac'd one; and this is a Matter of Fact which is easily cleard and ascertained" (*MOL*, 615). The challenging tone is softened by the exaggerated term "funeral Oration"—his *Life* has clearly been neither funereal nor oratorical—but the hint of defiance is still noticeable.

More telling and convincing is Hume's resolution to avoid the snare of vanity by controlling the unavoidable consequences of talking of oneself: if every such word is vain, then limit such talk to a bare minimum. This will be the condition under which Hume will write his *Life*, as he emphasizes from the start:

> It is difficult for a man to speak long of himself without Vanity: Therefore I shall be short. It may be thought an Instance of Vanity, that I pretend at all to write my Life: But this Narrative shall contain little more than the History of my Writings; as indeed, almost all my Life has been spent in literary Pursuits and Occupations. The first Success of most of my writings was not such as to be an Object of Vanity. (*MOL*, 611)

Anyone familiar with Hume's life, even any reader of the *Life* itself, realizes that the indifferent reception of his works scarcely made Hume think less of his achievement, but no one can dispute his claim concerning brevity. *My own Life* is unquestionably a short history, shorter indeed than most of Hume's admirers and perhaps even a few of his enemies might have wished for. In that respect it is at least minimally vain.

Admittedly, Hume could have avoided the imputation of vanity completely by not writing at all, but he took a great deal of care in specifying that this work would be prefixed to all posthumous editions of his writings, serving, as Jerome Christensen aptly observes, as both "epigraph and epitaph."[4] Thus the importance of this final statement should not be underrated. If one of the primary assumptions behind eighteenth-century critical thinking is that a man's life and his works are inextricably connected, that we want and need to know what sort of person a writer was, that his character is part of any consideration of what his works amount to, then here we have Hume putting the finishing touches on his own life's work. What kind of man was he? Though Hume's *Life* is brief, let no one doubt that Hume has taken pains to indicate precisely how that question ought to be answered. The impression must be as favorable as possible. In moral philosophy as much as in moral poetry, only the *vir bonus* can presume to teach.

Hence again the concern with vanity. If Hume is to reinforce an impression of himself as a good man, *le bon David*, as he was affectionately known, any hint that writing his life was self-serving and vain would be unthinkable. On the other hand, in his philosopical teaching Hume had boldly redefined virtue, insisting that greatness of mind and pride are more essentially virtuous than humility. Consider these statements in the *Treatise*, which anticipate exactly the problem Hume faced many years later in writing his *Life:*

> But tho' an over-weaning conceit of our own merit be vicious and disagreeable, nothing can be more laudable, than to have a value for ourselves, where we really have qualities that are valuable. . . . and 'tis certain, that nothing is more useful to us . . . than a due degree of pride, which makes us sensible of our own merit, and gives us a confidence and assurance in all our projects and enterprizes. . . . [But] that impertinent, and almost universal propensity of men, to over-value themselves, has given us such a *prejudice* against self-applause, that we are apt to condemn it, by a *general rule,* wherever we meet with it; and 'tis with some difficulty we give a privilege to men of sense, even in their most secret thoughts. At least, it must be own'd, that some disguise in this particular is absolutely requisite; and that if we harbour pride in our breasts, we must carry a fair outside, and have the appearance of modesty and mutual deference in all our conduct and behaviour. (*T,* 596–98)

Thus vanity is a good thing, if decorously masked. Vanity is also a good thing if it results in virtuous action: "NERO had the same vanity in driving a chariot, that TRAJAN had in governing the empire with justice and ability. To love the glory of virtuous deeds is a sure proof of the love of virtue" (*E,* 86). It is with this justifiable and even noble kind of vanity that Hume would prefer to be associated. It would be necessary for him only to demonstrate a reality of personal virtue in *My own Life.* In that sense the record would speak for itself, as indeed he avers in the final sentence of his *Life.*

Fashioning *Le Bon David*

In what ways is an image of *le bon David* projected in the few pages of *My own Life?* The Hume of this narrative is everywhere polite and well-intentioned, pursuing his studies and his writing—his "ruling Passion" (*MOL,* 615)—for some reason unaccountably exciting the resentment of some very clamorous factions. One almost forgets just how explosive many of Hume's ideas were, or how easily offended some understandably were by those ideas. Hume does not dwell on this facet of his publications. They are his innocent progeny who do not merit the disregard or antagonism they receive. We pity the father and his unfortunate family: the *Treatise of Human Nature* "fell *dead-born from the Press*" (*MOL,* 612); the second volume of the *History of England* "helped to buoy up its unfortunate Brother" (*MOL,* 614). Their father was himself an orphan, a "younger Brother" with but a slender patrimony, who looks back on his infancy: "My Father, who passed for a man of Parts, dyed, when I was an Infant; leaving me, with an elder Brother and a Sister under the care of our Mother, a woman of singular Merit, who, though young and handsome, devoted herself entirely to the rearing and educating of her Children" (*MOL*, 611). Here speaks the grateful son in a passage capable of stimulating a faint heartthrob in an eighteenth-century reader. Yet Hume, ever industrious, persevering, and cheerful, accepts his lot. We cannot miss the engaging self-deprecation when he boasts, "My Appointments, with my Frugality, had made me reach a Fortune, which I called independent, though most of my Friends were inclined to smile when I said so: In short I was now Master of near a thousand Pound" (*MOL*, 612).

But the unassuming "younger Brother" does have friends; he is always surrounded by company who know how to value such a man. The concluding character sketch—"My Company was not unacceptable to the young and careless, as well as to the Studious and literary: And as I took a particular Pleasure in the Company of modest women, I had no Reason to be displeased with the Reception I met with from them" (*MOL*, 615)—merely underscores that acceptance by polite society made clear throughout Hume's narrative. Hume does not neglect to highlight his reception in Paris. He may affect embarrassment at the adulation—"The more I recoiled from their excessive Civilities, the more I was loaded with them"—yet the next remark surely indicates what this lionization meant for Hume: "There is, however, a real Satisfaction in living at Paris from the great Number of sensible, knowing, and polite Company with which the City abounds above all places in the Universe" (*MOL*, 614). For Hume virtue is always to be associated with civilized company, and acceptance by the highly civilized, as here, is no trifling endorsement.

This sense of a man being appreciated by the knowing is also strengthened by the many instances of Hume's being sought after by important and influential people for help. The "Friends and Family" of the Marquess of Annandale "were desirous of putting him under my Care and Direction: For the State of his Mind and Health required it"; "I then received an Invitation from General St clair to attend him" (*MOL*, 612); "the Faculty of Advocates chose me their Librarian" (*MOL*, 613); "I received . . . an Invitation from Lord Hertford, with whom I was not in the least acquainted, to attend him on his Embassy to Paris" (*MOL*, 614); "I received from Mr Conway an invitation to be Under-Secretary; and this Invitation both the Character of the Person, and my Connexions with

Lord Hertford, prevented me from declining" (*MOL*, 615). Hume is willing to interrupt his studies to engage in public service; one imagines that he had no other motive than to be obliging and to do his duty. There is no mention that Hume may have needed the money and in fact had been receptive to efforts by his friends to secure him positions, preferment, and pensions. Nor is there any mention of efforts that did not succeed, such as the two fruitless bids for professorial appointments.

Hume makes sure that the facts he presents speak in his favor; the others are passed by or played down. Thus we are told that he was invited to go with General St. Clair on an expedition first directed against Canada and finally against France, but not of the farcical misadventures of that expedition; we are told that he was chosen by the Faculty of Advocates as their librarian, but not of the careful engineering it took his friends to get him this appointment. And there is no hint of the troubles Hume experienced in the chaotic household of the mad marquess, or of the highly vexacious and character-threatening aftermath of his break with Rousseau.[5] Anything that might sully the image of the man of the world and philosopher is downplayed or ignored. Thus Victor Wexler is right in observing that Hume's tone is deceptive, softening "the recollections of an unhappy youth, a distressing adolescence, and a frustrating middle age."[6] A sentence Hume struck out in manuscript is revealing in that regard. The sentence deleted follows the one quoted earlier concerning his being loaded with civilities in Paris: "Dr Sterne told me, that he saw I was [two words illegible] *Town* in the same manner that he himself had been in London: But he added, that his Vogue lasted only one Winter."[7] For one thing, there would seem a certain pettiness, not to mention foppish vanity, in measuring one's "vogue" alongside someone else's. Perhaps more damaging still, what credit would there be in suggesting any kind of association with the notorious Lawrence Sterne? However he may have liked Sterne, Hume had no desire to intimate that he was in any way a mere wit or trifler, as Sterne was often unfairly perceived to be in his day.

Rather, Hume was presenting himself as dignified and modest, as well-loved and socially accepted, as sensitive and virtuous—as a man of feeling above all. It is no accident that the most rhetorical sentence in the *Life* portrays Hume in this capacity. It records his *History*'s initial reception. Because of the subject itself and his impartiality, Hume confesses that he was "sanguine" in his expectations. "But miserable was my Disappointment: I was assailed by one Cry of Reproach, Disapprobation, and even Detestation: English, Scotch, and Irish; Whig and Tory; Churchman and Sectary, Freethinker and Religionist; Patriot and Courtier united in their Rage against the Man, who had presumed to shed a generous Tear for the Fate of Charles I, and the Earl of Strafford" (*MOL*, 613). Hume's presentation is hyperbolical, for the reception was hardly one of universal detestation; moreover, all these disparate groups would have had little reason equally to condemn the treatment of Charles I in itself. In this case, however, Hume's intention is to contrast his own benevolence with the selfish malice of the world. The point here is that Hume had not actually sided with King Charles so much as he had pitied him. "To shed a generous Tear" gives it all away: it is the grand gesture of the man of feeling. The sentimental catchword "generous" is particularly noteworthy, for it stresses the highmindedness, the magnanimity of the act. Threatening the man of feeling is a mob, united only in their irrational hatred, an image nicely intensified by Hume's piling up of "English, Scotch, and Irish; Whig and Tory" and so on into as unlikely a collection of bedfellows as one can imagine. It is a picture calculated to win sympathy.[8] Indeed, because autobiography is history, we see again and again in his *Life* that Hume is scripting himself a modestly heroic role (the oxymoron here seems appropriate). Linking himself to Charles I, he becomes a rather unassuming but no less genuine hero of feeling.

Besides the heightening and exaggeration involved, the rhetorical function of this passage becomes clear in another respect. For the passage ends, "And after the first Ebullitions of this Fury were over, what was still more mortifying, the Book seemed to sink into Oblivion" (*MOL*, 613). Hume apparently intends to enjoy the benefits of being identified as a man of feeling without giving the opposition the satisfaction of thinking he suffers on their account. If it is worse to be ignored than attacked by the mob, then their rage must be impotent against a good man, whose feelings are stirred only by objects worthy of his generosity. Thus to punish the ill-natured as they deserve, Hume suggests throughout that he is not affected in the least by "their senseless Clamour" (*MOL*, 614). Like his benevolence, this equanimity is the gift of nature: "I was ever more disposed to see the favourable than the unfavourable Side of things; a turn of Mind, which it is more happy to possess than be born to an Estate of ten thousand a Year" (*MOL*, 613); and he knows how to cultivate those gifts: "I was now callous against the Impressions of public Folly; and continued very peaceably and contentedly in my Retreat at Edinburgh" (*MOL*, 614); so that by the end, in the character sketch, benevolence seems appropriately fused with equanimity into a sweetness of temper that looks with pity and forgiveness on the ill-natured mob: "In a word, though most men any wise eminent, have found reason to complain of Calumny, I never was touched, or even attacked by her baleful Tooth: And though I wantonly exposed myself to the Rage of both civil and religious Factions, they seemed to be disarmed in my behalf of their wonted Fury" (*MOL*, 615). This is surely to make light of the vilification he suffered throughout his life. If it would not be rather inappropriate for Hume, one could almost see in this attitude true Christian charity.

Playfulness and Satire

Hume's forgiveness of his enemies is more a satirical strategy than it is Christian charity. Hume can well afford to appear indifferent or even charitable at this point, for he has had a number of previous opportunities to twit his enemies on their fecklessness. Hume has paid them again and again the supreme insult of not taking them seriously, and they are not taken seriously because they are so small and contemptible. In places the atmosphere seems almost mock-heroic, as a crowd of dunces clamors in vain for a chance to inflict some mean and gratuitous injury on the invulnerable hero. It is an atmosphere of "literary Squabbles" (*MOL*, 613), with each dunce scribbling an impotent pamphlet to be consigned to oblivion. "Answers, by Reverends and Right Reverends, came out two or three in a Year: And I found by Dr Warburtons Railing that the Books were beginning to be esteemed in good Company" (*MOL*, 612). The Warburtonians are especially malicious—and amusing. "I published at London, my natural History of Religion. . . . Its public Entry was rather obscure, except only that Dr Hurd wrote a Pamphlet against it, with all the illiberal Petulance, Arrogance, and Scurrility, which distinguishes the Warburtonian School. This Pamphlet gave me some Consolation for the otherwise indifferent Reception of my Performance."[9] Such attacks were apparently the consolation of philosophy. In the next sentence Hume seems to echo the title of his friend Gibbon: "In 1756, two Years after the fall of the first Volume, was published the second Volume of my History" (*MOL*, 613). My association of Hume's phrasing with Gibbon's title is not as fanciful as it might first appear. Hume wrote this sentence within a month after reading the initial volume of *The Decline and Fall of the Roman Empire*, and in a letter to Gibbon (18 March 1776), in that strain of bitterness toward the factious public typifying his later correspondence, he uses the memorable words of the title to predict the same hostile reaction to Gibbon that his own works had received: "among many other marks of Decline, the Prevalence of Superstition in England, prognosticates the Fall of Philosophy and Decay of Taste" (*L*, 2:310). At any rate, the phrase "fall of the first Volume" in the *Life* shows Hume playfully indifferent (or so he might like to pretend) to public hostility, and it may slyly hint that his enemies, like those of the Roman Empire, were barbarians and Christians.

It is apparent that Hume enjoyed writing his own *Life*. An *apologia pro vita sua*, it allowed him to vindicate himself and to indulge that sportive humor for which he was well known among his friends. In fact, much of the *Life* is aimed at two different readers—one an outsider, the other an insider. The outsider might be sympathetic; he would be instructed and inspired by this story of a true philosopher triumphing over ignorance and malice. The unsympathetic outsider would be looking for something damaging, for evidence of Hume's unsavory character or of his suffering and regret, and looking in vain. The insider, on the other hand, knowing Hume intimately, would read between the lines. He would recognize the suppressions of detail and the understatement.

The insider would know the full meaning of Hume's saying "I received little or no Emolument" (*MOL*, 613) from being librarian of the Faculty of Advocates, because he would know that Hume had arranged for the blind poet Thomas Blacklock to receive the stipend in bond of annuity.[10] He might smile when he read of Hume's tutelage of the insane marquess of Annandale—"the Friends and Family . . . were desirous of putting him under my care and Direction: For the State of his Mind and Health required it" (*MOL*, 612)—for he would notice not only the understatement but also remember the vexations of that whole experience for Hume, except for the satisfaction of netting him a profit (of which part was disputed for years). The insider would surely recognize the wag when Hume magnifies his disgust with the world:

I was discouraged; and had not the War been at that time breaking out between France and England, I had certainly retired to some provincial Town of the former Kingdom, have changed my Name, and never more returned to my native Country. But as this Scheme was not now practicable, and the subsequent Volume was considerably advanced, I resolved to pick up Courage and to persevere. (*MOL*, 613)

The seriousness of the threat is considerably undercut by the practical impossibility, and of no little importance to Hume the writer, the attraction of completing and publishing another work—not to mention his genuine love of Scotland. But the real drollery is in the resolve to change his name: Hume had done that long since, altering his name from "Home" to "Hume," somewhat to the disapproval of several relatives and friends.[11]

Another joke Hume's friends would be certain to appreciate is the remark on the reception of the first *Enquiry:* "On my return from Italy, I had the Mortification to find all England in a Ferment on account of Dr. Middletons Free Enquiry; while my Performance was entirely overlooked and neglected" (*MOL*, 612). What is not stated is that Conyers Middleton had created an uproar by questioning the authenticity of miracles since the time of the apostles—boldly latitudinarian, perhaps, but not likely to shake the church, even as it was not intended to. In outrageous contrast, Hume, who had suppressed his iconoclastic essay "Of Miracles" for ten years, had at last brought it out in his own very "free" *Enquiry,* only to find the whole work ignored! Whereas Middleton had questioned some miracles, which were not necessary to support Christianity, Hume had undermined a belief in all miracles, and accordingly he had done, one would think, considerable damage to the Christian system. Could anyone have predicted such a strange turn of events, Hume might have said (and probably did say) to his friends? And they would have laughed with him at the folly of the world, as indeed Hume invites them to at this moment as he reminisces on his life.

Ars Moriendi

One further dimension of *My own Life* needs to be considered. It is a vindication of Hume's character and a revelation of his engaging personality, to be sure. It is also Hume's parting shot at the narrow-minded religionists who had been his chosen adversaries throughout his life. We have seen them disappointed in their efforts to discredit or vanquish Hume. If they looked in the *Life* for anything to support their prejudices, they would be utterly frustrated. Realizing that the zealots, as Hume calls them, would be looking so hard, Hume has gone out of his way to bait them. He would remember the fondness of the pious for deathbed conversions of the wicked; it was a staple, after all, of seventeenth- and eighteenth-century religious literature. In this light, James

Boswell's delightful "deathbed" interview of Hume can be read as if Hume were deliberately toying with his interviewer, who like a good reporter was angling for a sensational story, fully as significant as Bishop Gilbert Burnet's conversion of the dissolute Lord Rochester, perhaps the most iconoclastic poet of the Restoration period. And in this case it is the "pious" Boswell, not the infidel, who has his philosophy shaken.[12] As Hume sketched out his *Life*, so it would be with others concerned for his immortal soul.

In what manner is divine providence or judgment manifest in Hume's *Life*—or life? There is of course no direct reference to this order of reality that the pious would consider as a sine qua non; the course of Hume's life seems not only devoid of providential order but is indeed antiprovidential. That Hume's life is a success story might ordinarily suggest some providential interpretation. In Hume's case, on the contrary, the ending is wrong, for the infidel should be punished, not rewarded. Hume was probably happy to tease the self-righteous with this unpoetic justice, but the major emphasis in the *Life* is on the total absence of evidence for divine intervention or plan. Essentially, nothing ever happens as one might have expected it to, nor does any turn of events suggest purpose and order. Without doubt the good things that happen to Hume stem from his natural abilities, industry, and sobriety, yet Hume does not pretend to account for why his successes come when they do. Usually he is surprised. Why, in the same year, would his *Political Discourses* be well received while his *Enquiry Concerning the Principles of Morals*, in his opinion "incomparably the best" of all his writings, come "unnoticed and unobserved into the World"? (*MOL*, 613) Why, amid the furor over the initial appearance of the *History*, would the primates of England and of Ireland alone react kindly? (*MOL*, 613) Who can explain why the second volume "happened to give less Displeasure to the Whigs, and was better received?" (*MOL*, 614) How did it happen that in spite of the "Variety of Winds and Seasons, to which my Writings had been exposed"—an image sufficiently antiprovidential—"the Copy Money, given me by the Booksellers, much exceeded any thing formerly known in England: I was become not only independent, but opulent"? (*MOL*, 614) Hume does not know and does not presume to guess. Admittedly, God may move in mysterious ways, but the wonders unfolded here have no tendency to show the infidel his errors and make him welcome salvation. As far as the narrative is concerned, these wonders are purposeless, except that they enforce a contrary lesson: man is necessarily ignorant of what passes beyond his ken of immediate experience, about which no certitude or regularity can be posited either; his business is not to invent systems and preach dogmas but rather to live with dignity and compassion—and with good humor—in a chaotic world. This is the lesson of Hume's philosophy, and of his *Life*.[13]

Nowhere does that lesson become more apparent than in the penultimate paragraph, in which Hume describes in some detail his state of mind in facing death. It is the doctrine that so upset Boswell, here presented with chilling—or reassuring, depending on one's state of mind—artfulness. This is the passage in full:

> In spring 1775, I was struck with a Disorder in my Bowels, which at first gave me no Alarm, but has since, as I apprehend it, become mortal and incurable. I now reckon upon a speedy Dissolution. I have suffered very little pain from my Disorder; and what is more strange, have, notwithstanding the great Decline of my Person, never suffered a Moments Abatement of my Spirits: Insomuch, that were I to name the Period of my Life which I shoud most choose to pass over again I might be tempted to point to this later Period. I possess the same Ardor as ever in Study, and the same Gaiety in Company. I consider besides, that a Man of sixty five, by dying, cuts off only a few Years of Infirmities: And though I see many Symptoms of my literary Reputation's breaking out at last with additional Lustre, I know, that I had but few Years to enjoy it. It is difficult to be more detached from Life than I am at present. (*MOL*, 615)

The fortitude Hume shows becomes all the more remarkable when we consider how the prospect of death has been introduced. Neither the reader nor the hero is prepared for it. In the immediately preceding sentence Hume has written, "I returned to Edinburgh in 1769, very opulent (for I possessed a Revenue of 1000 pounds a year) healthy, and though somewhat stricken in Years, with the Prospect of enjoying long my Ease and of seeing the Encrease of my Reputation" (*MOL*, 615). It is not the prospect of death but rather of long ease and satisfaction that is before us. Hume intensifies the shock of the other frightening prospect by shrinking a six-year span of time into a shift of paragraphs: it is not a gradual decline in health but a sudden change. Even the early signs are dismissed, "at first" giving "no Alarm," only to "become mortal and incurable." No shred of hope can be clung to. And there is a studied determination to emphasize Hume's complete awareness of his mortality and to heighten the awful connotations of finality, of the grave. "I apprehend it. . . . I now reckon upon a speedy Dissolution." To use such a word as "Dissolution" seems a terse affirmation of that argument put forth in Hume's essay "Of the Immortality of the Soul"; here is a man for whom the decay of the body, the materiality of the soul, and the imminence of the grave strike no terror. No terror but rather cheerful acceptance—"what is more strange," to say the least! To those who might have hoped for Hume's exasperating peace of mind, unsupported by religion, to be shaken at the moment of the final accounting, Hume throws the contrary in their face: "Insomuch, that were I to name the Period of my Life which I shoud most choose to pass over again I might be tempted to point to this later Period." Hume may have thought that his performance before Boswell were deserving of a wider audience.

In a sense Hume has put himself into a tragedy that becomes a comedy instead, though no divine comedy. There is the sudden reversal from the height of health, recognition, and success to the nothingness of "speedy Dissolution." Yet the hero becomes more optimistic than ever. And it is not the happiness of being well-deceived, but instead a well-reasoned attitude toward death: "I consider besides, that a Man of sixty five, by dying, cuts off only a few Years of Infirmities." One might think Hume were speaking of taking a stroll. "It is difficult to be more detached from Life than I am at present." Hume has demonstrated ataraxia with consummate skill. If the true philosopher makes a poor tragic hero, he is the hero of a much larger drama of life subsuming death. How fitting that Gibbon should pronounce, "[Hume] died at Edinburgh the death of a Philosopher."[14]

The character sketch of the final paragraph brings into sharp focus those personal traits that have informed the entire narrative:

> To conclude historically with my own Character—I am, or rather was (for that is the Style, I must now use in speaking of myself; which emboldens me the more to speak my Sentiments) I was, I say, a man of mild Dispositions, of Command of Temper, of an open, social, and cheerful Humour, capable of Attachment, but little susceptible of Enmity, and of great Moderation in all my Passions. Even my Love of literary Fame, my ruling Passion, never soured my humour, notwithstanding my frequent Disappointments. My Company was not unacceptable to the young and careless, as well as to the Studious and literary: And as I took a particular Pleasure in the Company of modest women, I had no Reason to be displeased with the Reception I met with from them. In a word, though most men any wise eminent, have found reason to complain of Calumny, I never was touched, or even

attacked by her baleful Tooth: And though I wantonly exposed myself to the Rage of both civil and religious Factions, they seemed to be disarmed in my behalf of their wonted Fury: My Friends never had occasion to vindicate any one Circumstance of my Character and Conduct: Not but that the Zealots, we may well suppose, wou'd have been glad to invent and propagate any Story to my Disadvantage, but they coud never find any which, they thought, woud wear the Face of Probability. I cannot say, there is no Vanity in making this funeral Oration of myself; but I hope it is not a misplac'd one; and this is a Matter of Fact which is easily cleard and ascertained. (*MOL*, 615)

It is the portrait of a man who was successful in every way Hume would have valued; he claims no more than is strictly called for—note the preponderance of negatives—but it is enough. Like the skeptical moralist discussed in chapter 4, Hume here escapes from his writing, escapes from any dogmatic version of himself. One almost detects in the sense of modest sufficiency a faint echo of the closing epitaph in Gray's famous *Elegy*, except that the role of Heaven is nowhere appropriate:

> Large was his bounty, and his soul sincere,
> Heav'n did a recompence as largely send:
> He gave to Mis'ry all he had, a tear,
> He gain'd from Heav'n ('twas all he wish'd) a friend.

I would not mention Gray's *Elegy* at all, for I do not pretend that Hume was alluding to it, were it not for the way in which Hume's character sketch resembles in its function the epitaph in Gray. They both extrude from the body of the work that has occasioned them to serve as a final earthly memorial and account of an individual life whose significance is now bound up with the significance of all human life. The implication in Gray is that man's standards no longer apply, inasmuch as the final judgment now rests with God. For Hume, in marked contrast, the human assessment is all that can matter, and the individual himself pronounces his own "funeral Oration" from the grave. Hume calls our attention to the immediacy of death, perhaps even the instant of death, by shifting tenses with an unmistakable flourish: "I am, or rather was (for that is the Style, I must now use in speaking of myself) I was, I say . . ." Hume has stepped, as he himself would say, into Charon's boat at this very moment. He now speaks beyond the grave. In a farewell *jeu d'esprit*, Hume has granted himself a kind of immortality, after all.[15]

Hume's Benediction

J. C. A. Gaskin closes his book on Hume's religious philosophy with these words:

> There is in the Carlton Cemetary in Edinburgh an austere monument over the tomb of the Great Sceptic. At his own request it records only his name and dates of birth and death, posterity being left to add the rest. Posterity has added a great deal . . . [and] within the limitations of human existence, . . . has already fulfilled the promise of Colonel Edmondstoune in his last letter to the dying philosopher: "You can't die, you must live in the memory of all your friends and acquaintances, and your works will render you immortal."[16]

We have seen that, like the austere monument itself, Hume preferred a rigorously understated autobiography as a memorial, as a document for those he left behind to interpret more fully. And we have seen that Hume's last words speak to us far beyond the unassuming surface of his text.[17]

Hume regarded himself preeminently as a man of letters, and *My own Life* is quintessentially such a man's last words. It is in every way commensurate with the remarkable life it presents. Though far different from the autobiographies of Rousseau, Franklin, and Gibbon, most obviously in its dearth of anecdote and intimate detail, it is no less artful, and finally, no less revealing. It is surely the man, as much as we would say those other famous memoirs embody their subjects.

As we have seen, Hume must have intended for the zealots to read *My own Life* with disappointment, and yet some more friendly to Hume have probably read it with disappointment as well, sorry that it did not at least tell more. When we read it, however, fully aware of Hume's thought, the details of his life, and his reputation, perceived so differently among so many people of his day, then his purpose in writing his own *Life* becomes clearer, and its pervasive art and good humor that much more evident. Writing of "this small piece" to Adam Smith (3 May 1776), Hume once again speaks of more than might first meet the eye: "You will find among my Papers a very inoffensive Piece, called *My own Life*, which I composed a few days before I left Edinburgh, when I thought, as did all my Friends, that my Life was despaired of. There can be no Objection, that this small Piece should be sent to Messrs Strahan and Cadell and the Proprietors of my other Works to be prefixed to any future Edition of them" (*L*, 2:318)

Unlike the *Dialogues Concerning Natural Religion*—or the suppressed essays on suicide and the immortality of the soul—there need be no solicitude on Smith's or any other friend's account about publishing this little work.[18] That it would be "very inoffensive" Hume may have had other thoughts. The zealots could surely not take comfort in its lessons. To Hume's friends, though, and to all generous men and women, *My own Life* would prove "very inoffensive" only by the most extravagant understatement. It would delight.[19]

Notes

Preface

1. One recent instance is David Fate Norton in *David Hume: Common-Sense Moralist, Sceptical Metaphysician* (Princeton: Princeton University Press, 1982), but despite the title, Norton is not concerned with the details of Hume's moral teaching.

2. Ernest C. Mossner, "The Religion of David Hume," *Journal of the History of Ideas* 39 (1978): 653–64; Donald W. Livingston, *Hume's Philosophy of Common Life* (Chicago: University of Chicago Press, 1984), 174; J. C. A. Gaskin, *Hume's Philosophy of Religion* (London: Macmillan, 1978), 170.

3. Two recent exceptions, however, are Jerome Christensen, *Practicing Enlightenment: Hume and the Formation of a Literary Career* (Madison: University of Wisconsin Press, 1987); and Robert Ginsberg, "The Literary Structure and Strategy of Hume's Essay on the 'Standard of Taste,' " in *The Philosopher as Writer: The Eighteenth Century*, ed. Robert Ginsberg (Selinsgrove, Pa.: Susquehanna University Press, 1987), 199–237.

Introduction: Hume's Shaping Moral Imagination

Epigraph: *EHU*, 9.

1. *The Moral and Political Philosophy of David Hume* (New York: Columbia University Press, 1963), 10.

2. *The English Moralists* (New York: W. W. Norton, 1964), 259.

3. Most Humeans appear to view Hume as an ethicist rather than as a moralist. Thus James T. King writes: "his is decidedly not a doctrine about moral behavior. Hume says little about how men in general behave; he offers a theory based on an analysis of language, not on a survey of practices." See "The Place of the Language of Morals in Hume's Second *Enquiry*," in *Hume: A Re-Evaluation*, ed. Donald W. Livingston and James T. King (New York: Fordham University Press, 1976), 347.

4. The word "metaphysician" was itself highly pejorative in seventeenth- and eighteenth-century English.

5. Michael Morrisroe, Jr., has usefully reminded philosophers to find Hume's meaning in his writing itself rather than in restatements or summaries of his writing. Nonetheless he uses this passage to Hutcheson to claim that Hume typically writes as "an anatomist, a clinical observer unaffected by imaginative visions and prejudice." See "Linguistic Analysis as Rhetorical Pattern in David Hume," in *Hume and the Enlightenment*, ed. William B. Todd (Edinburgh and Austin: Edinburgh University and the University of Texas Presses, 1974), 78. In

this book I shall take considerable exception to Morrisroe's view of an unemotional Hume.

6. This work appeared originally in six volumes but assumed an eight-volume format in 1763.

7. I am referring to the deathbed conversation that Adam Smith reported having with Hume. See Hume's *Works*, 3: 11.

8. See Hayden White, *The Content of the Form: Narrative Discourse and Historical Representation* (Baltimore: Johns Hopkins University Press, 1987), 180–81, 20–21. It will become apparent that my own approach to literary criticism and historiography—perhaps I should say textual hermeneutics—is more conservative and traditional than that espoused in much "postmodern" critical theory; still, I am indebted to many insights on the part of these theorists.

9. *The Whole Duty of Man, Laid down in a Plain and Familiar Way, for the Use of All, but especially the Meanest Reader* . . . (1658; rpt. London, 1716), 223. Subsequent references will be cited parenthetically in the text.

10. Cicero, *De Officiis*, in the Loeb Classical Library, vol. 21, translated by Walter Miller (Cambridge: Harvard University Press, 1913), 338–39.

Chapter 1. In Search of the Hero of Feeling

Epigraphs, respectively: *L*, 1: 47; *EPM*, 181; *L*, 1: 210. A somewhat different and abbreviated version of this chapter, "The Sentimental Sublime in Hume's *History of England*," appears in the August 1989 issue of *The Review of English Studies* and is used with permission.

1. Whether or to what degree Hume was a naturalist has been the topic of much disagreement. Norman Kemp Smith's much-admired and seminal study, *The Philosophy of David Hume* (London: Macmillan, 1941), argues convincingly for Hume's naturalism. David Fate Norton's *David Hume: Common-Sense Moralist, Sceptical Metaphysician* (Princeton: Princeton University Press, 1982) is the most recent lengthy study questioning Smith's emphasis on the primacy of the passions in Hume's philosophy, particularly his metaphysics.

2. A very useful discussion of sensibility or sentimentalism is to be found in R. F. Brissenden, *Virtue in Distress: Studies in the Novel of Sentiment from Richardson to Sade* (London: Macmillan, 1974), 11–55. Louis I. Bredvold's *The Natural History of Sensibility* (Detroit: Wayne State University Press, 1962) is also helpful.

3. Ernest Campbell Mossner, *The Life of David Hume*, 2d ed. (Oxford: Clarendon Press, 1980), 253–54, 380–81, 396–99.

4. Hume does not provide a source for either story; of the first, he says it is "commonly told," suggesting that it is the material of legend, which in this case he wants to take advantage of.

5. For a discussion of the youthful indiscretion of the *Treatise*, see my " 'Ardor of Youth': The Manner of Hume's *Treatise*," a chapter in Robert Ginsberg, ed., *The Philosopher as Writer: The Eighteenth Century*, 177–98, in which several observations in the previous paragraph first appeared and are used here with permission.

6. Brissenden calls "the notion that the spontaneous moral responses of the individual, despite their basic subjectivity, possess some special and general authority" one of "the deepest fantasies of the age." See Brissenden, *Virtue in Distress*, 5.

7. As David Miller explains, "Sympathy as Hume understands it is best

described as a mechanism which allows emotions to be transferred from one mind to another. His use of the term remains close to its sense in physics, where we speak of a vibrating string communicating its resonance sympathetically to a neighboring string. The second string will duplicate the vibration of the first." See David Miller, *Philosophy and Ideology in Hume's Political Thought* (Oxford: Clarendon Press, 1981), 52. Barry Stroud's account is also quite lucid. See his *Hume* (London: Routledge & Kegan Paul, 1977), 196–98. Stroud observes, "If we were not 'sympathetic' beings then almost none of the things we now regard as virtuous or as vicious would be so regarded. Certainly the variety of things we approve of would not be as great as it is. In that sense, sympathy might be described as the foundation of morality—not as something that can provide us with, or serve as a basis for, a rational proof of the moral quality of an act or character, but as a fundamental human characteristic that is responsible for morality being what it is" (p. 198). The importance of sympathy in Hume's philosophy is widely recognized. Thus Donald Livingston says: "In the end, Hume's most important philosophical contribution is not his famous analysis of causation but his doctrine of sympathy. As Kemp Smith first pointed out, it is the central doctrine of the *Treatise* and the governing idea behind Hume's favorite work, the *Enquiry* on morals." See Livingston, *Hume's Philosophy of Common Life*, 84.

To be sure, Hume's reliance on sympathy is vulnerable to accusations of vagueness and inconsistency. Philip Mercer in his detailed critique finds that Hume's notion of "sympathy as a kind of emotional infection" is not a very satisfactory basis for beneficence. See Mercer, *Sympathy and Ethics: A Study of the Relationship Between Sympathy and Morality with Special Reference to Hume's Treatise* (Oxford: Clarendon Press, 1972), 21. And Alasdair MacIntyre calls Hume's concept of sympathy a mere invention to attempt to bridge a logical gap between a search for general rules of conduct and idiosyncratic desires and interests. According to MacIntyre, Hume's sympathy is "the name of a philosophical fiction." See *After Virtue: A Study in Moral Theory* (Notre Dame: University of Notre Dame Press, 1981), 47.

8. Critics point to problems in Hume's optimistic account of sympathy. As D. C. Yalden-Thomson reminds us, a disinterested spectator at a funeral may find his sympathies pulled in counterdirections by a weeping widow and a rejoicing heir. See his "Recent Work on Hume," *American Philosophical Quarterly* 20 (1983): 8. But Hume would probably not view this situation as problematic. His spectator's sympathy would surely be with the person in greatest need, the conventional object of pity, and although he would otherwise appreciate the heir's joy, the heir's callous indiscretion would overpower any sympathetic response to his new prosperity. Hume might well sympathize with a rejoicing heir of a miserly wretch with no grieving widow or dependents.

9. See Michel Foucault, *Discipline and Punish: The Birth of the Prison*, trans. Alan Sheridan (New York: Vantage Books, 1979), 9, 59–61, et passim.

10. The entire essay "Of Tragedy" should be consulted.

11. Hume goes on to detail the reciprocal enthusiasm of actor and audience and the strong communication of emotion that the theater allows the dramatist to exploit.

12. Note the similar statement made later: "Absolute, unprovoked, disinterested malice has never perhaps place in any human breast; or if it had, must there pervert all the sentiments of morals, as well as feelings of humanity" (*EPM*, 227). In both statements Hume's assurance seems rather like wish fulfillment.

13. Likewise Hume says later: "And though this affection of humanity may not be generally esteemed so strong as vanity or ambition, yet, being common to all men, it can alone be the foundation of morals." (*EPM*, 273).

14. Stephen Greenblatt has argued that stretegies of self-fashioning mark the private-public dichotomy in the literary personae of great Renaissance figures. See his *Renaissance Self-Fashioning from More to Shakespeare* (Chicago: University of Chicago Press, 1980).

15. In his surveys of history and comparisons of cultures, Hume always notes a progress of sensibility from ancient times to modern and a general superiority in sensibility among the Europeans. See *EPM*, 256–57; or the remark in the *History* on the wicked Colonel Kirk, mentioned earlier as the villain who robbed a young maid of her virtue and hanged her brother: Kirk was "a soldier of fortune, who had long served at Tangiers, and had contracted, from his intercourse with the Moors, an inhumanity less known in European and in free countries" (*H*, 6: 462).

16. The passage is quoted at greater length and discussed in the opening section of chapter 3.

17. Hume's treatment of these qualities in the second *Enquiry* would seem to anticipate Burke's famous discussion in *A Philosophical Enquiry into . . . the Sublime and Beautiful* (1757). Later, in 1759, he called Burke's essay "a very pretty treatise" (*L*, 1: 303).

18. See the discussion of this sentimental catchword in J. C. Hilson, "Hume: The Historian as Man of Feeling," in *Augustan Worlds*, ed. J. C. Hilson, M. M. B. Jones, and J. R. Watson (Bristol: Leicester University Press, 1978), 211–12. Hilson's essay is a useful study, though I take some exception to his conclusions, as noted later. On the same subject Geoffrey Carnall observes, "Hume's *History* is everywhere informed with a generous if ironical appreciation of innocence, good-nature, and benevolence, wherever these qualities are to be found. It is one of the great, and now unduly neglected, monuments in the Age of Sensibility." See Geoffrey Carnall, "Historical Writing in the Later Eighteenth Century," in *The History of Scottish Literature*, vol. 2, ed. Andrew Hook (Aberdeen: Aberdeen University Press, 1987), 2:210–11.

19. See *L*, 1: 315, 344, and E. C. Mossner's "New Hume Letters . . . ," *Texas Studies in Literature and Language* 4 (1962): 449.

20. Thus I take some exception to the view of John B. Radner that Hume "isolates the importance of a deliberate effort of imagination to a compassionate (hence benevolent) life, but leaves it to others to translate this awareness into a call for sustained exercise and development of this power." See his "Sympathy in British Moral Thought," *Studies in Eighteenth-Century Culture* 9 (1979): 199. Radner's article, however, is a very useful study.

21. In *Absalom and Achitophel* (1681) (11. 817–63), Dryden had used the examples of Ormond and Ossory, respectively the ideal courtier and the ideal son, to counter examples of seditious and perverted talent. See *The Works of John Dryden* (Berkeley and Los Angeles: University of California Press, 1972), 2: 30–31.

22. I cannot agree with Leo Braudy's view that Hume suppresses his personal voice and attempts to speak with as much detachment as possible: "he does not speak enough in his own voice. . . . Like an 'ideal observer' in his ethics, . . . Hume's voice remains cool and remote." See Leo Braudy, *Narrative Form in History and Fiction: Hume, Fielding, and Gibbon* (Princeton: Princeton University Press, 1970), 88. Passages like the one just cited, or indeed like those quoted throughout this book, reflect a very personally involved Hume. Even Braudy

recognizes the sympathetic element in the *History* when he admits, "Although he does not want to personalize the historian, history has become a study which is valuable in itself for its ability to extend sympathies and perceptions beyond the immediate" (p. 33). For further discussion of the involved versus the detached Hume, see the first section of chapter 4 in this book.

23. Quoted in Mossner, *Life of Hume*, 479.

24. Quoted in *L*, 2: 366ff. See Mossner, *Life of Hume*, 425ff, for the translation.

25. *Boswell's London Journal: 1762–1763*, ed. Frederick A. Pottle (New York: McGraw-Hill, 1950), 173, 161.

26. Braudy argues that Hume's interest in great personalities fades as his work recedes into the medieval period, Hume coming to believe that a structure of time and events, not personality, informs history: "The 'character' as a literary method and character as a concept for understanding history drop out completely in the medieval volumes" (p. 75; see also pp. 31–80). However, it is just as plausible to follow Hume's opinion and say that the seventeenth century was simply richer in interesting personalities that were well-documented and thus available for analysis.

Christensen ingeniously suggests in *Practicing Enlightenment* (p. 110) that Hume's writing history backwards (that is, Stuart, Tudor, medieval) makes "the ancients as *effects* of Hume's method, which is derived and developed in encounters with more proximate and less prepossessing historical figures." While I agree that seventeenth-century figures may pale alongside certain mythic ancients, by contrast in Hume's own *History* the figures in his initial volume are the emotional giants of the whole set.

27. Here is Hume's character sketch of Mary:

> Ambitious and active in her temper, yet inclined to chearfulness and society; of a lofty spirit, constant and even vehement in her purpose, yet polite, and gentle, and affable in her demeanour; she seemed to partake only so much of the male virtues as to render her estimable, without relinquishing those soft graces, which compose the proper ornament of her sex. In order to form a just idea of her character, we must set aside one part of her conduct, while she abandoned herself to the guidance of a profligate man; and must consider these faults, whether we admit them to be imprudences or crimes, as the result of an inexplicable, though not uncommon, inconstancy in the human mind. . . . An enumeration of her qualities might carry the appearance of a panegyric; an account of her conduct must, in some parts, wear the aspect of severe satire and invective (*H*, 4: 251–52)

28. John Strype, *Annals of the Reformation and Establishment of Religion* (London, 1728), 3: 383–88; I quote from the *Annals . . .* (Oxford: Clarendon, 1824), 3: 557–64. William Camden, *Annales rerum Anglicarum et Hibernicarum regnante Elizabetha . . .* (London, 1615); Camden is available in a modern text and translation, edited by Wallace T. MacCaffrey (Chicago: University of Chicago Press, 1970). Samuel Jebb, *De Vita et rebus gestis serenissimae principis Mariae Scotorum Reginae . . .* 2 vols (London, 1725); I am quoting from Jebb's translated version, *The History of the Life and Reign of Mary Queen of Scots* (London, 1725).

29. Mossner, "New Hume Letters . . . ," 449.

30. Compare Jebb, for example: "And then covering her face with a linen handkerchief, in which the Holy Eucharist had formerly been inclos'd, she resolutely kneel'd down upon the cushion, and without any sign of fear repeated the Psalm in *Latin, In thee, O Lord, do I trust*. . . . And laying her head on the block, and stretching forth her body, and repeating three or four times, *Into thy hands, O Lord, I commend my Spirit*, her head was cut off. (pp. 356–57).

31. William Robertson, *The History of Scotland* (1759; rpt. London, 1794), 2: 178.

32. See the section on "Theoretical Assumptions" earlier in this chapter.

33. Foucault observes that the actual spectacle of torture and execution was significant because the spectators "could decipher crime and innocence, the past and the future, the here below and the eternal. It was a moment of truth that all spectators questioned: each word, each cry, the duration of the agony, the resisting body, the life that clung desperately to it, all this constituted a sign" (p. 46).

On the aesthetics of executions, see Samuel L. Edgerton, Jr., "*Maniera* and the *Mannaia*: Decorum and Decapitation in the Sixteenth Century," in *The Meaning of Mannerism*, ed. Franklin W. Robinson and Stephen G. Nichols, Jr. (Hanover, N.H.: University Press of New England, 1972), 67–99.

34. Jebb, *History of Mary, Queen of Scots*, 351 also shows Mary weeping with Melvil, but not "more from sympathy than affliction."

35. See, for example, Hilson, "Hume: The Historian as Man of Feeling," 205–22.

36. See, for instance, the letter quoted by Hilson, 219.

37. Quoted in Laurence L. Bongie, *David Hume: Prophet of the Counter-Revolution* (Oxford: Clarendon Press, 1965), 125–26; the source is J. B. A. Clèry, *Journal de ce qui s'est passé a la tour du Temple pendant la captivité de Louis XVI, Roi de France* (London, 1798), 203. As a nine-year-old boy, Louis had complimented Hume on his history of the Stuarts; see *L*, 1: 414, 416; *NL*, 75–76; and Bongie, *David Hume*, 120–26.

38. John J. Burke, Jr., sensibily discusses the various labels that have mistakenly been applied to Hume the historian. Burke shows that although Hume was often anti-Whig in order to shake English complacency, it does not follow that he was necessarily Tory. See John J. Burke, Jr., "Hume's *History of England*: Waking the English from a Dogmatic Slumber," *Studies in Eighteenth-Century Culture* 7 (1978): 235–50. J. G. A. Pocock says, "The ambiguity of the word 'Tory' in England, . . . coupled with its relative inapplicability in Scotland, should warn us against considering that Hume became a Tory in any eighteenth-century sense as his interpretation of the past became more Tory in a seventeenth-century one." See J. G. A. Pocick, *Virtue, Commerce, and History: Essays on Political Thought and History, Chiefly in the Eighteenth Century* (Cambridge: Cambridge University Press, 1985), 135.

39. For Hilson, this goodness is enough to make Charles Hume's sentimental hero. Hilson also claims, "Although he ascribes some aesthetic pleasure to the contemplation of what he calls 'sublime' characters, the men he admires most, both in his ethical writings and in the *History*, are those who display 'the merit of benevolence' " (pp. 212–13). Clearly, my interpretation of Hume is at odds with this view. Hilson (p. 214) even says that Hume admired Charles's passivity, but I have argued that passivity would never be attractive to Hume.

40. Hume's emphasis on the king's majestic self-control is evident throughout. Note this passage: "Such equability of temper did he possess, that, during all the variety of fortune, which he underwent, no difference was perceived in his countenance or behaviour; and though a prisoner, in the hands of his most inveterate enemies, he supported, towards all who approached him, the majesty of a monarch." (*H*, 5: 509).

41. Bulstrode Whitelocke, *Memorials of the English Affairs* (1682), 22; quoted in Hilson, "Hume: The Historian as Man of Feeling," 215.

42. Hume does not give a reference for this passage, but clearly his source is the *Eikon Basilike: The Portraiture of His Sacred Majesty in His Solitudes and Sufferings*

(1649). See the edition by Philip A. Knachel (Ithaca: Cornell University Press, 1966), 192–93.

Charles's signing the bill of attainder against Strafford might be seen to impugn his honor. As another instance of his shaping the character of Charles, Hume is careful to make the king feel this betrayal more keenly throughout the rest of his life than he did any other of his distresses. See *H,* 5: 325–26.

Hilson points out (pp. 215–16) that Hume adds to the pathos of the king's end by having "Charles spend the nights between sentence and execution at White-hall, where he can hear the sound of his scaffold being built," in spite of the doubtful historical authenticity of that legend.

43. Though many ardently Royalist historians record astounding repercussions of the beheading, Hume's source is obviously Richard Perrinchief's significantly titled *The Royal Martyr: or, The Life and Death of King Charles I.* (London, 1676), 211. Indeed, Hume copies Perrinchief almost verbatim: "When the news of his Death was divulged, Women with Child for grief cast forth the untimely Fruit of the Womb. . . . Others, both Men and Women, fell into Convulsions and swounding Fits, and contracted so deep a Melancholy as attended them to the Grave. Some unmindful of themselves, as though they could not, or would not, live when their beloved Prince was slaughtered, (it is reported) suddenly fell down dead." Long before Hume wrote his version, stories of such prodigies had been scoffed at. See, for example, [John Oldmixon], *The History of England . . .* (London, 1730), 369–70.

44. Hume's main source for the execution is John Rushworth, *Historical Collections* (London, 1721–22), 4: 269, where in fact Strafford is recorded as reading in the Book of Common Prayer with his chaplain "almost a quarter of an Hour" and then praying without the Book "as long or longer."

45. The poem is quoted in John Buchan, *Montrose* (1928; rpt. London: Hodder and Stoughton, 1938), 322. Livingston has argued that Hume viewed the cultivation of literature as "the ultimate standard of progress" and thus of civilization (pp. 267–69). Montrose's poetical flight surely befits this greatest of heroes.

Chapter 2. Religion and the "Peace of Society"

Epigraphs, respectively: *L,* 1: 34, 153, 154; *NL,* 43. A small part of this chapter originally appeared as "Hume on Idolatry and Incarnation," *Journal of the History of Ideas* 45 (1984): 379–96, and is incorporated with permission.

1. The most complete treatment of the subject is by J. C. A. Gaskin in *Hume's Philosophy of Religion;* also among the better general discussions are James Noxon, "Hume's Concern with Religion," in *David Hume: Many-Sided Genius,* ed. Kenneth R. Merrill and Robert W. Shahan (Norman: University of Oklahoma Press, 1976), 59–82; Keith E. Yandell, "Hume on Religious Belief," in *Hume: A Re-Evaluation,* 109–25; and Norman Kemp Smith in his edition of the *Dialogues Concerning Natural Religion,* 2d ed. (London: Thomas Nelson and Sons, 1947), 1–75. Ernest C. Mossner's monumental *Life of David Hume* should also be consulted, along with his article "The Religion of David Hume," *Journal of the History of Ideas* 39 (1978): 653–64.

2. David Berman explains why Hume could sincerely deny the existence of atheists: Hume defines God in such a way that no one could deny his existence, but by the same token no one can find very much to believe in. "The conception of God is so vague and dilute that no past or present atheist would bother to

attack it. Atheism is defeated and God is rescued: but both victories are only verbal." See David Berman, "David Hume and the Suppression of Atheism," *Journal of the History of Philosophy* 21 (1983): 385.

3. *Boswell in Extremes, 1776–1778,* ed. Charles McC. Weis and Frederick A. Pottle (New York: McGraw-Hill, 1970), 11.

4. Victor Wexler, *David Hume and the History of England,* (Philadelphia: American Philosophical Society, 1979), "Preface."

5. *The Poems of Alexander Pope; A One-Volume Edition of the Twickenham Text,* ed. John Butt (London: Methuen, 1963), 808.

6. The entire discussion in *H,* 6: 140–46, is revealing; see also Hume's remarks on presbyterian government (*H,* 4: 45).

7. Two paragraphs earlier Hume writes, "superstition sate so easy and light upon them" (*NHR,* 78), and at the very end of this section he uses the same figure: mythology "sits also so easy and light on men's minds" (*NHR,* 81).

8. The section titles do not appear in the first edition (*Four Dissertations,* 1757). Hume added them to "help the Reader to see the Scope of the Discourse," hoping to answer an objection to *NHR* "that it wants order" (*L,* 1: 250–51).

9. It is difficult to understand Gaskin's observation that Hume never speaks favorably of polytheism, even though later Gaskin admits that for Hume "the effects of polytheism are in many ways preferable to those of monotheism." See Gaskin, *Hume's Philosophy of Religion,* 18, 145ff.

10. Hume, of course, was not alone among Enlightenment thinkers in harking back to pagan culture for normative values and in preferring ancient polytheism to modern monotheism. This preference is the controlling thesis of volume 1 of Peter Gay's great study, *The Enlightenment: An Interpretation,* 2 vols. (New York: Alfred A. Knopf, 1966–69). J. G. A. Pocock puts it this way: "In Voltaire and Hume, as well as in Gibbon, we find an avowed preference for Greco-Roman polytheism as permitting philosophy to develop independently of the gods, whereas the assertion—whether Platonic or Semitic—of a single godhead condemned it to the embrace of theology." See "Gibbon's *Decline and Fall* and the World View of the Late Enlightenment," *Eighteenth-Century Studies* 10 (1977): 288–89.

11. This sentence, amongst others, was omitted in the versions of 1768 and later. Duncan Forbes notes that much of Hume's distinction between superstition and enthusiasm, save for the political dimension Hume gives it, can be found in an essay in the *Old Whig* of 9 March 1738. See *Hume's Philosophical Politics* (Cambridge: Cambridge University Press, 1975), 214.

12. This sense of a despicable, perverted kind of learning assuming superiority over total ignorance is amusingly captured in the following remark. Concerning Pope Pascal's reference to the barbarous English, Hume observes, "Nothing can be a stronger proof of the miserable ignorance in which that people were then plunged, than that a man, who sat on the papal throne, and who subsisted by absurdities and nonsense, should think himself intitled to treat them as barbarians" (*H,* 1: 267).

13. See *H,* 1: 286; 2: 14, 258.

14. Throughout his account of the Reformation, Hume seems eager to juxtapose one type of absurdity with another. Later on we hear of one Puritan who in a zeal to destroy crosses went so far as not allowing "one piece of wood or stone to lie over another at right angles," and immediately following, of a dean "zealous for ecclesiastical ceremonies" who opposed the Puritans' insistence on breaking sacramental bread with their fingers by maintaining that nought but a

specially consecrated knife could "perform that sacred office, and must never afterwards be profaned by any vulgar service" (*H*, 5: 302).

15. When Hume describes the efforts of French Catholics to oppose Scottish Protestants, he does so in a similar battle-of-the-books manner, with a similar satirical reference to the superiority of brute force: "More French troops soon after disembarked under the command of La Brosse, who was followed by the bishop of Amiens, and three doctors of the Sorbonne. These last were supplied with store of syllogisms, authorities, citations, and scholastic arguments, which they intended to oppose to the Scottish preachers, and which, they justly presumed, would acquire force, and produce conviction, by the influence of the French arms and artillery" (*H*, 4: 27).

16. *John Knox's History of the Reformation in Scotland*, ed. William Croft Dickinson (New York: Philosophical Library, 1950), 1: 79.

17. See chapter 1 for a discussion of Hume's own response to Mary.

18. See, for example, Dickinson's edition of Knox, 2: 33–36; and *H*, 4: 42–43. It is interesting that one of Hume's few reservations to his otherwise enthusiastic praise of Robertson's *History of Scotland* concerns his fellow historian's too respectful treatment of Knox. Hume speaks with pride of his own effort to make "John Knox and the Reformers . . . very ridiculous" (*L*, 1: 300), and he requests of Adam Smith, "Flatter my Vanity, by telling me, that all the Godly in Scotland abuse me for my Account of John Knox & the Reformation &c" (*NL*, 54–55). David R. Raynor has argued persuasively that Hume was the reviewer who puffed Robertson's book in the *Critical Review* for February, 1759; there the writer, though lauding Robertson in general, deplores his prejudices in favor of Knox. See David R. Raynor, "Hume and Robertson's *History of Scotland*," *British Journal of Eighteenth-Century Studies* 10 (1987): 59–63.

19. *Virtue, Commerce, and History*, 136.

20. *Lives of the English Poets*, ed. George Birkbeck Hill (Oxford: Clarendon, 1905), 1: 215. Johnson had little sympathy for the "libertine" bent of Hume's writings, but in his description of the seventeenth-century enthusiasts (pp. 214–15), he agrees exactly with Hume: "[We] do not know the sour solemnity, the sullen superstition, the gloomy moroseness, and the stubborn scruples of the ancient Puritans. . . . It is scarcely possible . . . to image the tumult of absurdity and clamour of contradiction which perplexed doctrine, disordered practice, and disturbed both publick and private quiet in that age, when subordination was broken and awe was hissed away; when any unsettled innovator who could hatch a half-formed notion produced it to the publick; when every man might become a preacher, and almost every preacher could collect a congregation."

21. *Joseph Andrews* and *Shamela*, ed. Martin Battestin (Boston: Houghton Mifflin, 1961), 319.

22. Hilson (p. 216) describes Hume's Cromwell as "at once villain and clown." See also Hilson, "Hume: The Historian as Man of Feeling," 216–18.

23. These comments on the Parliamentary leaders, found in a letter to the passionately Whiggish historian Catherine Macaulay, are relevant:

> I grant, that the cause of liberty, which you, Madam, with the Pyms and Hampdens have adopted, is noble and generous; but most of the partizans of that cause, in the last century disgraced it, by their violence, and also by their cant, hypocrisy, and bigotry, which, more than the principles of civil liberty, seem to have been the motive of all their actions. Had those principles always appeared in the amiable light which they receive both from your person and writings, it would have been impossible to resist them; and

however much inclined to indulgence towards the first James and Charles, I should have been the first to condemn those monarchs for not yielding to them. (NL, 81–82)

24. *The Prose Works of Jonathan Swift*, ed. Herbert Davis (Oxford: Basil Blackwell, 1939–68), 1: 88. See also *H*, 6; 181ff.

25. Gay, like Gaskin and other commentators on Hume's "sociology of religion," concludes that "all houses of faith were houses of infection" (*Enlightenment*, 1: 412). But as we have seen, some houses were more infected than others.

26. See Mossner, *Life of Hume*, 306–307, for the complete text of the rejected passage.

27. Wexler notes that the passages deleted had offended two contemporary reviewers (Wexler, *David Hume*, 27).

28. Carl Becker, *The Heavenly City of the Eighteenth-Century Philosophers* (New Haven: Yale University Press, 1932), 110.

29. Gay notes that "the medical metaphor [was] always a favorite with the philosophers" (*Enlightenment*, 2: 379).

30. There are, to be sure, many other instances of religion's *poisoning, infecting*, and the like, scattered throughout Hume's writings.

31. Many of these quotations specifically concern the persecutions during the reign of Bloody Mary, but Hume clearly blames the Protestants equally: "Though the protestant divines had ventured to renounce opinions, deemed certain during many ages, they regarded, in their turn, the new system so certain, that they would suffer no contradiction with regard to it, and they were ready to burn in the same flames, from which they themselves had so narrowly escaped, every one that had the assurance to differ from them" (*H*, 3: 366).

32. See the passage fully quoted in chapter 1.

33. Among the literature on this aspect of Hume's religious philosophy, the essay by Kenneth R. Merrill and Donald G. Wester, "Hume on the Relation of Religion to Morality," *Journal of Religion* 60 (1980): 272–84, is particularly helpful.

34. The story of William Parry's plot to assassinate Elizabeth is almost as striking. See *H*, 4: 210–11.

35. See Mossner, *Life of Hume*, 233, 319.

36. Livingston (pp. 313–23) appears to say that Hume attributed Puritan immorality to its excessively theoretical radicalism, but I will show that Hume was more specific in his analysis.

37. The first *Enquiry* also reflects Hume's contempt for religious ceremonies, but he never makes them a principal object of concern. Discussing "the effect of resemblance in enlivening . . . ideas," Hume rehearses the reasons that Roman Catholics "usually plead in excuse for the mummeries, with which they are upbraided" (*EHU*, 51–52). Hume's reference to these ceremonies is scornful, but his main purpose here is merely to exemplify his argument concerning the power of resemblance.

38. Gaskin writes (p. 182): "In a discussion of this subject it might seem desirable to distinguish between what Hume has to say about religious observances and ceremonies on the one hand and frivolous species of merit or 'monkish virtues' on the other. But the subjects are not consistently separated by Hume and any attempted distinction by another on his behalf would be tenuous and of questionable value." I shall demonstrate that Hume does separate the two, and I hope that the resulting distinction is of considerable value.

39. I am omitting more than a page of detailed description. It is significant to note that the whole passage is a fairly close paraphrase of Hume's source—Rushworth, 2: 76–77—except that Hume tends to dramatize the episode and to

exaggerate a few details. For example, whereas in Rushworth, Laud on two occasions bows "several" times, in Hume he bows "frequently" or makes "many lowly reverences." Other dramatic touches such as the clause "he suddenly let fall the napkin" are Hume's interpolation. And in addition to the final sarcastic remark, the tone of the passage reflects Hume's lack of sympathy with the entire affair. Thus Rushworth: "When the Curses were ended, he pronounced a number of Blessings . . ."; and Hume: "The imprecations being all so piously finished, there were poured out a number of blessings. . . ."

40. Although nearly all of Hume's corrections in this passage are stylistic, the wording of the first edition, compared with the corrected version, may suggest a continuing shift in Hume's attitude toward sacred rites from one of antagonism to toleration: the first version's "popish superstition" is mollified into "popish ceremonies," a change consistent with Hume's desire here to recommend rather than condemn these practices.

41. There are numerous passages in the *History* that support this argument. Consider this endorsement of Queen Elizabeth's policy:

> But the princess herself, so far from being willing to despoil religion of the few ornaments and ceremonies which remained in it, was rather inclined to bring the publick worship still nearer to the Romish ritual; and she thought that the reformation had already gone too far in shaking off those forms and observances, which, without distracting men of more refined apprehensions, tend, in a very innocent manner, to allure, and amuse, and engage, the vulgar. (*H*, 4: 122–23)

One should remember that this passage was written *after* the Stuart volumes.

Livingston observes (*Hume's Philosophy of Common Life*, 315–16) that Hume was more friendly to conservative Catholic-Anglican ritualism than to the metaphysical abstraction represented by the Protestant-Puritan tradition, but he does not go very far in accounting for why. Likewise, Paul H. Meyer refers to an "emotional satisfaction" for the masses that prompted Hume "to insist on the need for an attractive and inspiring ceremonial," but he does not explore this "psychological consideration" any further. See Paul H. Meyer, "Voltaire and Hume as Historians: A Comparative Study of the *Essai sur Les Moeurs* and the *History of England*," *PMLA* 73 (1958): 65.

42. Hume next relates another blasphemous story concerning a converted Turk who so confuses his catechism that he concludes there is no God because yesterday he ate him during the Eucharist (NHR, 67–68).

43. Kemp Smith regards this insistence on the literalness or concreteness of images in the thought process as one of the "chief defects in Hume's teaching in Book I of the *Treatise*," namely, "his professed denial of abstract ideas, and his consequent not infrequent assumption that all intellectual processes have to be carried on in terms of images which are in all respects as specific and detailed as the happenings they recall." See Smith, *The Philosophy of David Hume*, 427–48.

Whether or not it is a defect, this tendency in Hume's thought does support the argument that Hume considered concrete referents as essential to ratiocination and conceivably then as antidotes to theogenic fantasy. Consider, for example, these confident assertions in the *Treatise:* "A person, who desires us to consider the figure of a globe of white marble without thinking on its colour desires an impossibility" (*T*, 25); "We can form no idea of a vacuum, or space, where there is nothing visible or tangible" (*T*, 53); or consider this statement in the first *Enquiry:* "An extension, that is neither tangible nor visible, cannot possibly be conceived; and a tangible or visible extension, which is neither hard nor soft, black nor white, is equally beyond the reach of human conception" (*EHU*, 154–55).

Livingston's discussion of this issue (pp. 72–84) is helpful. John P. Wright in *The Sceptical Realism of David Hume* (Minneapolis: University of Minnesota Press, 1983) stresses the mechanistic, psychophysical character of imagination in Hume. Also see Peter Jones, "Cause, Reason, and Objectivity in Hume's Aesthetics," in *Hume: A Re-Evaluation*, 323–42.

44. Cf. this observation in Hume's essay "Of National Characters" (1748): "all wise governments will be on their guard against the attempts of a society [the priesthood], who will for ever combine into one faction, and while it acts as a society, will for ever be actuated by ambition, pride, revenge, and a persecuting spirit" (*E*, 201n.).

45. "But it was found by fatal experience, that after spilling an ocean of blood in those theological quarrels, that the evil was of a peculiar nature, and was both inflamed by violent remedies, and diffused itself more rapidly throughout the whole society. Hence, though late, arose the paradoxical principle and salutary practice of toleration" (*H*, 5: 130).

46. Hume's use of summarized arguments may derive from his familiarity with Clarendon, who was fond of what Martine Brownley calls the "abbreviated dialectic." See Martine Brownley, *Clarendon and the Rhetoric of Historical Form* (Philadelphia: University of Pennsylvania Press, 1985), 56–57.

47. John B. Stewart rightly observes (p. 284) the irony of "a clash in which the politician, Gardiner, and the devout Pole took views opposite to what one might expect." But I am suggesting that both views reflect Hume's tendentious phrasing and that Gardiner's are by no means so especially devout and nonpolitical.

48. Stewart, *The Moral and Political Philosophy of David Hume*, 283.

49. Gibbon, *Decline and Fall of the Roman Empire*, ed. Bury, 7: 215; quoted by Gay, *Enlightenment*, 2: 377n.

50. *History of the Reformation of the Church of England*, 2d ed. (London, 1681), 1: 244.

51. At one point Hume footnotes a long and hilarious passage from Bulstrode Whitelock recounting a Hudibrastic rout of the clergy by the women of Perth (*H*, 6: 547). The passage can be found in Whitelock, *Memorials of the English Affairs from the Beginning of the Reign of Charles the First to the Happy Restoration of King Charles the Second* (Oxford: University Press, 1853), 3: 432–33. In this instance Hume copies Whitelock almost verbatim, adding only minor touches of his own to heighten the absurdity. Still, this borrowed anecdote is a good example of Hume's seizing a good opportunity for sacrilegious ridicule.

52. See Wexler's discussion of Hume's treatment of Joan (*David Hume*, 88–89); also Meyer's comparison (p. 63) of Voltaire's and Hume's versions: Meyer says that both historians are rigorously skeptical and rationalistic but that Voltaire goes further in insisting that the story was "a deliberate fraud . . . put over on Joan's contemporaries, either by her or by those who used her to further their own designs."

53. Stephen Greenblatt's penetrating discussion of the complexities of More's persona should be consulted. See Greenblatt, *Renaissance Self-Fashioning*, 11–76.

54. Hume's sources for More's persecution of Bainham are John Foxe, *Acts and Monuments of Matters most speciall and memorable . . .* (London, 1632), 2: 297; and Gilbert Burnet, *History of the Reformation of the Church of England* (London, 1681), 1: 342. Hume is faithful to these accounts, yet it is interesting that the Protestant clergyman Burnet is more skeptical in this case than the great skeptic Hume:

"But *Fox* adds a passage that seems scarce credible, the thing is so extraordinary, and so unlike the Character of the Lord Chancellor, who though he was fiercely zealous for the old Superstition, yet was otherwise a great person. . . . If [the story] was true, it shews the strange influence of that Religion, and that it corrupts the Noblest natures." On More and Bainham, see Greenblatt, *Renaissance Self-Fashioning*, 74–76.

55. Gaskin, *Hume's Philosophy of Religion*, 170.

56. Hume refers to a letter from Charles I discovered by Catharine Macaulay and quoted in her *History of England*, vol. 4, dated 1768. Wexler comments on the irony of Hume's using Mrs. Macaulay's "researches to further his own interpretation"—one diametrically opposed to her staunchly Whiggish view. "Hume's use, in a new edition of his own work, of the letter she had discovered must have infuriated Mrs. Macaulay. She had maintained that the letter showed that a 'passion for power was Charles' predominant vice,' and that his religious convictions were insincere, 'a secondary and subordinate affection.' " See Victor Wexler, "David Hume's Discovery of a New Scene of Historical Thought," *Eighteenth-Century Studies* 10 (1976/77): 200–201; see also Wexler's *David Hume*, 23ff.

Chapter 3. The Things of This World

Epigraphs, respectively: *T*, 330; *EPM*, 179; *L*, 2: 232; *EPM*, 319n.

1. Thus note in the *Treatise:*

If we consider the causes of love and hatred, we shall find they are very much diversify'd. . . . The virtue, knowledge, wit, good sense, good humour of any person, produce love and esteem; as the opposite qualities, hatred and contempt. The same passions arise from bodily accomplishments, such as beauty, force, swiftness, dexterity; and from their contraries; as likewise from the external advantages and disadvantages of family, possessions, cloaths, nation and climate (*T*, 330)

2. Paschal Larkin, *Property in the Eighteenth Century with Special Reference to England and Locke* (London: Longmans, Green and Company, 1930), 98.

3. Gaskin, *Hume's Philosophy of Religion*, 152.

4. James T. King says (pp. 343–615) that Hume "locates morality in language." On the limitations of Hume's verbal-catalogue approach to defining virtue, see William Davie, "Hume's Catalogue of Virtue and Vice," in *David Hume: Many-Sided Genius*, 45–57. Also see Livingston, *Hume's Philosophy of Common Life*, 68–69. A more favorable view is that of Ronald J. Glossop, "Hume, Stevenson, and Hare on Moral Language," in *Hume: A Re-Evaluation*, 362–85. Gaskin notes (p. 152), "The analysis is Aristotelian in tone but with a very strong utilitarian bias."

5. *The Autobiography of Benjamin Franklin*, ed. Leonard W. Labaree, et al. (New Haven: Yale University Press, 1964), 148–50.

6. Mossner, *Life of Hume*, 477.

7. Quoted in *L*, 1: 127n. Hume playfully boasts of his skill in cookery to Gilbert Elliot, *L*, 1: 208.

8. There are many more details revealing Hume's appreciation of opulence than I mention, but the following "press release," written while Hume was private secretary to the British ambassador to France, is to the point:

Paris. On Tuesday the fourth of June, being the Anniversary of his Majesty's Birth day, the Earl of Hertford, Ambassador from England, invited all the English of Rank and

Condition to this Place, to the Number of seventy Persons, who dind with him and celebrated that Solemnity. The Company appeard very splendid, being almost all drest in new and rich Cloaths on this Occasion; the Entertainment was magnificent, and the usual Healths were drunk with great Loyalty and Alacrity by all present (L, 1: 505)

9. Christensen, *Practicing Enlightenment*, 151.

10. To be sure, Hume does speak of the "fictitious value" of money—that is, its arbitrary and conventional value—but that point supports his contention that industry and commerce, not the money supply, control the rate of interest (E, 297).

Christensen discusses this problem in Hume's economics, maintaining that Hume theoretically sees no real value in gold but conceding that to Hume gold retains a priority over paper money because its weight beneficially keeps the economy from becoming too volatile: "Gold's weightiness is the last sense of a locus of value on which one can take a stand" (pp. 171–72). Of course that is the point: the weight of gold appeals to Hume's economic imagination.

11. Peter Jones, *Hume's Sentiments: Their Ciceronian and French Context* (Edinburgh: Edinburgh University Press, 1982), 7, 17; Robert F. Anderson, *Hume's First Principles* (Lincoln: University of Nebraska Press, 1966), 163; Livingston, *Hume's Philosophy of Common Life*, 167–86; and Wright, *The Sceptical Realism of David Hume*, 211, 221, 209.

12. L, 1: 114–33 is the source of the citations in this section. This section and a summary of this chapter's argument originally appeared as "Hume as Philosophical Traveler: From 'Wild Agreeable Prospects' to a 'Very Pretty Machine,' " *Studies in Eighteenth-Century Culture* 18 (1988): 187–98, and is reprinted with permission.

13. See Mossner, *Life of Hume*, 209–13.

14. Note Hume's use of a gothic vs. classic metaphor: "By means of [the Glorious Revolution], a more uniform edifice [of government] was at last erected: The monstrous inconsistence, so visible between the ancient Gothic parts of the fabric and the recent plans of liberty, was fully corrected: And . . . king and people were finally taught to know their proper boundaries" (H, 6: 475–76).

15. In order to reinforce his argument concerning the appeal of utility itself, Hume, like Shaftesbury and Hutcheson before him, is usually careful to insist that ownership has nothing to do with the perception of this kind of beauty. After listing "tables, chairs, scritoires, chimneys, coaches, sadles, ploughs, and indeed . . . every work of art"—not all objects, we might note, that most people would classify as beautiful—he says, "But this [utility] is an advantage, that concerns only the owner, nor is there any thing but sympathy, which can interest the spectator" (T, 364). Nonetheless, in the next paragraph that sympathy becomes strong enough to enable the perceiver to "share" these valuable possessions with the proprietor. See also Jones, *Hume's Sentiments*, 127. James Engell confirms, by the way, that "Hume uses fancy and imagination synonymously." See James Engell, *The Creative Imagination: Enlightenment to Romanticism* (Cambridge: Harvard University Press, 1981), 385n.

16. We might also remember the list in the preceding note that includes "chimneys, coaches, sadles, ploughs" among beautiful objects.

17. Gay, *Enlightenment*, 2: 359.

18. Larkin, *Property in the Eighteenth Century*, 98.

19. For a fascinating history of the idea from ancient times to the eighteenth century, see John Sekora, *Luxury: The Concept in Western Thought, Eden to Smollett* (Baltimore: Johns Hopkins University Press, 1977), 1–131. The headnote to

"Luxury" in Diderot, D'Allembert, et al., *Encyclopedia: Selections*, ed. Nelly S. Hoyt and Thomas Cassirer (Indianapolis: Bobbs, Merrill, 1965), 203–204, provides a succinct introduction, and Joseph A. Schumpeter, *History of Economic Analysis* (New York: Oxford University Press, 1954), 324–26n., provides a long note on the various meanings of the term and their economic implications.

20. In the Tudor volumes of the *History*, appearing in 1759, Hume provides some clarification of his reasons for the change of title. He defends affluence " . . . in spite of those who declaim so violently against refinement in the arts, or what they are pleased to call luxury." (*H*, 3: 76). Clearly he views "luxury" as a pejorative word to most people. However, in this discussion I shall refer to the essay by its original and more accurate little "Of Luxury." Of Hume's change in title, Sekora comments (p. 110), "Confident that his own view . . . would soon hold the day, he was willing to forego at least part of the taunting edge of his earlier position."

21. Sekora lists (p. 2) the following participants in England alone: "Mandeville, Addison, Steele, Defoe, Pope, Swift, Bolingbroke, Fielding, Chesterfield, Hume, Johnson, Pitt father and son, Walpole father and son, Goldsmith, Gibbon, Ferguson, Steuart, Wesley, and Adam Smith"—and of course Smollett, the focal author of his study. Sekora also notes (p. 66), "For the period of Smollett's lifetime, 1721–71—roughly the time between the enlarged edition of the *Fable of the Bees* and the *Wealth of Nations*—the British Museum and London School of Economics possess more than 460 books and pamphlets in English that discuss luxury; for the whole century the number would nearly double."

22. Actually Hume says as much himself: see *E*, 275ff.

23. Sekora thinks (p. 122) that Hume's response to libertines like Mandeville is "rather weak," but overall he praises (p. 110) Hume's essay as a "devastating" and "prescient" commentary on the subject.

24. Forbes, *Hume's Philosophical Politics*, 87–88.

25. See Lawrence Klein, "The Third Earl of Shaftesbury and the Progress of Politeness," *Eighteenth-Century Studies* 18 (1984–85): 186–214, esp. 213. David Miller notes that "Hume inverts the arguments of those republicans who defended simple agricultural societies on the grounds that they fostered virtue and military prowess," for in Hume it is the "civilized, commercial societies" that foster these characteristics (p. 192).

26. See *E*, 80–82. Peter Jones points to the influence of "Cicero's discussion of the similarities and differences between man and other animals" in this essay. See Peter Jones, " 'Art' and 'Moderation' in Hume's Essays," in *McGill Hume Studies*, ed. D. F. Norton, Nicholas Capaldi, and Wade L. Robison (San Diego: Austin Hill Press, 1979),166. The general assumptions resemble those common in various eighteenth-century moralists such as Shaftesbury, Addison (e.g., *Tatler* No. 108), and Chesterfield.

27. Schumpeter looks down on Hume's glib utilitarianism and self-worship: "Hume modeled the moral world to his own image. It is plain that, with delightful naïveté, he thoroughly approved of this image: the schema of his own preferences was the reasonable schema" (p. 129). Regarding Hume's distaste for "any kind of primitivist romanticism," Pocock notes that Hume "was never happy with his friend Adam Ferguson's *Essay on the History of Civil Society*, and . . . his emotions discharged themselves on the evident fraud of Macpherson's *Ossian* with something like relief." See Pocock, *Virtue, Commerce, and History*, 130.

28. Folkenflik, *Samuel Johnson, Biographer* (Ithaca: Cornell University Press, 1978),30; Livingston, *Hume's Philosophy of Common Life*, 245.

29. In a statement such as this Hume is very close to his great English counterpart Samuel Johnson; see, for example, *Rambler* No. 60 and *Idler* No. 84. John A. Vance compares the two men in this respect; see his "Johnson and Hume: Of Like Historical Minds," *Studies in Eighteenth-Century Culture* 6 (1986): 241–56.

30. J. B. Black regards Hume's appendices as "his most signal failure," separated as they are from the narrative. They are "ragbags . . . specifically invented to receive whatever odds and ends cannot be utilized in the main body of the history. . . . [L]ittle, if any, advantage can be drawn from these curious chapters." See J. B. Black *The Art of History* (New York: F. S. Crofts, 1926), 115–16. John Laird, in *Hume's Philosophy of Human Nature* (London: Methuen, 1932), 269, contrasts Hume's "desultory notes at the end of a reign" quite unfavorably with Voltaire's successful depiction of manners. Leo Braudy is less severe, although he still views the mass of factual detail in the appendices as signs of Hume's inability to find an adequate narrative form for his history: "Despite a minimal coherence, the appendices are like huge compendia, which threaten to split apart at the slightest unbalancing of their loads of disparate elements" (p. 89). Even Constant Noble Stockton, who fully appreciates the economic significance of Hume's details, describes these sections as "haphazard," as "somewhat disjointed digressions." See his "Economics and the Mechanism of Historical Progress in Hume's *History*," in *Hume: A Re-Evaluation*, 298.

31. Hume's laissez-faire economics is always squarely opposed to price controls. Of the attempts to promote archery by fixing the price of bows during the reign of Henry VII, he observes, "The only effect of this regulation must be either that the people would be supplied with bad bows or none at all" (*H*, 3: 78).

32. Stockton substantiates that Hume often uses his lists of prices to develop "a broader hypothesis concerning the economic, social, or political life of the past." More generally, "Hume's *History of England* reflects his interests in historical demography, in the theory of money, in the fiscal history of the English government. . . , in his theories on the question of mercantilism *vs.* economic liberty, of prices, of interest, of economic cycles, and of the relation between a nation's economic development and its social and political development." Stockton also suggests that Hume moves from "a more idealist analysis" of economics in his *Essays* to "a more materialist analysis" in the *History*. See Stockton, "Economics in Hume's *History*," 307, 303, 313.

33. In letters to his printer William Strahan, Hume speaks of Thomas Percy's having unfortunately seen an advance copy of this new footnote and of Percy's complaint that Hume seemed to be satirizing the old earl, an ancestor of Percy. Hume protests to Strahan that he intended no "Satyre on that particular Nobleman . . . [but] only meant to paint the manners of the Age." However, Strahan "must reprint all of that Note," even though a few minor alterations have been made to placate Dr. Percy. From the note as it now stands, it is hard to imagine that Hume softened his remarks very much; nonetheless, these letters confirm how important this material was to Hume. See *L*, 2: 267–68. See also Victor G. Wexler, *David Hume and the History of England*, 55–57.

34. Forbes, *Hume's Philosophical Politics*, 297; J. G. A. Pocock, *The Machiavellian Moment: Florentine Political Thought and the Atlantic Republican Tradition* (Princeton: Princeton University Press, 1975), 495. This magisterial study develops the larger intellectual background of Hume's own views on the relationship of commerce to civilization. According to Pocock, Hume and the other propounders, mainly Scottish, of the doctrine of commerce as the parent of social good never recognized the "contradictions between virtue and culture," that "by its nature society

humanized man and by the same processes distracted and alienated him again."
Rousseau, who was only too ready to point out this contradiction, was thus "the
Machiavelli of the eighteenth century" (p. 504).

35. Hume was not one to regard colonialism as anything malign. What if, in
Ireland, British planters took away the land of the natives? The advantages of
progress outweigh all other considerations: "a more than equal return had been
made [the slothful and barbarous Irish], by [the planters'] instructing the natives
in tillage, building, manufactures, and all the civilized arts of life" (*H*, 5: 336).

36. See the article on "Art" in the *Encyclopedia: Selections*, 6, 15.

37. Much of the material in this and the following two paragraphs comes from
my article "Hume on Idolatry and Incarnation" and is reprinted with permission.

38. A superb analysis is that of Ralph Cohen, "The Transformation of Passion:
A Study of Hume's Theories of Tragedy," *Philological Quarterly* 41 (1962): 450–64;
and his "The Rationale of Hume's Literary Inquiries," a contribution to *David
Hume: Many-Sided Genius*, 97–115.

39. Christopher MacLachlan cleverly reads the whole essay as an ironical
exposure of a true standard of taste, and so he questions Hume's belief in any
correspondence between physical taste and aesthetic taste. Though MacLachlan
makes some interesting points, I am not convinced that Hume's inconsistencies
and inadequacies on such a nebulous subject as taste prove that he therefore
must have intended an extended irony. See Christopher MacLachlan, "Hume
and the Standard of Taste," *Hume Studies* 12 (1986): 18–38.

40. In his ambitious and revealing study, Robert Ginsberg seems to consider
Hume's connection of taste and morality as an aberration: "Smuggled into this
essay on taste is a critique of the immorality of religion. . . . Hume oversteps the
boundaries of good taste by making an occasion in the course of a discussion of
aesthetic matters to attack a religion and its adherents." But Ginsberg makes a
virtue of Hume's supposed defects—"The weaknesses of the essay are among its
strengths"—arguing that Hume is demonstrating the process of developing and
exercising taste as he writes, and Ginsberg concludes, "Cautious and wandering,
committed and inconclusive, confounding and clear, circular and skeptical, this
curious conjunction of writing and philosophizing is the most engaging and
ingenious essay in the history of aesthetic thinking." See Ginsberg, "The Literary Structure and Strategy of Hume's Essay . . ." 205, 227, 232, 234. I believe that
Ginsberg underestimates the significance of morality in Hume's aesthetics, but
his conclusion is much in agreement with my portrayal in the next chapter of
Hume's skeptical empiricism.

41. Gay, *Enlightenment*, 1: 181.

42. In his wide-ranging study, *The Creative Imagination*, James Engell credits
Hume with being a "pivotal figure" in the movement from a mechanistic to a
more organic view of the imagination: "he shows the extent to which thought
and feeling—under the sway of the imagination—are intrinsically connected" (p.
56). However, Engell apparently still sees Hume's concept of the imagination as
being fairly distant from Coleridge's.

Chapter 4. Moral Skepticism

Epigraphs, respectively: *E*, 169; *L*, 1: 265; *L*, 2: 323.

1. John V. Price has explored this aspect of Hume's exposition in *The Ironic
Hume* (Austin: University of Texas Press, 1965). In his discussion of Hume the

historian, Leo Braudy emphasizes (p. 88) Hume's detachment: "Hume's voice remains cool and remote, and his humor is Olympian irony." Basil Willey makes (p. 248) Hume's "unruffled calm of manner" into a key for understanding Hume and his age. John B. Stewart remarks (p. 263): "the unvaried courtly measure and high polish of his prose seem incongruent with the earnestness of his thought. . . . Nothing that might be taken for wild, thoughtless rapture erupts to disturb the urbane equipoise, the calculated balance of this circumspect, elegant prose." John J. Richetti also sees Hume, in contrast to Locke and Berkeley, as the exemplar of clear and controlled philosophic prose: "In part, Hume's distinctiveness is a matter of essayistic fluency, a careful tonal control and delicate sense of audience his predecessors to some extent neglected"—John J. Richetti, *Philosophical Writing: Locke, Berkeley, Hume* (Cambridge: Harvard University Press, 1983), 185. The entire discussion in his chapter 4 deserves attention.

2. For significance of style in the *Treatise*, see my essay " 'Ardor of Youth': The Manner of Hume's *Treatise*," in *The Philosopher as Writer, 177–98*. The discussion of the *Treatise* at the beginning of this chapter originally appeared in this essay and is reprinted with permission.

3. Hume may never have sent the letter, the writing itself being therapy enough, it would seem; also we cannot be sure that Arbuthnot was Hume's intended consultant, though the evidence provided by Mossner is persuasive. See Mossner's *Life of David Hume*, 83–88, and idem, "Hume's Epistle to Dr. Arbuthnot, 1734: The Biographical Significance," *Huntington Library Quarterly* 7 (1944): 135–52.

4. Mossner, *Life of Hume*, 86.

5. John Sitter, *Literary Loneliness in Mid-Eighteenth-Century England* (Ithaca: Cornell University Press, 1982), 28.

6. Richetti, *Philosophical Writing*, 227; James Noxon, *Hume's Philosophical Development* (Oxford: Clarendon, 1973), 22. See also Richetti on Noxon, p. 217, and Christensen on Richetti, *Practicing Enlightenment*, 79. Christensen (pp. 89–90) basically sees Hume always playing at philosophy with a loaded deck, gambling because he has ensured that there is no chance of any significant loss: "crisis has been written out of the official version of philosophy that Hume proposes." Overall, Christensen's is a subtly and pervasively hostile reading of Hume. See, for example, p. 5, or his entire last chapter.

7. Sitter, *Literary Loneliness*, 28–29.

8. See the excellent discussion by Terence Penelhum in "Hume's Skepticism and the *Dialogues*," in *McGill Hume Studies*, 253–78, esp. 258 and 263.

9. Peter Jones makes a similar observation, though he is not concerned with Hume's strategy of disengagement: "It is worth remarking that Hume never again gives the impression, conveyed at the end of Book I of the *Treatise*, of half-succumbing to the intoxication of limitlessly wielding the sceptical tool. Certainly, his decision to set aside puzzles apparently irresolvable by thought, is a decision based on his view about the proper balance between thought, feeling and action, and further grounded in the fact that basic human responses effectively block undisciplined indulgence in sceptical reasoning" (Jones, *Hume's Sentiments*, 6–7).

10. John Sitter's approach to Hume and belief is different from mine; see Sitter, *Literary Loneliness*, 35–49, 148–50, 174–75.

11. Another good reason, consistent with my arguments concerning Hume's worldly morality, is that the dialogue is preeminently a social, hence worldly,

philosophical activity. Lawrence Klein's discussion of Shaftesbury's fondness for the dialogue applies just as well to Hume: Shaftesbury preferred "a worldly moralism: a moral discourse situated precisely in the *world*. His aim of a polite philosophy expressed the concern for moral worldliness. One of the appeals of ancient dialogue to him was its secular localization" (p. 210). Hume's Pamphilus says that a good dialogue "carries us, in a manner, into Company, and unites the two greatest and purest Pleasures of human Life, Study and Society" (*D*, 144).

12. This whole question is admirably treated in Gaskin, *Hume's Philosophy of Religion*, 159–66. Mossner's discussion is also helpful; see E. C. Mossner, "Hume and the Legacy of the *Dialogues*," in *David Hume: Bicentenary Papers*, ed. G. P. Morice (Edinburgh: Edinburgh University Press, 1977), 1–22. See also James Noxon, "Hume's Agnosticism," *Philosophical Review* 73 (1964): 248–61; reprinted in *Hume: A Collection of Critical Essays*, ed. V. C. Chappell (New York, 1966), 361–83.

13. Duncan Forbes supports the argument of A. Jeffner, *Butler and Hume on Religion* (Stockholm, 1966), 192–209, that no one represents Hume and that "*all* the arguments are destroyed, and all three positions are untenable" (p. 62n.).

14. Smith, *The Philosophy of David Hume*, 59.

15. Gaskin, *Hume's Philosophy of Religion*, 161.

16. Ibid., 32.

17. Peter Jones's observation on the contrast between Hume and one of his chief philosophical mentors, Cicero, is relevant here: "Cicero's own views . . . are not always stated; he cannot be identified completely . . . with any single spokesman in the *Tusculan Disputations* or even in *De Natura Deorum*. It is significant that in his last philosophical work, *De Officiis*, . . . Cicero abandons the dialogue form in the urgency of stating his own position. . . . In contrast, Hume's own last work represents the apogee of philosphical dialogue" (Jones, *Hume's Sentiments*, 39). Livingston agrees (pp. 39–44):

> Indeed, we may say that in the *Dialogues* Hume's dialectical intelligence finds its true literary form, a form the analogues of which are discernible in some shape or other in most of his works from the *Treatise* on. . . . Hume solved the problem of stumbling over himself by eliminating himself as a character in the inquiry in favor of other characters. No character may be taken to represent entirely Hume's views. The result is, perhaps, the purest expression of philosophical inquiry in literature.

18. Gay, *Enlightenment*, 1: 171.

19. Ibid., 405.

20. Sitter, *Literary Loneliness*, 149.

21. Noxon, *Hume's Philosophical Development*, 178.

22. Lionel Gossman, "Literary Scholarship and Popular History," *Eighteenth-Century Studies* 7 (1973/74): 139–40. For a detailed study of Hume's irony, see Price, *The Ironic Hume*. Though not speaking directly about irony, Richetti accurately describes this suspension of commitment that Hume's style typically enforces: "Resolved not to be an 'enthusiast' in anything, Hume seeks a language that matches the complex neutrality of his philosophic stance and avoids the implicit self-satisfaction of rigid positions or even of fixed attitudes. He is sometimes accused of lacking a true position or of occupying so fluid and shifting a set of positions that it is nearly impossible to pin him down" (p. 217).

23. See Willey, *The English Moralists*, 253. Alasdair MacIntyre (*After Virtue*, 45) pronounces Hume a moral conservative.

24. See Johnson's *Dictionary* under "sensible," especially senses three and

four. "Sensible"'s current meaning of "reasonable" was still colloquial when Hume wrote this passage. See Brissendon, *Virtue in Distress*, 18.

25. Barry Stroud has discussed the problem of the sensible knave and has concluded that on this score Hume's whole attempt to make the artificial virtue of justice inevitable is flawed:

> The point is not that Hume's theory is inadequate because it makes it possible for men to be unjust. No theory could make that impossible. The point is rather that we regard justice as a virtue, and so even when we act against it there must be something that recommends it to us, even if we allow it to be outweighed by other factors. Hume thinks he can explain what recommends it to our avidity or self-interest alone, and that is what I think he fails to do.

Stroud goes on to suggest that Hume should have based his explanation of justice more on an innate human disposition, an explanation that would be in keeping with Hume's general tendency towards naturalism: "It may well be that an elaborate scheme of justice does not serve merely to channel or direct our acquisitive 'avidity' in more mutually beneficial directions, but that a more or less disinterested concern for justice and fairness is a natural outgrowth of outward-looking or socially-oriented emotional needs that human beings inevitably develop" (pp. 205–18.)

26. This of course is a major difficulty of Hume's catalogue ethics. See Davie, "Hume's Catalogue of Virtue and Vice," 45–57.

27. Livingston, *Hume's Philosophy of Common Life*, 220–22; Forbes, *Hume's Philosophical Politics*, 110. Interestingly, Livingston misreads the reference to the amoral French as that of Palamedes, when in fact the speaker is the "I." Peter Gay, although he does not go further than to see in "A Dialogue" a "still fairly rudimentary relativism," at least recognizes it as displaying some degree of relativism as well as "the germs of historicism" (Gay, *Enlightenment*, 2:381).

28. As Gay notes, in the second *Enquiry* Hume reduces the problem of incest to a relative matter of public utility: "Hume's analysis, in contrast [to Christian social thought], is cool, secular, and relativistic" (*Enlightenment*, 2: 201).

29. Quoted in Hume's *Works*, 3: 52.

30. Peter Jones points out: "The quartet of essays, taken as a group, constitutes one of Hume's earliest attempts at the dialogue form. . . . Hume's immediate model was Cicero, who, having outlined and rejected Epicureanism, Stoicism, and Platonism, presented his own skeptical position" (Jones, "'Art' and 'Moderation' in Hume's Essays," 176).

31. Jones briefly discusses these four essays with the aim of contending that "The Sceptic" is the culminating and thus the only true expression of proper Ciceronian moderation, Hume's actual viewpoint. See Jones, *Hume's Sentiments*, 158–60, and idem., "'Art' and 'Moderation,'" 172–79. Though the last essay need not be viewed as the true and final position, synthesizing all the others, Livingston's assessment is plausible, if somewhat different from mine: "they are so contrived that the reader experiences the seeds of each position in himself and, as he passes through them, views the earlier positions which seemed acceptable at the time in a different and critical light. The last essay . . . emerges as the true position which reconciles the earlier conflicting positions into a new perspective without entirely destroying them. The solution is a dialectical one and is achieved narratively" (p. 40).

32. See R. S. Crane, "Suggestions toward a Genealogy of the 'Man of Feeling,'" *ELH* 1 (1934): 205–30.

33. Indeed in his discussion Jones simply brushes "The Platonist" aside (Jones, " 'Art' and 'Moderation,' " 173).

34. John Laird calls "The Sceptic" "rather more sceptical than Hume generally permitted himself to be" (p. 245).

35. Larkin, *Property in the Eighteenth Century,* 100.

36. Gay, *Enlightenment,* 1: 418–19.

37. Mossner, *Life of Hume,* 485–86. Hume's philosophical kinsman Gibbon has this to say: "nor could I approve the intolerant zeal of the philosophers and Encyclopaedists the friends of d'Olbach and Helvetius: they laughed at the scepticism of Hume, preached the tenets of Atheism with the bigotry of dogmatists, and damned all believers with ridicule and contempt." See Edward Gibbon, *Memoirs of My Life,* ed. Georges A. Bonnard (London: Thomas Nelson and Sons, 1966), 127.

38. I basically agree with David Fate Norton's definition and defense of Hume's eminently "sane, normally functioning believing" skepticism. See David Fate Norton, *David Hume: Common-Sense Moralist, Sceptical Metaphysician,* 290, et passim. Robert Ginsberg's remark that Hume "is the foremost philosopher of 'but' " (p. 202) encapsulates much of what I have been arguing in this chapter.

Chapter 5. David Hume's Last Words

Epigraphs, respectively: *T,* 598; *L,* 2: 323. An earlier version of this chapter appeared in *Studies in Scottish Literature* 19 (1984): 132–47, and is used with permission.

1. T. E. Jessop, "The Misunderstood Hume," in *Hume and the Enlightenment,* ed. William B. Todd (Edinburgh: Edinburgh University Press, 1974), 9.

2. Gibbon, *Memoirs of My Life,* 208. I am probably being too severe with Gibbon, for he was no doubt sincerely affected by his youthful romance, however defensive he might have been much later in life: "I need not blush at recollecting the object of my choice, and though my love was disappointed of success, I am rather proud, that I was once capable of feeling sure a pure and exalted sentiment" (p. 84).

3. *The Autobiography of Benjamin Franklin,* 160.

4. See Hume's letters to Adam Smith and William Strahan (*L,* 2: 317–18, 323); Christensen, *Practicing Enlightenment,* 200. See Christensen's interesting discussion (pp. 46–52) of Hume's *Life,* which parallels my own on a few points, though mine was written independently and published three years prior to his (see the initial note to this chapter).

5. Mossner, *Life of Hume,* 187–204, 249–51, 163–76, 507–32. For the Rousseau scandal, also see Christensen (pp. 51–52, 243–73), who makes Hume into something of a hypocritical cad in his interesting but quite fanciful reading of the whole "text." Regarding Hume's statements late in the autobiography that he never was touched by calumny or that his "Friends never had occasion to vindicate . . . [his] Character and Conduct" (*MOL,* 615), Lewis White Beck points out in a letter to me that on these issues Hume "comes close to outright lying. . . . Hume's French friends, who attempted to answer the scurrilities of Rousseau, seem . . . to be little rewarded for their efforts in Hume's behalf."

6. Wexler, *David Hume and the History of England,* 2.

7. See the text in *L,* 1: 6n.

8. On Hume's sentimental treatment of Charles, see chapter 1; also Hilson, "Hume: The Historian as Man of Feeling," 205–22.

9. Mossner expresses surprise over this passage: "In view of the tumult occasioned by *Four Dissertations*, it is not easy to interpret the remark of Hume in his autobiography concerning the 'indifferent reception of my Performance.' Certainly he could not have meant that it went unnoticed." And Mossner goes on to document the angry attention Hume got on this occasion (Mossner, *Life of Hume*, 331–32). When we consider the overall impression of personal serenity that Hume has endeavored to create, then his remark is not at all hard to interpet.

10. Mossner, *Life of Hume*, 253–55, 382.

11. Ibid., 6–7, 276. See also the deathbed letter to Hume's favorite nephew David Home or Hume, with its avuncular banter: "I doubt not but my Name woud have procured you Friends and Credit, in the Course of your Life, especially if my Brother had allowd you to carry it: For who will know it, in the present Disguise?" (*L*, 2: 333).

12. A convenient reprinting of Boswell's interview with Hume is in Norman Kemp Smith's edition of the *Dialogues* (Indianapolis: Bobbs-Merrill, 1947), 76–79.

13. It is revealing that Hume praised *Candide* as a sprightly and impious "Satyre upon Providence, under Pretext of criticizing the Leibnitian System" (*NL*, 53). Livingston observes: "It was difficult [for Hume's detractors] to appreciate the view that events of great historical significance were not intended by anyone (neither individuals nor Providence). This thesis is not a quirk of Hume's historical thinking; it is at the center of his philosophical vision" (Livingston, *Hume's Philosophy of Common Life*, 257).

14. Gibbon, *Memoirs of My Life*, 169.

15. Christensen (*Practicing Enlightenment*, 46–47) calls this shifting of tenses "a posthumous style . . . that seals off a 'life' and a fame exempt from all infirmities." See my comment on his discussion of Hume's *Life* in note 4.

16. Gaskin, *Hume's Philosophy of Religion*, 174.

17. Richetti describes (*Philosophical Writing*, 183) this work as "a short autobiography whose calm introspection and ironic modesty strike comically against the fervor of youthful ambition by which he was 'seized very early.' "

18. *L*, 2: 318; Mossner, *Life of Hume*, 328–32.

19. The reception of *My own Life* turned out to be exactly as Hume might have expected and intended, delighting his friends and confounding his enemies. For a survey of the negative reaction, see Hume, *Works*, 3: 80–84. I am indebted to Professor Ernest Mossner for reading this chapter and offering suggestions for its improvement, and in particular for calling my attention to this revealing observation by Adam Smith in a letter to Alexander Wedderburn (14 August 1776): "Poor David Hume is dying very fast, but with great chearfulness and good humour and with more real resignation to the necessary course of things, than any Whining Christian ever dyed with pretended resignation to the will of God." See *The Correspondence of Adam Smith*, ed. Ernest Campbell Mossner and Ian Simpson Ross (Oxford: Clarendon Press, 1977), 203.

Bibliography

Included are all works cited except those by David Hume, which are listed in the Abbreviations for Hume's Works.

[Allestree, Richard.] *The Whole Duty of Man, Laid down in a Plain and Familiar Way, for the Use of All, but especially the Meanest Reader. . . .* 1658. Reprint. London, 1716.

Anderson, Robert Fendal. *Hume's First Principles.* Lincoln: University of Nebraska Press, 1966.

Beck, Lewis White. Letter to author, 12 May 1988.

Becker, Carl. *The Heavenly City of the Eighteenth-Century Philosophers.* New Haven: Yale University Press, 1932.

Berman, David. "David Hume and the Suppression of Atheism." *Journal of the History of Philosophy* 21 (1983): 375–87.

Black, J. B. *The Art of History.* New York: F. S. Crofts, 1926.

Bongie, Laurence L. *David Hume: Prophet of the Counter-Revolution.* Oxford: Clarendon Press, 1965.

Boswell, James. *Boswell in Extremes, 1776–1778.* Edited by Charles McC. Weis and Frederick A. Pottle. New York: McGraw-Hill, 1970.

———. *Boswell's London Journal.* Edited by Frederick A. Pottle. New York: McGraw-Hill, 1950.

Braudy, Leo. *Narrative Form in History and Fiction: Hume, Fielding, and Gibbon.* Princeton: Princeton University Press, 1970.

Bredvoid, Louis I. *The Natural History of Sensibility.* Detroit: Wayne State University Press, 1962.

Brissenden, R. F. *Virtue in Distress: Studies in the Novel of Sentiment from Richardson to Sade.* London: Macmillan, 1974.

Brownley, Martine Watson. *Clarendon and the Rhetoric of Historical Form.* Philadelphia: University of Pennsylvania Press, 1985.

Buchan, John. *Montrose.* 1928. Reprint. London: Hodder and Stoughton, 1938.

Burke, Edmund. *A Philosophical Enquiry into the Origin of our Ideas of the Sublime and Beautiful.* London, 1757.

Burke, John J., Jr. "Hume's *History of England:* Waking the English from a Dogmatic Slumber." *Studies in Eighteenth-Century Culture* 7 (1978): 235–50.

Burnet, Gilbert. *History of the Reformation of the Church of England.* 2d ed. 3 vols. London, 1681–1715.

Camden, William. *The History of . . . Princess Elizabeth. . . .* Edited by Wallace MacCaffrey. Chicago: University of Chicago Press, 1970.

Carnall, Geoffrey. "Historical Writing in the Later Eighteenth Century." In *The History of Scottish Literature*, vol. 2. Edited by Andrew Hook. Aberdeen: Aberdeen University Press, 1987.

Christensen, Jerome. *Practicing Enlightenment: Hume and the Formation of a Literary Career.* Madison: University of Wisconsin Press, 1987.

Cicero. *De Officiis.* Loeb Classical Library, vol. 21. Translated by Walter Miller. Cambridge: Harvard University Press, 1913.

Clèry, J. B. A. *Journal de ce qui s'est passé a la tour du Temple pendant la captivité de Louis XVI, Roi de France.* London, 1798.

Cohen, Ralph. "The Rationale of Hume's Literary Inquiries." In *David Hume: Many-Sided Genius.* Edited by Kenneth R. Merrill and Robert W. Shahan. Norman: University of Oklahoma Press, 1976.

———. "The Transformation of Passion: A Study of Hume's Theories of Tragedy." *Philological Quarterly* 41 (1962): 450–64.

Crane, R. S. "Suggestions toward a Genealogy of the 'Man of Feeling.' " *ELH* 1 (1934): 205–30.

Davie, William. "Hume's Catalogue of Virtue and Vice." In *David Hume: Many-Sided Genius.* Edited by Kenneth R. Merrill and Robert W. Shahan. Norman: University of Oklahoma Press, 1976.

Diderot, Denis, et al. *Encyclopedia: Selections.* Edited by Nelly S. Hoyt and Thomas Cassiser. Indianapolis: Bobbs, Merrill, 1965.

Dryden, John. *The Works of John Dryden.* Edited by H. T. Swedenberg et al. 19 vols. Berkeley and Los Angeles: University of California Press, 1956–79.

Edgerton, Samuel L., Jr. "*Maniera* and the *Mannaia:* Decorum and Decapitation in the Sixteenth Century." In *The Meaning of Mannerism.* Edited by Franklin W. Robinson and Stephen G. Nichols, Jr. Hanover, N.H.: University Press of New England, 1972.

Eikon Basilike: The Portraiture of His Sacred Majesty in His Solitudes and Sufferings. 1649. Reprint. Edited by Philip A. Knachel. Ithaca: Cornell University Press, 1966.

Engell, James. *The Creative Imagination: Enlightenment to Romanticism.* Cambridge: Harvard University Press, 1981.

Fielding, Henry. *Joseph Andrews* and *Shamela.* Edited by Martin Battestin. Boston: Houghton Mifflin, 1961.

Folkenflik, Robert. *Samuel Johnson, Biographer.* Ithaca: Cornell University Press, 1978.

Forbes, Duncan. *Hume's Philosophical Politics.* Cambridge: Cambridge University Press, 1975.

Foucault, Michel. *Discipline and Punish: The Birth of the Prison.* Translated by Alan Sheridan. New York: Vantage Books, 1979.

Foxe, John. *Acts and Monuments of Matters most speciall and memorable. . . .* 3 vols. London, 1632–41.

Franklin, Benjamin. *The Autobiography of Benjamin Franklin.* Edited by Leonard W. Labaree, Ralph L Ketchem, Helen C. Boatfield, and Helene H. Fineman. New Haven: Yale University Press, 1964.

Gaskin, J. C. A. *Hume's Philosophy of Religion.* London: Macmillan, 1984.

Gay, Peter. *The Enlightenment: An Interpretation.* 2 vols. New York: Alfred A. Knopf, 1966–69.

Gibbon, Edward. *History of the Decline and Fall of the Roman Empire.* Edited by J. B. Bury, 3 vols. New York: Heritage Press, 1946.

———. *Memoirs of My Life.* Edited by Georges A. Bonnard. London: Thomas Nelson and Sons, 1966.

Ginsberg, Robert. "The Literary Structure and Strategy of Hume's Essay on the 'Standard of Taste.' " In *The Philosopher as Writer: The Eighteenth Century.* Edited by Robert Ginsberg. Selinsgrove, Pa.: Susquehanna University Press, 1987.

Glossop, Ronald J. "Hume, Stevenson, and Hare on Moral Language." In *Hume: A Re-Evaluation.* Edited by Donald W. Livingston and James T. King. New York: Fordham University Press, 1976.

Gossman, Lionel. "Literary Scholarship and Popular History." *Eighteenth-Century Studies* 7 (1973/74): 133–42.

Greenblatt, Stephen. *Renaissance Self-Fashioning from More to Shakespeare.* Chicago: University of Chicago Press, 1980.

Hilson, J. C. "Hume: The Historian as Man of Feeling." In *Augustan Worlds.* Edited by J. C. Hilson, M. M. B. Jones, and J. R. Watson. Bristol: Leicester University Press, 1978.

Jebb, Samuel. *The History of the Life and Reign of Mary Queen of Scots.* London, 1725.

Jeffner, Anders. *Butler and Hume on Religion: A Comparative Analysis.* Stockholm: Diakonistyrelsens bokforlag, 1966.

Jessop, T. E. "The Misunderstood Hume." In *Hume and the Enlightenment.* Edited by William B. Todd. Edinburgh: Edinburgh University Press, 1974.

Johnson, Samuel. *Lives of the English Poets.* Edited by George Birkbeck Hill. 3 vols. Oxford: Clarendon Press, 1905.

Jones, Peter. " 'Art' and 'Moderation' in Hume's Essays." In *McGill Hume Studies.* Edited by David Fate Norton, Nicholas Capaldi, and Wade L. Robison. San Diego: Austin Hill Press, 1979.

———. "Cause, Reason, and Objectivity in Hume's Aesthetics." In *Hume: A Re-Evaluation.* Edited by Donald W. Livingston and James T. King. New York: Fordham University Press, 1976.

———. *Hume's Sentiments: Their Ciceronian and French Context.* Edinburgh: Edinburgh University Press, 1982.

King, James T. "The Place of the Language of Morals in Hume's Second *Enquiry.*" In *Hume: A Re-Evaluation.* Edited by Donald W. Livingston and James T. King. New York: Fordham University Press, 1976.

Klein, Lawrence. "The Third Earl of Shaftesbury and the Progress of Politeness." *Eighteenth-Century Studies* 18 (1984/85): 186–214.

Knox, John. *John Knox's History of the Reformation in Scotland.* 2 vols. Edited by William Croft Dickinson. New York: Philosophical Library, 1950.

Laird, John. *Hume's Philosophy of Human Nature.* London: Methuen, 1932.

Larkin, Paschal. *Property in the Eighteenth Century with Special Reference to England and Locke.* London: Longmans, Green and Co., 1930.

Livingston, Donald W. *Hume's Philosophy of Common Life.* Chicago: University of Chicago Press, 1984.

Macaulay, Catherine. *History of England.* 8 vols. London, 1763–83.

MacIntyre, Alasdair. *After Virtue: A Study in Moral Theory.* Notre Dame: University of Notre Dame Press, 1981.

MacLachlan, Christopher. "Hume and the Standard of Taste." *Hume Studies* 12 (1986): 18–38.

Mercer, Philip. *Sympathy and Ethics: A Study of the Relationship Between Sympathy and Morality with Special Reference to Hume's Treatise.* Oxford: Clarendon Press, 1972.

Merrill, Kenneth R. and Donald G. Wester. "Hume on the Relation of Religion to Morality." *Journal of Religion* 60 (1980): 272–84.

Meyer, Paul H. "Voltaire and Hume as Historians: A Comparative Study of the *Essai sur Les Moeurs* and the *History of England*." *PMLA* 73 (1958): 51–68.

Miller, David. *Philosophy and Ideology in Hume's Political Thought.* Oxford: Clarendon Press, 1981.

Morrisroe, Michael, Jr. "Linguistic Analysis as Rhetorical Pattern in David Hume." In *Hume and the Enlightenment.* Edited by William B. Todd. Edinburgh and Austin: Edinburgh University Press and the University of Texas Press, 1974.

Mossner, Ernest Campbell. "Hume and the Legacy of the *Dialogues*." In *David Hume: Bicentenary Papers.* Edited by G. P. Morice. Edinburgh: Edinburgh University Press, 1977.

———. "Hume's Epistle to Dr. Arbuthnot, 1734: The Biographical Significance." *Huntington Library Quarterly* 7 (1944): 135–52.

———. *The Life of David Hume.* 2d ed. Oxford: Clarendon Press, 1980.

———. "New Hume Letters to Lord Elibank, 1748–1776." *Texas Studies in Literature and Language* 4 (1962): 431–60.

———. "The Religion of David Hume." *Journal of the History of Ideas* 39 (1978): 653–64.

Norton, David Fate. *David Hume: Common-Sense Moralist, Sceptical Metaphysician.* Princeton: Princeton University Press, 1982.

Noxon, James. "Hume's Agnosticism." *Philosophical Review* 73 (1964): 248–61.

———. "Hume's Concern with Religion." In *David Hume: Many-Sided Genius.* Edited by Kenneth R. Merrill and Robert W. Shahan. Norman: Unversity of Oklahoma Press, 1976.

———. *Hume's Philosophical Development.* Oxford: Clarendon Press, 1973.

[Oldmixon, John.] *The History of England. . . .* London, 1730.

Penelhum, Terence. "Hume's Skepticism and the *Dialogues*." In *McGill Hume Studies.* Edited by David Fate Norton, Nicholas Capaldi, and Wade L. Robison. San Diego: Austin Hill Press, 1979.

[Perrinchief, Richard.] *The Royal Martyr: or, The Life and Death of King Charles I.* London, 1676.

Pocock, J. G. A. "Gibbon's *Decline and Fall* and the World View of the Late Enlightenment." *Eighteenth-Century Studies* 10 (1977): 287–303.

———. *The Machiavellian Moment: Florentine Political Thought and the Atlantic Republican Tradition.* Princeton: Princeton University Press, 1975.

———. *Virtue, Commerce, and History: Essays on Political Thought and History, Chiefly in the Eighteenth Century.* Cambridge: Cambridge University Press, 1985.

Pope, Alexander. *The Poems of Alexander Pope; A One-Volume Edition of the Twickenham Text.* Edited by John Butt. London: Methuen, 1963.

Price, John V. *The Ironic Hume.* Austin: University of Texas Press, 1965.

Radner, John B. "Sympathy in British Moral Thought." *Studies in Eighteenth-Century Culture* 9 (1979): 189–210.

Raynor, David R. "Hume and Robertson's *History of Scotland. British Journal of Eighteenth-Century Studies* 10 (1987): 59–63.

Richetti, John J. *Philosophical Writing: Locke, Berkeley, Hume.* Cambridge: Harvard University Press, 1983.

Robertson, William. *The History of Scotland.* 1759. Reprint. 2 vols. London, 1794.

Rushworth, John. *Historical Collections.* 8 vols. London, 1721–22.

Schumpeter, Joseph A. *History of Economic Analysis.* New York: Oxford University Press, 1954.

Sekora, John. *Luxury: The Concept in Western Thought, Eden to Smollett.* Baltimore: Johns Hopkins University Press, 1977.

Siebert, Donald T. "'Ardor of Youth': The Manner of Hume's *Treatise.*" In *The Philosopher as Writer: The Eighteenth Century.* Edited by Robert Ginsberg. Selinsgrove, Pa.: Susquehanna University Press, 1987.

———. "David Hume's Last Words: The Importance of *My Own Life.*" *Studies in Scottish Literature* 19 (1984): 132–47.

———. "Hume as Philosophical Traveler: From 'Wild Agreeable Prospects' to a 'Very Pretty Machine.'" *Studies in Eighteenth-Century Culture* 18 (1988): 187–98.

———. "Hume on Idolatry and Incarnation." *Journal of the History of Ideas* 45 (1984): 379–96.

———. "The Sentimental Sublime in Hume's *History of England.*" *Review of English Studies,* New Series 40 (1989): 350–72.

Sitter, John. *Literary Loneliness in Mid-Eighteenth-Century England.* Ithaca: Cornell University Press, 1982.

Smith, Adam. *The Correspondence of Adam Smith.* Edited by Ernest Campbell Mossner and Ian Simpson Ross. Oxford: Clarendon Press, 1977.

Smith, Norman Kemp. "Introduction" to David Hume, *Dialogues concerning Natural Religion.* London: Thomas Nelson and Sons, 1947.

———. *The Philosophy of David Hume.* London: Macmillan, 1941.

Stewart, John B. *The Moral and Political Philosophy of David Hume.* 1963. Reprint. Westport, Conn.: Greenwood Press, 1973.

Stockton, Constant Noble. "Economics and the Mechanism of Historical Progress in Hume's *History.*" In *Hume: A Re-Evaluation.* Edited by Donald W. Livingston and James T. King. New York: Fordham University Press, 1976.

Stroud, Barry. *Hume.* London: Routledge and Kegan Paul, 1977.

Strype, John. *Annals of the Reformation and Establishment of Religion.* 1728. Reprint. 19 vols. Oxford: Clarendon Press, 1812–24.

Swift, Jonathan. *The Prose Works of Jonathan Swift.* Edited by Herbert Davis. 14 vols. Oxford: Basil Blackwell, 1939–68.

Vance, John A. "Johnson and Hume: Of Like Historical Minds." *Studies in Eighteenth-Century Culture* 16 (1986): 241–56.

Wexler, Victor. *David Hume and the History of England.* Philadelphia: American Philosophical Society, 1979.

———. "David Hume's Discovery of a New Scene of Historical Thought." *Eighteenth-Century Studies* 10 (1976/77): 185–202.

White, Hayden. *The Content of the Form: Narrative Discourse and Historical Representation*. Baltimore: Johns Hopkins University Press, 1987.

Whitelock, Bulstrode. *Memorials of the English Affairs from the Beginning of the Reign of Charles the First to the Happy Restoration of King Charles the Second*. 1682. Reprint. 4 vols. Oxford: Oxford University Press, 1853.

Willey, Basil. *The English Moralists*. New York: W. W. Norton, 1964.

Wright, John P. *The Sceptical Realism of David Hume*. Minneapolis: University of Minnesota Press, 1983.

Yalden-Thomson, D. C. "Recent Work on Hume (A Survey of Hume Literature 1969–1979)." *American Philosophical Quarterly* 20 (1983): 1–22.

Yandell, Keith E. "Hume on Religious Belief." In *Hume: A Re-Evaluation*. Edited by Donald W. Livingston and James T. King. New York: Fordham University Press, 1976.

Index